Principles-Based Counselling and Psychotherapy

Many current approaches to the treatment of psychological problems focus on specific disorders and techniques that are purported to be effective and distinct. Recent advances in knowledge and theory, however, have called into question this approach. The conceptual framework of transdiagnostic, rather than disorder-specific, processes is gaining traction. Alongside this has been the call to focus on evidence-based principles rather than evidence-based practices and techniques. The rationale behind this is that many apparently unique and innovative practices are usually the reflection of common underlying principles. This book describes three foundational principles that are key to understanding both the rise and the resolution of psychological distress.

Principles-Based Counselling and Psychotherapy promotes a Method of Levels (MOL) approach to counselling and psychotherapy. Using clinical examples and vignettes to help practitioners implement a principles-based approach, this book describes three fundamental principles for effective therapeutic practice and their clinical implications. The first chapter of the book provides a rationale for the principles-based approach. The second chapter describes the three principles of control, conflict, and reorganisation, and how they relate to each other from within a robust theory of physical and psychological functioning. The remainder of the book covers important aspects of psychological treatment such as the therapeutic relationship, appointment scheduling, and the change process from the application of these three principles.

With important implications for all therapeutic approaches, *Principles-Based Counselling and Psychotherapy* will be an invaluable resource for psychotherapists, counsellors, and clinical psychologists in practice and training. It provides clarity about their role, and a means for providing a resolution to psychological distress and improving the effectiveness of their practice.

Timothy A. Carey is a Professor and Director of the Centre for Remote Health, a joint centre of Flinders University and Charles Darwin University, Alice Springs, Australia. Tim is a clinician, researcher, and teacher, and has authored over 100 publications. He has used MOL in clinical practice for more than 10 years, and has conducted MOL training in Australia, the United Kingdom, and Canada.

Warren Mansell is Reader in Clinical Psychology at the University of Manchester, UK, and the author of over 100 publications, including *A Transdiagnostic CBT Using the Method of Levels Therapy: Distinctive Series* (Routledge, 2012) with Tim Carey and Sara J. Tai. He has provided workshops on MOL therapy to health professionals in the UK, Europe, and Australia.

Sara J. Tai is a senior lecturer at the University of Manchester and practising Consultant Clinical Psychologist. She works internationally as a researcher, trainer, and supervisor of the MOL. She has published on psychological interventions for people with long-term mental health problems and is author of *A Transdiagnostic CBT Using the Method of Levels Therapy: Distinctive Series* (Routledge, 2012) with Warren Mansell and Tim Carey.

'This new book from Carey, Mansell, and Tai is a refreshing reading. My enthusiasm with this new perspective is that central features of MOL approach are important bridges between several methods of therapy, from cognitive-behaviour, to constructivist and process-oriented, to experiential therapies. Therapists focus in understanding clients' meaning-making processes, center in clients' distress (not in their symptoms), emphasise the therapeutic relationship, conceive clients as experts into their own lives, and highlight the therapeutic power of each individual session. A must read for all psychotherapists, both experienced and trainees.'

—**Miguel M. Gonçalves**, PhD, Professor, Director – Psychology Research Center (CIPsi), Vice-President – School of Psychology, University of Minho, Braga, Portugal

'This book notes in its introduction that it hopes to intrigue, challenge and excite the reader. In a refreshing text, which slices therapeutic work in a novel direction by advocating a principles-based approach, it certainly achieved these goals for me.'

—**Terry Hanley**, Director of the Doctorate in Counselling Psychology at the University of Manchester, UK

'Carey, Mansell, and Tai lay out a set of principles that will help you cut through the morass of conflicting therapeutic techniques and approaches and deliver more effective and consumer-friendly treatment.'

—**Scott D. Miller**, PhD, www.centerforclinicalexcellence.com. Chicago, Illinois, USA

'This book offers a reader-friendly, example-packed account of the Method of Levels (MOL), an innovative therapy grounded in the principles of Perceptual Control Theory (PCT). PCT holds that people control their lives by acting to match their perceptions with their goals. MOL suggests that when clients' goals conflict with each other, a path out of conflict is stepping up a level to view the conflicting goals from a broader perspective. The therapy is radically person-centered without being nondirective. It focuses on articulating clients' goals and perceptions, facilitating – but not imposing – a productive reorganisation. A valuable book for clinicians seeking a fresh perspective.'

—**William B. Stiles**, Professor Emeritus, Miami University, Oxford, Ohio, USA

Principles-Based Counselling and Psychotherapy

A Method of Levels approach

Timothy A. Carey,
Warren Mansell,
and Sara J. Tai

Routledge
Taylor & Francis Group
LONDON AND NEW YORK

First published 2015
by Routledge
2 Park Square, Milton Park, Abingdon, Oxon, OX14 4RN

and by Routledge
711 Third Avenue, New York, NY 10017

Routledge is an imprint of the Taylor & Francis Group, an informa business

British Library Cataloguing in Publication Data
A catalogue record for this book is available from the British Library

Library of Congress Cataloging in Publication Data
Carey, Timothy A.
Principles-based counselling and psychotherapy: a method of levels approach/Timothy A. Carey, Warren Mansell, and Sara J. Tai.
pages cm
Includes bibliographical references.
1. Psychotherapy. 2. Counseling psychology. I. Mansell, Warren.
II. Tai, Sara. III. Title.
RC480.C298 2015
616.89′14 – dc23
2014046348

ISBN: 978-0-415-73877-4 (hbk)
ISBN: 978-0-415-73878-1 (pbk)
ISBN: 978-1-315-69577-8 (ebk)

Typeset in Times New Roman
by Florence Production Ltd, Stoodleigh, Devon, UK

Contents

Introduction

It is a tremendous privilege to be able to provide counselling and psychotherapy services to people experiencing psychological distress. We are continually humbled at the strength of the human spirit that people with psychological troubles demonstrate through their resilience and endurance. People place an enormous amount of trust in counsellors and psychotherapists when they bare their souls to them during programmes of psychological treatment. Sometimes, in only just a few minutes of meeting them, these people tell their counsellors or psychotherapists things that they have told no one else.

Given how debilitating psychological distress can be, we think it is important to constantly seek to improve the services provided by counsellors and psychotherapists. Unfortunately, despite the regular appearance of new and seemingly innovative approaches on the psychotherapy scene, there has not been a steady advance in the effectiveness or efficiency of our treatments. Many innovations are often only innovative at a superficial level and actually turn out to be recycled versions of well-established, more fundamental methods. Exposure is a good example of this. Exposure, in its broadest sense, occurs when people maintain an awareness of distressing images, thoughts, feelings, and objects for a prolonged period of time, and arrive at a different, less upsetting, understanding of these experiences than they had previously. Much of the stock available in the marketplace of psychotherapy techniques is, at its core, a way of promoting exposure, even though it might be packaged very differently (Carey, 2011a).

The approach we offer in this book is an invitation to focus less on the tools you might collect for your toolbox and to focus more on the principles behind why you might use each tool, and when and how it is used. We invite you to do this regardless of your therapeutic orientation – whether it originates in psychodynamic therapy, client-centred counselling, or cognitive behavioural therapies, for instance. We also recognise that the principles we describe will have relevance to wider disciplines that are concerned with mental health and well-being, such as psychiatry, nursing, social work, occupational health, and education. The principles will provide new insights and directions for working with people experiencing distress even for those who are not directly providing psychological therapies – such as support workers or advocates.

The aim of our book is to help to distil the underlying principles of alleviating psychological distress, rather than to add yet another therapy to the plethora of approaches available. There is a strong reason to believe that most psychotherapies 'work' on average (in the sense of helping people reduce psychological distress). Our goal is to distil the key principles of any form of counselling or psychological therapy that help it maximise its effects for each client. In this way, our book is designed to enhance reflective practice. For more than 40 collective years, we have been studying an explanation of behaviour that we think provides the key to significant and sustained improvements in the provision of counselling and psychotherapy treatments. The explanation is perceptual control theory (PCT; www.pctweb.org). We outline PCT in detail in this book, as well as its relevance to addressing human misery and internal mayhem.

Three fundamental principles are at the core of PCT, and our contention is that by understanding these principles, counsellors and psychotherapists will be able to work effectively and efficiently with a wide range of people experiencing a variety of manifestations of psychological distress. We think that successful approaches can be built from these principles, and we describe the Method of Levels (MOL; www.methodoflevels.com.au) that can be considered a transdiagnostic therapy that is based entirely on the three principles we present in this book.

The initial idea of MOL was suggested by William T. Powers (the originator of PCT), but this idea was then developed and refined in routine therapeutic practice. It has now been used successfully in different health-care contexts by different therapists with different clients and in different countries with different health systems. On the one hand, MOL lends itself particularly well to services in which there is an impetus for an effective and efficient method to get started earlier without a long assessment period, such as clients in primary care or in acute inpatient psychiatric wards, often where people might only attend a small number of sessions, or may wish to use therapy as a 'drop-in' service. On the other hand, it is particularly flexible for people who want therapy to be available for longer than the 'average' client (e.g. people with long-term conditions or complex interpersonal problems) or for people who wish to use therapy to make a long-term recovery and circumvent the problems of mental health diagnoses (e.g. recovery from psychosis). It is an intervention that can be used for everyday problem-solving, irrespective of mental health problems, and therefore also serves as a model for settings such as therapy supervision, teacher training, and co-counselling. In this book, we particularly focus on how a principles-based approach can refine clinical practice and serve as a training resource. It helps us to think about *why* we ask our clients a question at a particular moment about a particular topic, and *how* might be the most pertinent and simplest ways to ask these questions from the clients' perspectives.

Evaluations of MOL have consistently demonstrated that it is experienced helpfully by many clients. We provide detailed explanations of MOL throughout this book, as well as an abundance of examples from therapeutic practice to demonstrate and highlight important features of the approach.

In Chapter 1, we begin with a broad overview of mental health generally, and we present our rationale for why we think a principles-based approach to counselling and psychotherapy is overdue. We explain what we mean by a 'principles-based approach' and we describe some of the advantages of this way of working, as well as some of the difficulties that might be encountered in adopting this approach. When you get to the end of Chapter 1, you will be in a good position to assess how ready you might be to undertake working from this perspective.

We explain and explore the three fundamental principles that form the basis of the book in Chapter 2. Our stance is that control is what people do, conflict is what interferes with control, and reorganisation is what resolves conflict and restores control. Control, conflict, and reorganisation, therefore, are the cornerstone principles of our approach. The control that is the basis of PCT has a robust scientific foundation but, conceptually, it is nothing more than the process of making things be the way you want. Despite its conceptual simplicity, the phenomenon of control has profound implications for the life sciences, and none more so than in the area of understanding and treating psychological distress.

Some of the implications of these principles are explored in Chapter 3. PCT and its approach to control, for example, influences the way that ideas such as 'empathy' and 'objective' are understood. PCT also helps to clarify the change process in therapy and, in doing so, permits a more nuanced understanding of both the role of the therapist and the role of the client in facilitating change. 'Relativity' is not often discussed when psychological distress is being considered, but we explain its importance and relevance to any form of distress.

After discussing some of the general implications for therapeutic practice, we begin to focus on the specifics of therapy provision. In Chapter 4, we spend time clarifying the roles of both the therapist and the client from a PCT perspective. We illustrate, with a simple activity, how therapists might be able to become more aware of their own motivations in therapy by examining their inclination towards the different techniques and routines they use. We also describe the two fundamental goals an MOL therapist focuses on in each session and we consider the experience of the client in a programme of MOL therapy.

In Chapter 5, we extend the discussion from the previous chapter by shifting from considering the therapist and the client individually to focusing on the relationship they create together. We explain how the therapeutic relationship can be understood from a PCT perspective and we offer what might be the minimum requirement for therapeutic success in the context of the therapeutic relationship. To assist in learning, we also provide some short scripts of what a therapist might say to explain different points and we spend some time addressing how you might deal with potential difficulties in the therapeutic relationship.

Chapter 6 discusses some practicalities of therapeutic service provision in terms of how appointments are scheduled. We advocate for a client-led approach to appointment scheduling and we explain the benefits of this approach as well as how it can be implemented. While the way in which we decide how appointments are scheduled might seem like a fairly mundane aspect of therapy provision, it can uncover important assumptions and beliefs that therapists hold about how much therapy a client should have and who should decide when enough is enough in terms of therapy provision.

The thesis of Chapter 7 is that the therapeutic value of any technique can be enhanced by an understanding of the three principles we expound in this book. We illustrate this point using well-known examples such as activity scheduling, thought diaries, and mindfulness. Each of these techniques is helpful and meaningful for some people and inert for others. To magnify therapeutic potency, we suggest four components that we maintain are the necessary and sufficient ingredients whenever any technique is effective therapeutically. By focusing on these components rather than the strategy itself, therapists will be able to become more effective more of the time.

As we near the end of the book, we spend some more time addressing the nature of psychological distress and the general unhelpfulness of the current diagnostic categories in understanding disruptions to psychological functioning. Our contention in Chapter 8 is that it is important to focus on the distress underlying any particular symptom constellation rather than the symptoms themselves. We demonstrate, by reference to some widely used questionnaires, how implicitly symptoms are assumed to be distressing without this assumption ever really being verified. Formulation can be a valuable alternative to a diagnostic approach but formulation has problems of its own, so we propose that the principles-based approach that is offered in this book can even help to improve formulation.

While change is the basic remit of all approaches to counselling and psychotherapy, it is very difficult to find unambiguous definitions of change. Understanding change more clearly and then considering how it might be promoted most efficiently and effectively is the purpose of Chapter 9. We explain change from a PCT perspective that characterises the change process as non-linear and unpredictable. Lasting and satisfying change is not constrained by the time frames that counsellors and psychotherapists devise. Persistent psychological distress can be thoroughly resolved in any number of sessions. Sometimes a successful reorganising occurs after only a session or two, and on other occasions it takes many more sessions. A principles-based approach understands this and accommodates it. Recognising change as reorganisation has serious implications for counselling and psychotherapy, and we explore some of these in this chapter.

In the final chapter, we discuss some practicalities such as monitoring client progress and self-reflection but we also synthesise the information from previous chapters by providing an example of what an actual programme of MOL might look like. We discuss how MOL might be introduced in the first session and the way questionnaires might be used and integrated into therapy. We then discuss subsequent sessions and explain, in practical terms, how aspects such as client-led appointment scheduling can be implemented.

We hope you like this book but, more than that, we hope you are intrigued by it, challenged by it, and excited by it. For us, learning PCT and providing MOL has been a professional trip like no other. We think MOL is an excellent demonstration of what can happen when the principles of robust, accurate, and elegant scientific theories are applied with sensitivity and diligence. While it is exhilarating to be standing on the shore, with our backs to the familiar world of mental health disorders and psychological treatments, and to be contemplating the brave new PCT world of psychological well-being and human relationships, we have but yet dipped our toes in the water. The destination is clear but the journey is not. We would love it if we met up with you along the path.

Chapter 1

A principles-based approach to therapy

The what and why

By reading this chapter, you will learn:

1 what a principles-based approach is;
2 why a principles-based approach is important; and
3 what the advantages of a principles-based approach are.

Compromised states of mental health are a growing problem in society. National surveys, for example, estimate that as many as one in five people report experiencing symptoms of a mental health disorder in a 12-month period (e.g. Slade, Johnston, Oakley Browne, Andrews, & Whiteford, 2009). The mental health difficulties that people experience are costly to both the individual and society. They are costly to individuals in terms of miserable lives and unfulfilled potential, and they are costly to society in terms of lost productivity and an increasing demand for health services. The significance of mental health troubles is magnified if one considers the interrelatedness of mental health and physical health. Mental health issues are increasingly being recognised as important factors in chronic diseases, terminal illnesses, degenerative conditions, and substance use disorders.

The concept of disease burden is a way of quantifying the impact of disease and injury. The World Health Organization (WHO, 2008) estimates that mental health disorders make up '3 of the 10 leading causes of disease burden in low- and middle-income countries, and 4 of the leading 10 in high-income countries' (p. 46). For women, depression is the leading cause of disease burden in high-, middle-, and low-income countries (WHO, 2008). From a global perspective to national examples: in Australia, mental health disorders are the third most important determinant of burden (Andrews, Sanderson, Slade, & Issakidis, 2000), and they make the largest contribution to health-related nonparticipation rates in the labour force (Whiteford & Groves, 2009), while in Britain the picture is similar, with mental illness reported to account for over one-third of the burden of illness (London School of Economics, 2006). The Improving Access to Psychological Therapies (IAPT) initiative was prompted largely by a report in 2006 by the London School of Economics in which it was stated that mental illness had usurped unemployment as Britain's largest social problem. In the report, estimates were provided for potential savings to the government by treating people's mental health problems and thereby returning them to work and reducing the expenditure on incapacity benefits (London School of Economics, 2006).

Given the increasing prevalence of mental health problems, it is not surprising that demand for effective therapies for these problems is increasing. Consequently, there has been an unprecedented and unabated promulgation of new therapeutic options available to counsellors, psychotherapists, psychologists, cognitive behavioural therapists, psychiatrists, mental health nurses, and other mental health clinicians. Although the range of treatment options is expanding, this growth does not necessarily represent progress in terms of increased understanding or enhanced treatment effectiveness. Some research, for example, indicates that many bona fide therapies show equal effectiveness in terms of client outcomes when pooled across studies (e.g. Wampold, 2001). Furthermore, meta-analyses indicate that psychotherapy effect sizes may be declining over time or, at most, staying stable (Collins & Carey, 2015), which is the opposite of what would be expected if substantial progress was being realised in understanding and addressing psychological maladies. Additionally, while it has been estimated that the average person is better off than 80 per cent of untreated people (Asay & Lambert, 1999), this also means that 20 per cent of people who do not receive treatment are better off than 50 per cent of people who do receive treatment (Carey, 2006a). So, while researchers and therapists continue to develop new treatment options for people, we are not necessarily making great strides in enhancing the effectiveness or efficiency of the treatments we offer.

While the effectiveness and efficacy of psychological therapies is often, but not always, clearly demonstrated through various research programmes, a frequently overlooked aspect of therapy effectiveness is efficiency. It is rare to find studies that explicitly investigate the efficiency of psychological therapies, as well as their effectiveness or efficacy. To quantify just how scarce efficiency studies are in the literature, a database search was conducted in June 2014 of two of the most prominent journals in the field with regard to the evaluation of psychological treatments: *Journal of Consulting and Clinical Psychology* and *British Journal of Clinical Psychology*. Combining the search term 'efficien*' along with the title of the journal yielded a total of 93 articles but, of these, perusal of abstracts indicated that only four articles included an investigation of treatment efficiency as one of the main aims of the study.

We find this lack of empirical attention to treatment efficiency perplexing because we think efficiency should be regarded as a fundamental component of therapy effectiveness. Suppose that two therapies are equally effective in assisting people to resolve their psychological distress as assessed, perhaps, by changes in scores on standardised outcome measures. To achieve this change, however, people use an average of six sessions of Therapy A and an average of 11 sessions of Therapy B. In this situation, we would consider Therapy A to be a more effective treatment than Therapy B because it is more efficient. The difference in people requiring either six sessions (on average) or 11 sessions (on average) to achieve the same state of desired functioning has important implications for both the time it takes to function the way one would like to, and the difference in cost required to provide treatment of an average of either six or 11 sessions.

By including efficiency as an essential component of therapy effectiveness, we are not advocating for 'quick and dirty' approaches. Nor are we recommending a purely 'economic' attitude with regard to service provision. We believe therapy should be as long as necessary and no longer. We also believe 'as long as necessary' will be different for different clients: even clients who are ostensibly experiencing the same kinds of problems. If therapy remains focused on helping clients live the sort of lives they want to live, and if therapists see their role as, ultimately, to help the client get along without the therapist, then, all other things being equal, we do not think clients generally want to be 'in therapy' for long periods of time or even indefinitely. Ultimately, we think clients want to be 'out there' in the 'real world' living a life they value. Efficient therapists, therefore, might have an attitude of, ultimately, making themselves redundant to their clients. These therapists provide only as much therapy as the client requires and they understand that individual clients will determine what 'only as much' is. While therapists might be aware of how much improvement is *possible* for clients, they can never know (except by asking the client) how much improvement is *desired* by any particular client.

Therapies are needed, therefore, that can flexibly adapt to the various requirements of different clients. Focusing on the application of important principles of therapy rather than the utilisation of a range of specific therapeutic techniques and strategies can provide the required degree of flexibility while maintaining a high standard of effectiveness. To use a trivial example, someone who had a principle of 'eat a balanced diet' would be able to function effectively in a much broader range of contexts than someone who lived by the more specific directive of 'eat meat and three vegetables every day'. By basing one's practices on the application of foundational principles rather than the accumulation of different methods and activities, therapists will be able to be more helpful to more people more of the time.

Before discussing the way in which fundamental principles can be applied in therapy, it is necessary to explain what we understand a principles-based approach to counselling and psychotherapy to be and to outline why we think this approach is important. It will also be useful to describe some of the advantages of this approach, as well as trying to anticipate some of the difficulties you might encounter as you adopt this approach in your therapeutic practice. We will not be able to predict every possible problem of course, but we will discuss some typical concerns that might resonate with you. After beginning the book by considering what a principles-based approach is and why it is important, throughout the rest of the book we will describe the Method of Levels (MOL; Carey, 2006a, 2008a; Mansell, Carey, & Tai, 2012), which is a therapy based on three fundamental principles related to behaviour, psychological distress, and change.

What is a principles-based approach?

The online dictionary www.dictionary.com offers five explanations for the definition of 'principle'. Although the explanations are somewhat different, they all have something to do with a rule or a law that guides, or is the basis of, action or conduct. It seems that these rules can be professed or accepted but might also be fundamental or general laws, doctrines, or tenets.

Principles, then, can be accepted rules and norms or fundamental laws and tenets. They seem to be inherently involved in courses of action. Thinking of principles in this way suggests that principles are a ubiquitous and necessary, although sometimes perhaps unstated, aspect of day-to-day functioning. We think of principles as things such as honesty, respect, the laws of physics, or 'pursue a life worth living'. Sometimes, principles are expressed explicitly, such as 'Children should be seen and not heard', and sometimes they are more implicit. 'Wash your hands after you've patted the dog', for example, indicates a principle of hygiene. Sometimes, principles seem to be used to help achieve other principles. For instance, people might actually vary how tightly they adhere to their principle of honesty because, from time to time, it might be necessary to have a more relaxed approach to honesty in order to maintain respect and closeness (other principles) with a friend.

Principles are certainly involved in the conduct of counselling and psychotherapy. You might be able to remember conversations you have overheard or participated in where principles were discussed in some way. Statements such as 'It's a life-long illness', 'He's just not engaged in therapy', 'Your fluctuating moods are caused by a chemical imbalance', 'She's only doing it for attention', 'The client is the agent of change', 'Self-disclosure interferes with the process of therapy', and 'If we keep giving her more appointments, we're just reinforcing her behaviour' all reflect principles of one kind or another. Significantly, quite independently of the 'truth' or accuracy of any of these statements, they will have an important influence on the way therapists who subscribe to them interact with their clients. A therapist, for example, who believes that 'the client is the agent of change' will ask questions and introduce activities differently from the way in which a therapist who believes 'the treatment gets the client better' will ask questions and structure activities.

Surprisingly, despite the importance of principles to our general conduct and daily work, they seem not to be the focus of inspection when new therapies are being developed. In the field of counselling and psychotherapy, it is much more common to read books, attend workshops, and receive training in various techniques and strategies than it is to engage in professional development identifying and applying important principles. We think techniques and strategies are important but they are not important in and of themselves. The importance of techniques and strategies is in their ability to embody and apply particular principles. In fact, some techniques that appear quite different could well be informed by the same principle. Therapists who encourage their clients to paint or dance and therapists who encourage their clients to journal might all think that it is helpful to encourage the external expression of internal anguish even though the ways they promote this expression vary markedly.

So a principles-based approach to counselling and psychotherapy is one where the spotlight of attention shifts from techniques and strategies used in therapy to the principles underlying these methods. A principles-based approach is more interested in *why* counsellors and psychotherapists do what they do rather than *what* they do in any given session with any particular client. Paradoxically, by focusing on the principles underlying the practices of therapy, therapists will be able to be more creative and flexible with the techniques they use. After all, there are many different ways of achieving the same aim. Indeed, some therapists may even feel liberated since they will no longer be confined to particular courses of action by particular therapeutic modalities. Therapists who encourage clients to paint, for example, by recognising that they are actually applying a principle of 'expression', might be able to be more flexible and responsive to clients who seem reluctant to draw or paint. It could be that the way clients express themselves is less important than the actual expression occurring in some form. If clients shy away from painting or drawing, therefore, a responsive therapist could encourage clients to find their own best way of expressing those things they find difficult to think about. The challenge from this perspective is not to persuade the client to adopt the favoured activity of the therapist, but rather for the therapist to find the strategy preferred by the client that reflects the principle the therapist thinks is most relevant at that time.

As we discuss the importance of principles, we should qualify this information by explaining that we are not trying to lay down universal truths on stone tablets in this chapter. We are outlining *our* approach to principles-based psychotherapy and counselling. Other researchers and practitioners may consider principles differently. In 2006, for example, Castonguay and Beutler were the editors of an Oxford University Press publication titled *Principles of Therapeutic Change that Work*. The book has more than 40 chapter authors and presents the findings of a Joint Presidential Task Force of the Society of Clinical Psychology (Division 12 of the American Psychological Association) and of the North American Society for Psychotherapy Research. Information about the book on www.amazon.com states:

> This book transcends particular models of psychotherapy and treatment techniques to define treatments in terms of cross-cutting principles of therapeutic change. It also integrates relationship and participant factors with treatment techniques and procedures, giving special attention to the empirical grounding of multiple contributors to change. The result is a series of over 60 principles for applying treatments to four problem areas: depression, anxiety disorders, personality disorders, and substance abuse disorders.
>
> (www.amazon.com/dp/0195156846?tag=.asp-20)

In this book, principles are considered to be 'general statements that identify participant characteristics, relational conditions, therapist behaviours, and classes of intervention that are likely to lead to change in psychotherapy' (Beutler & Castonguay, 2006, p. 5). Table 1.1 provides a summary of the principles (Castonguay & Beutler, 2006a) that are described as 'empirically derived' or 'empirically grounded' (Beutler & Castonguay, 2006, p. 8).

While the depth and breadth of coverage of the research in the Castonguay and Beutler (2006b) text is impressive, our purpose in this book is somewhat different. The principles Castonguay and Beutler (2006b) offer are an eclectic mix of some specific, prescriptive statements and some global, indisputable statements (see Table 1.1). For example, principle 2.21 is 'Therapists should relate to their clients in an empathic way', principle 3.12 is 'Therapists should be able to skilfully use "nondirective" interventions', principle 1.212 is 'Client's expectations are likely to play a role in treatment outcome', and principle 3.21 is 'Time-limited therapy can be beneficial'. The principles we offer in this book, however, are different. Rather than over 60 principles, we offer just three, and we claim that these three principles are sufficient to develop a flexible, efficient, and effective therapy that can be used across a broad range of contexts and problems. These three integrated principles are based on a single, coherent, and robust theory, which articulates a rigorous explanation of human functioning. Throughout this book, you may be able to identify the way in which our three principles incorporate and accommodate the many more principles articulated in the Castonguay and Beutler (2006b) text.

Why is a principles-based approach important?

Perhaps the most basic reason for advocating a shift in attention from practices to principles is because the principles are there anyway. If principles are conceptualised as rules or guidelines describing how to go about our business, we contend that everyone has principles of some kind or another. Principles are part of the way we are designed. Principles are there all the time, mostly operating in the background, but nevertheless influencing goals for outcomes in important ways. Even something as vague as 'If what I'm doing isn't working, I just do something different' can be thought of as a rule or guide and, therefore, a principle. Therapists who attend numerous and varied workshops to keep up with the latest innovations, and amass collections of different strategies for their 'toolkit', may be following the 'do something different' rule.

If you reflect on your own practice and explore the reasons behind some of what you do, you might become aware of the principles you have developed regarding your own approach to therapy.

> *Do you conduct an assessment at the beginning of therapy?*
> Why do you do that?
>
> *Do you focus on building engagement and rapport?*
> Why do you spend time doing that?

Table 1.1 A summary of the common and unique principles of therapeutic change described by Castonguay and Beutler (2006a)

1.0 Participant characteristics	1.1 Observed characteristics	1.11 Common principles	1.111 Clients with a high level of impairment are less likely to benefit from therapy than those with a better level of impairment
			1.112 Clients who have been diagnosed with a personality disorder are less likely to benefit from treatment than those who are not
			1.113 Clients who face financial and/or occupational difficulties may benefit less from treatment than those who do not
		1.12 Unique principles	1.1201 Age is a negative predictor of a patient's response to general psychotherapy
			1.1202 Patients representing underserved ethnic or racial groups achieve fewer benefits from conventional psychotherapy than Anglo-American groups
			1.1203 If patients and therapist come from the same or similar racial/ethnic backgrounds, dropout rates are positively affected and improvement is enhanced
			1.1204 The most effective treatments are likely to be those that do not induce patient resistance
			1.1205 In dealing with the resistant patient, the therapist's use of directive therapeutic interventions should be planned to inversely correspond with the patient's manifest level of resistant traits and states
			1.1206 Patients with high levels of initial impairment respond better when they are offered long-term, intensive treatment, than when they receive non-intensive and brief treatments, regardless of the particular model and type of treatment assigned Patients with low impairment seem to do equally well in high- and low-intensive treatments
			1.1207 Patients whose personalities are characterised by impulsivity, social gregariousness, and external blame for problems benefit more from direct behavioural change and symptom reduction efforts, including building new skills and managing impulses, than they do from procedures that are designed to facilitate insight and self-awareness
			1.1208 Patients whose personalities are characterised by low levels of impulsivity, indecisiveness, self-inspection, and over-control tend to benefit more from procedures that foster self-understanding, insight, interpersonal attachments, and self-esteem than they do from procedures that aim at directly altering symptoms and building new social skills

		1.1209 Psychotherapy for anxiety is less likely to be successful if the client has low internal attributions of control or high negative self-attribution. Thus, rigid externalising or internalising coping styles are negative prognostic indicators
		1.1210 Therapists with, versus those without a history of substance use disorder appear to be equally effective in treating alcohol or illicit drug abuse
		1.1211 High-medical-risk smokers will be especially receptive to individual counselling for smoking cessation only if smoking plausibly contributed to their risk status
		1.1212 Although the evidence is not entirely consistent, cognitive behavioural therapy may be differentially effective with depressed smokers relative to comparison conditions. This prescriptive effect may apply especially to those smokers with chronic, recurrent depression
		1.1213 Therapists working with a specific personality disorder may increase their effectiveness if they receive specialised training with this population
1.2 Inferred characteristics	1.21 Common principles	1.211 Clients who experienced significant interpersonal problems during their early development may have difficulty responding to psychotherapy
		1.212 Client's expectations are likely to play a role in treatment outcome
	1.22 Unique principles	1.221 If psychotherapists are open, informed, and tolerant of various religious views, treatment effects are likely to be enhanced
		1.222 A secure attachment pattern in . . . therapist appears to facilitate the treatment process
		1.223 If patients have a preference for religiously oriented psychotherapy, treatment benefit is enhanced if therapists accommodate this preference
		1.224 Benefit may be enhanced when the interventions selected are responsive to and consistent with the patient's level of problem assimilation
		1.225 Therapy outcome is likely to be enhanced if the client is willing and able to engage in the treatment process
		1.226 The therapist is likely to increase his or her effectiveness if he or she demonstrates attitudes of open-mindedness, flexibility, and creativity
		1.227 The positive impact of therapy is likely to be increased if the therapist is comfortable with long-term emotionally intense relationships
		1.228 The benefits of therapy may be enhanced if the therapist is able to tolerate his or her own negative feelings regarding the patients and the treatment process

Table 1.1 Continued

		1.229 The therapist is likely to be more effective if he or she is patient 1.230 Smokers in more advanced stages of change, as defined in the transtheoretical model, are more likely to succeed in quitting smoking. Likewise, alcohol abusers reporting increased readiness to change face better in treatment
2.0 Therapeutic relationship	2.1 Quality of the therapeutic relationship	2.11 Therapy is likely to be beneficial if a strong working alliance is established and maintained during the course of treatment 2.12 Clients are likely to benefit from group therapy if a strong level of group cohesion is developed and maintained during therapy 2.13 Therapists should attempt to facilitate a high degree of collaboration with clients during therapy
	2.2 Therapist interpersonal skills	2.21 Therapists should relate to their clients in an empathic way 2.22 When adopted by therapists, an attitude of caring, warmth, and acceptance is likely to be helpful in facilitating therapeutic change 2.23 Therapists are likely to facilitate change when adopting an attitude of congruence or authenticity
	2.3 Therapist clinical skills	2.31 Therapists should be careful not to use relational interpretations excessively 2.32 When relational interpretations are used, they are likely to facilitate improvement if they are accurate 2.33 Therapists are likely to resolve alliance ruptures when addressing such ruptures in an empathic and flexible way 2.34 When working with depressed clients, therapists' use of self-disclosure is likely to be helpful. This may especially be the case for reassuring and supportive self-disclosures, as opposed to challenging self-disclosures 2.35 Providing feedback to the client is likely to be beneficial
3.0 Technique factors	3.1 Therapeutic stance and general interpersonal style	3.11 Positive change is likely if the therapist provides a structured treatment and remains focused in the application of his or her interventions 3.12 Therapists should be able to skilfully use 'non-directive' interventions 3.13 Therapists treating clients diagnosed with PD should be both honest and explicit about their limits 3.14 Therapists should not assume that clients diagnosed with PD possess the necessary cognitive or emotional capacities necessary for effective living

	3.15 The client's motivation for treatment is enhanced, and therapeutic change is most likely, if the therapist can address therapeutic impasses with non-confrontational strategies 3.16 The client's motivation for treatment is enhanced if the therapist is genuine and responsive 3.17 The client's motivation for treatment is enhanced when the therapist engages in strategic self-disclosure 3.18 The client's motivation for treatment is enhanced when the therapist conveys an understanding of how difficult it is for the client to change
3.2 Framework of intervention	3.21 Time-limited therapy can be beneficial 3.22 Therapeutic change may be facilitated by, or even require, intensive therapy 3.23 For the treatment of BPD, the therapist should plan to consistently apply treatment components over relatively long periods of time 3.24 Therapeutic change is most likely if the therapists treating the client in primary and auxiliary modes of therapy receive ongoing consultation and supervision 3.25 The client's motivation for treatment is enhanced if the individual therapist is flexible in his or her limits, being more available to the client during a period of crisis 3.26 Identify other social service or medical care needs and arrange for attention to these needs
3.3 Interpersonal/ systemic versus interpersonal/ individual procedures	3.31 A therapist may be more effective if he or she does not restrict him or herself to individual procedures: Being with others during treatment can be beneficial for some clients 3.32 Effective therapy may require therapists to address intrapersonal aspects of the client's functioning 3.33 Therapy outcome is likely to be enhanced if therapy addresses interpersonal issues related to clinical problems
3.4 Thematic/ insight-oriented versus symptom/ skill-building procedures	3.41 Therapy is likely to be beneficial if a therapist facilitates change in clients' cognition 3.42 The client is likely to benefit from therapy if the therapist helps him or her modify maladaptive behavioural, emotional, or physiological responses 3.43 Facilitating client self-exploration can be helpful
3.5 Abstract versus emotionally supportive procedures	3.51 Therapeutic change is likely if therapists help clients accept, tolerate, and, at times, fully experience their emotions 3.52 Interventions aimed at controlling emotions can be helpful

Do you set homework tasks?
Why?

When you see a client, do you book the next appointment with them?
Why?

It is likely to be the case that some principles are more robust and more useful than others; however, before decisions can be made about the value of any particular principle, it is first necessary to become aware of the principles that are currently followed.

Becoming aware of why you do what you do is an important aspect of working as a flexible and adaptive therapist rather than simply being a technician. In extreme circumstances, not being clear, accurate, and precise about why we are doing what we are doing or not having robust principles underpinning our practices can have disastrous consequences. The era of frontal lobotomies is perhaps the most relevant example to our work in counselling and psychotherapy. Superficially, it appeared that when people had part of their frontal lobes scrambled, they were no longer bothered by the troubles that had plagued them. We call this a superficial conclusion because the experience of the patients who underwent the procedure was not as straightforward as having their problems solved. Many of them became severely disabled and suffered irreversible changes to their personalities.

The thalidomide era is another chapter in medical history where a large number of children were born with malformed limbs because of a drug their mothers had taken to alleviate morning sickness during pregnancy. Although the development, administration, and consumption of the medication were all well intentioned, a lack of understanding about the full effects of the drug had devastating consequences. In time, will our current period of pharmacological treatment as the first, and sometimes only, option for people of all ages with a wide range of mental health difficulties be viewed in the same way that we now view frontal lobotomies and thalidomide? It is certainly the case that some people experience relief from their symptoms by taking medication, but it is also the case that the chemical imbalance principle, which guides the use of medication, is not supported by any scientific evidence (Moncrieff, 2009). Indeed, no physical or physiological anomaly that reliably identifies a psychiatric diagnosis has ever been discovered through scientific research (Timimi, 2011). Joanna Moncrieff (2009) is one of a growing number of psychiatrists who advocates for different principles to inform the practice of medication prescription for mental health afflictions.

In our own field, the panoply of techniques, strategies, and different therapies can be considered a consequence of a lack of attention to fundamental principles. Rosen and Davison (2003) insist that the field of psychotherapy should focus on empirically supported principles of change (ESPs), not empirically supported treatments (ESTs). The basis of their argument is that therapies that appear to be different may actually be applying the same principles. Any particular therapeutic protocol, therefore, could be thought of as being comprised of a component that is necessary for the clients to bring about change in their psychological state, and other components that may make the therapy unique but are not essential for change. Rosen and Davison (2003) suggest that this is the case with Eye Movement Desensitization and Reprocessing (EMDR). They cite evidence to suggest that the effectiveness of EMDR rests on well-established principles of exposure and that the unique elements of EMDR are inert aspects of treatment effectiveness.

Will we eventually learn the same lessons with other therapies? Therapists currently have a bountiful selection of therapeutic approaches to choose from. While the methods of each therapy and the scientific theories that inform them might vary considerably, how different are they *in principle*? Are mindfulness techniques and other attentional strategies simply novel and engaging ways of applying the principle of exposure? These methods are not currently described as applications of the exposure principle, but is it actually the fact that these therapeutic practices enable some people to examine experiential material they otherwise find difficult to focus on that is the key element of change?

Suppose five different people of about the same age all experienced depression following a long-term relationship break-up. As it happened, they all accessed a different therapy. The therapies they received were: Beck's cognitive behavioural therapy (CBT), behavioural activation (BA), acceptance and commitment therapy (ACT), cognitive analytic therapy (CAT), and interpersonal psychotherapy (IPT). At the beginning of therapy, they were all administered the same standardised depression questionnaire and they all scored in the severely depressed range. After 10 to 12 sessions provided over three to four months, they all scored in the normal range and they had all made a clinically significant change in their depressive symptomatology.

Each of the five therapies has quite different techniques, as well as different rationales for the manifestation and amelioration of depression. Is it likely to be the case that the five different people had five different variants of depression and yet, by some amazing stroke of good fortune, the person with the CBT type of depression saw the CBT therapist, the person with the BA type of depression saw the BA therapist, the person with the ACT type of depression saw the ACT therapist, and so on? There are 120 different ways that five people could be matched to five different therapies, so there was a 1 in 120 chance of getting the particular arrangement that occurred. Since counselling and psychotherapy has a much better chance than 1 in 120 of being effective, it seems probable that an explanation other than matching specific problems to specific therapeutic techniques is needed to account for the effectiveness that is achieved.

It is far more likely that each of the different therapies is comprised of an element that is necessary for therapeutic effectiveness and other elements that are not necessary. The element necessary for therapeutic effectiveness occurs whenever any therapy is effective and the other elements could be regarded as inert aspects of therapeutic change but important in the identity and demarcation of individual therapeutic modalities. So, for example, CBT is comprised of a 'bit' that is important for therapeutic effectiveness and a 'bit' that is important for identifying the therapy as CBT rather than some other therapy. Similarly, ACT and CAT have 'bits' that are key to their effectiveness and different 'bits' that demarcate them as ACT or CAT therapies.

Voltaire is attributed with saying that 'the art of medicine sometimes consists in amusing the patient while nature cures the disease' (Frances, 2013, p. 100). Perhaps the same could be said for psychotherapy. We may eventually discover that many of the techniques and strategies that demarcate different therapies are not crucial to the resolution of psychological distress but serve to 'amuse' the people accessing the therapy so that nature, in the form of an inbuilt error-reducing-balance-restoring mechanism, can remove the psychological distress.

We are going to suggest throughout this book that there are a small number of fundamental principles that are important to therapeutic effectiveness. All effective therapists incorporate these principles to some extent even though they may not be fully aware of them. We think therapists will be able to be much more effective and more efficient by increasing their awareness of these principles. Ironically, by shifting the focus from practices to general principles, therapists will have *more* options about the techniques they use. Rather than being tied to certain protocols, therapists can use their creativity and professional judgement to discover their own means of applying the principles that matter. Most importantly, this flexibility will make it easier to ensure that what you do therapeutically is more likely to fit with the range of needs that different clients have.

A more direct focus on fundamental principles of effective counselling and psychotherapy may, therefore, enhance progress for both research and practice. The evidence currently provides fairly clear information about what methods are likely to be most helpful to the greatest number of people, but we still cannot say with a great deal of confidence *why* these methods work when they do, and also why they are sometimes ineffective. Emphasising general principles that are linked congruently by a robust theory, rather than specific practices, could facilitate an unprecedented level of understanding and expertise.

In essence, then, a principles-based approach is an emphasis of focus, since all therapies are underpinned either explicitly or implicitly by principles. Our purpose in providing you with this book is to suggest that it is time to shift our attention away from techniques and strategies to the principles that underpin them. There have already been efforts to highlight the principles of various individual therapies (e.g. *General Principles and Empirically Supported Techniques of Cognitive Behavior Therapy*, O'Donohue & Fisher, 2009; *Introduction to Cognitive-Analytic Therapy: Principles and Practices*, Ryle & Kerr, 2002). There has also been work conducted to articulate therapy principles in general, such as the Castonguay and Beutler (2006b) publication we have already mentioned.

Our purpose here, however, is to demonstrate which principles of therapy are most appropriate through their alignment with a specific, robust theory of behaviour. Interestingly, the literature as a whole seems to allow a great deal of divergence between theory and principles. For example, the importance of reality testing is explicitly described in both Rogerian accounts of person-centred therapy and in Beck's cognitive therapy. Yet, their theories diverge considerably. Beck's cognitive theory clearly supports the principle of identifying negative thinking, but does not always support the principle of collaboration in practice, despite its vital importance to the effective delivery of cognitive therapy. Indeed, when one surveys a range of different theoretical accounts, it is principles rather than theories that seem to be shared across effective therapies (Mansell & Taylor, 2012). Indeed, Beutler and Castonguay (2006) 'believe that stepping outside of the box that is defined by our theories . . . may allow us to begin to better understand and help a wider range of patients' (p. 5). We are not sure if it is possible to step outside theories, but if it were, how would the terrain you would step into be negotiated? Surely a psychological theory should tell us which principles to focus on and which to disregard? Perhaps a desire to step outside current theories tells us something about the quality and utility of our existing explanatory frameworks. Rather than stepping outside theories, we embrace and endorse one particular, elegant, and sturdy theory of behavioural functioning. We would strongly advocate diving into this theory rather than stepping out of it.

So, which are the principles that we should use? We believe there are only a small number of foundational principles that are theoretically coherent and necessary to apply in counselling and psychotherapy. Our approach identifies, explains the rationale, and applies these principles to help people resolve their mental health issues effectively and efficiently.

The advantages of a principles-based approach

Counsellors and psychotherapists who adopt a principles-based approach will be able to work more flexibly with a wider variety of clients. By understanding important principles, therapists will have a greater sense of clarity about the necessary requirements for change and the way in which they can most efficiently and effectively contribute towards this. Issues of co-morbidity and complexity will not seem so daunting because fundamental principles are common to the diverse range of presenting problems and symptoms that people report, so they help to distil the essence of numerous, interconnected difficulties.

Attitudes of certainty and optimism may provide counsellors and psychotherapists with a renewed vitality for their work as they go about their business with greater precision. They will be much clearer about their role in the change process. Problems that were once seen as disruptive to the therapeutic process, such as lack of engagement, treatment resistance, or personality factors, may be considered differently and more constructively from a principles-based perspective. Therapists might feel more competent and confident providing their services.

Progress in the field generally could be expected to accelerate as the importance of underlying common properties is more widely appreciated. Research that provides useful information about therapeutically important principles of change will be highly relevant to therapists, and the findings of therapists from their routine daily practice will help to endorse research findings, as well as highlighting new areas for empirical investigation. Thus, a greater synergy between research and practice can be expected.

Therapists will become more discerning in their use of various therapeutic methods as they apply techniques more discriminately with greater awareness of the principles that are important. There may be a general loosening of allegiances to any particular therapeutic modality and greater communication and collaboration among therapists as the overlaps between different schools of therapy become more obvious. Even the distinction between specific and common factors may be de-emphasised in favour of greater interest in the links between principles and practices. Therapists and researchers may become interested in the different ways in which important principles can be applied in practice. There may even be an expansion of the variety of techniques available with a commensurate narrowing of the purposes for which these techniques are being used. Therapists may become less 'attached' to particular therapies and may be able to adapt more easily to the preferences and styles of different clients, so that if a client does not embrace a technique favoured by a therapist, a different way of applying the same principle can be adopted without disrupting the dynamics of the therapeutic process.

Adopting a principles-based approach might not be all plain sailing

While there are many advantages to a principles-based approach, learning to work in this way might not be completely problem-free. For some counsellors and psychotherapists, this could be a significant and uneasy transition. Learning anything new takes time, and sometimes during the learning process there can actually be an increase in uncertainty and confusion, and even a slight decrease in ability during the adjustment. When an accomplished tennis player begins to learn a new way of serving, their serve can become worse than it was before until they have reorganised and incorporated the new serve into their repertoire.

Some counsellors and psychotherapists might find it comforting to utilise specific strategies and techniques in a neatly prescribed sequence. It might feel daunting to be 'set free' from therapeutic protocols so that what to do in any particular session with any particular client is never entirely known beforehand. In some ways, a principles-based approach requires a greater level of independence and clinical judgement along with higher standards of professional conduct. It may be more desirable to be considered a therapist rather than a technician, but with this relabelling comes increased responsibility as well.

To some therapists, a principles-based approach might even feel somewhat 'messy' as answers are not known ahead of time. There will not be anyone to whom the therapist can turn to obtain the 'right answer' about what to do in any given situation. Therapists will not necessarily be able to plan specifically what they are going to do in upcoming sessions with clients. This uncertainty, however, also provides an increased ability to respond to the cues provided by the client. Over time, this ability to be responsive to different clients in order to achieve greater effectiveness may become even more treasured than the previous sense of surety that was gained from pre-planning sessions.

A principles-based approach, then, is not something to be entered into lightly. We are convinced it can transform the ways in which counselling and psychotherapy are conceptualised, designed, and delivered. We also think it will promote enhanced role clarity for therapists, as well as greater progress in the field. An increase in therapeutic effectiveness and efficiency, as well as a release for therapists from prescribed protocols, places a greater responsibility with therapists for the decisions they make. The difficulties that may be encountered in adopting this approach should therefore be considered before embarking on this adventure.

Summary of main points

- Principles are rules of conduct that influence goals for outcomes and are, therefore, an implicit but important aspect of counselling and psychotherapy. Principles can be specific and prescriptive rules for action or general laws that form the basis of conduct.
- Historical precedents indicate that there may be unrecognised but serious and even dangerous consequences when the important principles underlying particular practices are not well understood.
- A focus on a principles-based approach to counselling and psychotherapy could enhance the effectiveness and efficiency of current therapies and improve the clarity and certainty of therapists with regard to their role in the therapeutic process.
- Shifting the focus from practices to principles is a learning process that may be associated with increased uncertainty and confusion while concepts are being reorganised and integrated.

Topics for discussion

1 Therapies using quite different techniques could actually be applications of the same fundamental principles. Discuss.
2 If you were the Chief Advisor to the government for the establishment of an Institute for Expert Therapists, what would you insist were the two most essential things that the institute must include in their training? What would you make sure was never part of the curriculum of the institute? Why?

Activities for learning, consolidation, and fun!

1 Write down your five most important principles or ‘rules’ for providing effective and efficient therapy.
2 Think of a client you have worked with recently who you have seen more than once and expect to see again. What was the focus of the most recent

session you had with them? How many sessions have they seen you for already? What did you do in the session? Why did you choose these particular activities? What was the outcome? What will you do the next time you see this client? Why?

3 In a small group with some of your colleagues, generate a list of four or five things that you think make therapy effective (these could also be the things that are missing when therapy is ineffective). For each of these things, explain *how* they make therapeutic effective if 'effective' is considered to mean a reduction in psychological distress.

Chapter 2

The principles

Control, conflict, and reorganisation

By reading this chapter, you will learn:

1. what control is and why it is important;
2. how control can be disrupted;
3. just how common conflict is and why it can lead to problems; and
4. about a fundamental learning mechanism that helps keep everything in order.

In the first chapter, we explained the rationale for a principles-based approach to counselling and psychotherapy. We also explained that in our approach, we use a single, robust theory of psychological functioning that provides a small number of clearly defined and interrelated principles, rather than adopting a pragmatic collection of both general and specific principles from existing research (as carried out by Castonguay & Beutler, 2006b). We define our three principles in operational terms and in a significant amount of detail, but not as specific recommendations or instructions for particular therapeutic activities. The implications for conduct in therapy become apparent when the principles are considered in relation to individual clients and therapeutic situations. As you will see, the principles we use to guide therapy do not apply only to mental health and human beings; they are principles for how all living organisms function, survive, and thrive. Through a sequence of interviews across a wide range of contexts, we have found that these theoretically derived principles match closely with people's lived experiences of mental health problems and recovery (Alsawy & Mansell, 2013; Carey *et al.*, 2007; Gianakis & Carey, 2011; Higginson & Mansell, 2008; McEvoy, Schumann, Mansell, & Morris, 2012; Stevenson-Taylor & Mansell, 2012). We will define each of the principles in turn. The principles are: control, conflict, and reorganisation.

Control is ubiquitous in nature. It is unfortunate that, in recent times, the term 'control' has come to be associated with manipulation or coercion or the activity of tyrants. Although manipulation and coercion are forms of control, we mean something much more commonplace when we use the term. Cooperation and benevolence are just as clear examples of control as are bullying and intimidation. Standing upright is a control process, chopping tomatoes is a control process, cleaning teeth is a control process, tying shoelaces is a control process, blowing out birthday candles is a control process, and catching a bus is a control process. Autonomous control is a characteristic of living things. Tyrannical behaviour will certainly be included in our understanding of control, but so will admirable, altruistic, and even absent-minded behaviours. Winnie the Pooh is every bit as controlling as Attila the Hun.

What is control?

A colloquial understanding of control is conceptually very similar to a formal definition of the phenomenon. In everyday terms, 'control' could be thought of as: 'Making something happen the way you want'. Sometimes, that involves persuading other people to do things in a particular way, but it also includes keeping your car where you want it to be on the road, making sure your DVD player records your favourite show while you work late, and ensuring your lounge room stays as dust- and clutter-free as you prefer.

A formal definition of control is: 'Achievement and maintenance of a preselected perceptual state in the controlling system, through actions on the environment that also cancel the effects of disturbances' (Powers, 1973, p. 283). While this sentence might seem very different to the more casual definition offered in the paragraph above, three essential elements are the same. Two of these elements are directly stated and the third is implied.

Although we need to talk about these elements in a sequential way, it is important to realise from the beginning that the three elements all occur simultaneously. This realisation is important in order to accurately understand the process of control. Control is not a start-stop, cause-effect process. It is an ongoing, dynamic process in which the separation of causes and effects is often arbitrary and even unnecessary. The humble eye-blink reflex in relation to a puff of air illustrates the tightly coupled nature between effects and causes that reveals a process of circular, rather than linear, causality. In order for a puff of air to be followed by a blink, some preconditions need to be in place. First, the eye needs to be a living eye – dead eyes do not blink. Second, the puff of air needs to land on the surface of the eye. A puff of air on the elbow or ear lobe will not produce the same effect as a puff of air aimed directly at the eye. Why are these two preconditions important for the puff of air to 'work' in terms of producing a blink? It turns out that the surface of the eye has a particular moisture level that is maintained by blinking. When the puff of air lands on the surface of the eye it has the effect of changing the moisture of the eye's surface. The blink, however, has the effect of restoring the surface moisture to the pre-blinked level. So is the blink a cause? Well, yes. It is *both* cause and *caused*. It is *caused* by the puff of air and it causes a change in the moisture level on the surface of the eye. Is the blink an effect? Well, yes. It both *is* an effect and it *produces* an effect. The blink is the effect of the puff of air and the effect of the blink is a change in the moisture level on the surface of the eye.

Understanding the three elements of control enables us to make sense of the way in which the effects of causes and the effects of effects can actually be the same effects. With circular causality, something can be both a cause and an effect depending on your point of view and how you decide to analyse an event. Often, in order to identify causes and effects, one has to draw arbitrary lines that specify when a particular event starts and stops. On occasion, this can be helpful in analysing different aspects of behaviour, but in order to understand the behaviour as accurately as possible, the extracted segment must, at some time, be placed back into the context of the behaving creature. By focusing on the three elements we are introducing here, it becomes unnecessary to isolate samples of behaviour in order to identify causes and effects.

The first element that is obvious from both the colloquial and formal definitions is some 'desired state of affairs'. One definition calls it 'the way you want' and the other definition calls it 'a preselected perceptual state'. It is known by other names too. We could think of this element as a need, want, goal, dream, outcome, benchmark, desire, ideal, value, hope, directive, rule, standard, expectation, and so on. Each of these everyday terms implies subtly different kinds of 'wants'. For example, a 'hope' might be one that we feel strongly about but may struggle to achieve, whereas an expectation is typically achieved but not necessarily desired so strongly. A goal, such as to win a race, may be achieved over the space of a few hours whereas an 'ideal' may never be met fully over a lifetime. Yet, in every case, these words relate to the way in which some aspect of the world *should be.* Even the term 'should' is too restrictive, but we will use this term to stand for all of the above terms. The reason that we can include all of these different terms under one umbrella term is because of a focus on the mechanics of the process to which each of these terms point. Our stance is that the acts of observing a rule, maintaining a value, and chasing a dream all unfold the same way. Different actions will undoubtedly be involved in each case but the underlying process will be the same. For us, it is the way a process 'works' that is critical rather than the particular word labels used to name the process.

The second obvious element describes effort or activity. The casual definition specifies 'making something happen' while the formal definition describes 'actions on the environment'. Both statements therefore suggest that control does not happen serendipitously or by accident. Desired states of affairs are sculpted, fashioned, and hewn. So, control involves specifying the way in which we think some aspect of the world should be and also effort or activity to bring about this desired state of affairs. By the time we become adults, we are usually so good at controlling that we seldom notice the actions we use to maintain control. As a thought exercise, imagine what your appearance would look like in a week from now if you took absolutely no action whatsoever between now and then to affect your appearance. Spending time reflecting on the image that would greet you from the mirror in seven days' time if you suspended all appearance-directed activity might help you appreciate the subtle and ongoing ways in which we use actions to produce control.

The implied element that has been left unspecified so far is that of detecting, noticing, perceiving, sensing, or experiencing. In order to be able to act to make the world be as it should be, we have to know how the world currently *is*. Control, in fact, could be described as a process of making what *is* match what we think *should be* – or keeping the difference between *is* and *should be* as small as possible. So, we have to remain aware of how the world *is* – or at least that aspect of the world we are controlling – constantly. If we take our eye off the ball, control will be compromised. We cannot control the volume of the television or the al dente-ness of pasta if we cannot tell what the volume of the television is or how firm the pasta currently is.

The process of acting to make the world we experience match some internally specified standard is, quite literally, a matter of life and death, for all living things. Even a single cell will only survive for as long as it can keep its internal state stable in the midst of fluctuations in the external conditions surrounding it. The phenomenon of control is so fundamental it can be thought of as a defining feature that separates living from non-living things. Living things control autonomously – that is, their standards are internally calibrated – whereas non-living things do not.

Some non-living things, such as temperature control systems in buildings or cruise control devices in cars, are organised to control, and mimic very closely the way living things behave. Non-living control systems, however, have their standards set by an external controller. When you push on a rock, it moves in direct proportion to the force applied to it. When you push on a living creature, however, the result is not nearly so predictable. Non-living things do not care what happens to themselves, but living things do.

A temperature control system does not decide for itself how warm or cool it will be inside the doors of the Grand National on the corner of 16th and Main, and a cruise control device does not have its own preference for the speed at which the Volkswagen Eos 155TSI motors down the M5. Living things, however, set their own standards for those things they like to experience. Brand new babies have preferences for how dry or how fed they like to feel, and adults have their own unique standards for how fast they like their car to travel, how long they like their fingernails to be, how overdrawn they like their bank account to be, how tanned they like their skin to be, and so on.

All living things control, and they control using the three essential elements we have described. For single cells to exist and to continue existing in the chemical soups they inhabit, they have to be able to act on their very limited environments to ensure that certain internal quantities and conditions remain in particular states. Even a single cell has a *should be*, a way of detecting what *is*, and the ability to keep the difference between the two at a minimum. The Princess cichlid that swims around its tropical aquarium has to be able to control the way it experiences the variable states of its aquatic environment, such as the speed with which it locates and ingests food and the distance between it and its aquatic cohabiters. If the cichlid is not able to control these important variables, or if the conditions of the tank change so that control is impossible, the fish will perish.

Emperor penguins at the South Pole control, Bactrian camels of the Gobi Desert control, giraffe-necked weevils of the Amazon rainforest control, and cats and rats and elephants control. In fact, all living things control for as long as they continue living.

How does control work?

Given the importance of control, it is not surprising that the topic is discussed widely in the psychology and mental health literature. In 1996, for example, Ellen Skinner published a paper listing over 100 different constructs of control. Included in the list were terms such as behavioural control, instrumental control, and control beliefs, as well as less obvious control-related concepts such as expectancy, agency beliefs, responsiveness, and learned helplessness (Skinner, 1996).

Noticeably absent from Skinner's (1996) paper, however, was any suggestion of how control works. We think understanding how something works is an essential prerequisite to using that something effectively and efficiently. Since we are in the business of helping people solve problems and reduce psychological distress so that they can live their lives more as they would like to, and since 'living their life more as they would like to' is fundamentally a control process, we think it is important to understand how control works. In fact, we think it is important to understand how anything works when one is attempting to modify or improve that thing. A car mechanic who did not understand how car engines worked would not be able to fix cars regularly and routinely. A computer repairer who did not know how computers worked would not be able to address the problems of a broken computer efficiently. An electrician who did not have a sound knowledge of the way in which electricity worked would actually be a dangerous tradesman to have in your house. Because these people understand the workings of the objects to which they apply their trade, they are able to work systematically and successfully to restore optimal functioning. Much of the field of psychotherapy and counselling, however, is not based on an accurate understanding of how people function, so while many therapists are very successful with their clients, we think they are successful serendipitously rather than systematically. We say serendipitously because, when therapy does not go according to plan, we do not have a robust and uniform approach to analysing and correcting the problem. The many hundreds of different therapies that are currently available is strong evidence of the fact that we currently have no clear idea of the best way to go about helping people experiencing psychological distress. If we are to help people systematically to resolve psychological distress and live more of the life they would like to, we think it is important to understand the way in which the process of living actually 'works'. In this sense, we think of the process of living as a process of control.

Although control is discussed just as frequently in the mental health literature as it is in the more general psychology literature, an explanation for how control works is also missing here. It is widely recognised that attentional control, behavioural control, emotional control, impulse control, and so on are all important aspects of mental health. What is not so clear is how control actually occurs.

The working explanation of control that we use is described in perceptual control theory (PCT; Powers, 1973, 2005; Powers, Clark, & McFarland, 1960a, 1960b). PCT explains the way in which the three components we have described – specifying the way the world *should be*, noticing the way the world *is*, and acting to make sure *is* matches *should be* – fit together to produce the phenomenon of control. Figure 2.1 (from Carey, 2008b) illustrates the way in which these components are connected to produce a negative feedback loop. This little loop is known as a control system and is regarded as the basic building block of life from a PCT perspective.

Figure 2.1 is a particular kind of diagram, and not the kind we might be familiar with from clinical formulations – it is not based on self-reports, for example. In Figure 2.1, you will also notice single letters such as '*r*' and '*e*' and '*p*', as well as two simple equations: $e = r - p$; and $qi = a + d$. We will not go into the technical details here (and there are many more details such as 'leaky integrators' and 'delays'), but it is important to realise that the diagram in Figure 2.1 is regarded as the beginnings of a blueprint for making something that works. When an

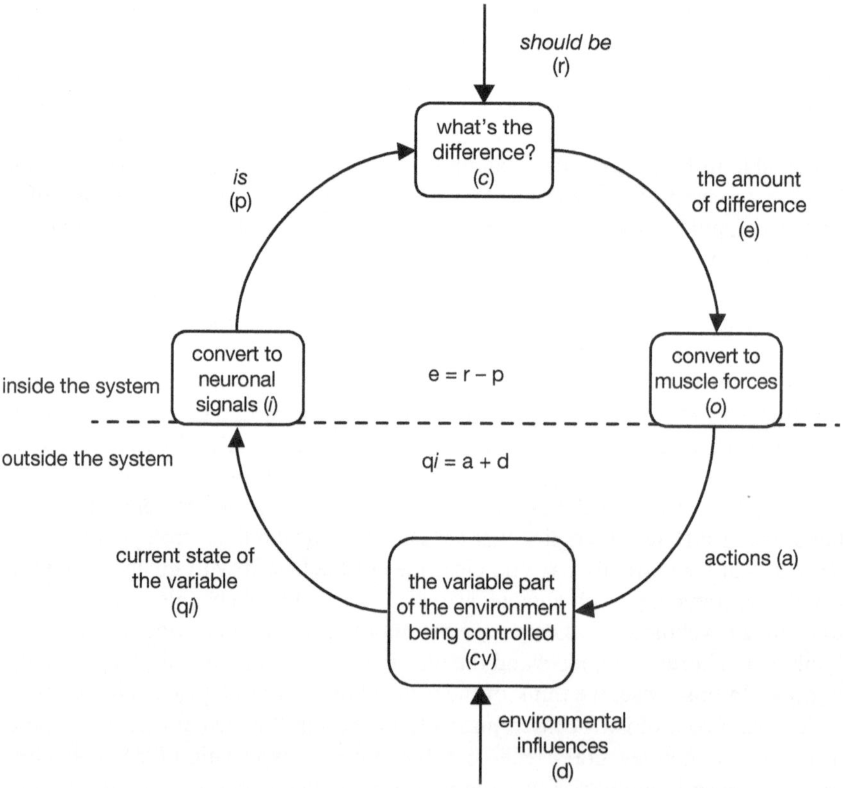

Figure 2.1 The basic unit of PCT: a closed causal negative feedback loop
Source: Copyright © *International Journal of Cognitive Therapy*, 2008, reproduced with permission

architect draws a plan of a house, it is with the intention of constructing an actual dwelling from the plan. This is a very different perspective from the way models and diagrams are usually considered in psychology. Models in psychology are generally hypothetical – *conceptual* or *statistical*, but they are hardly ever *functional*. Functional models have to resemble what actually happens in real life, so they are much more robust and are tested far more rigorously than conceptual or statistical models (Marken & Mansell, 2013). A functional model is more accurate and more precise. It is this exacting and stringent nature of model building that is the primary reason that we prefer the PCT model to other models that might try to explain one or more aspects of control. In this sense, it is even hard to compare PCT with other theories because it requires comparing a functional model to a statistical or conceptual model. A comparison of that nature is a bit like comparing a teaspoon with a satellite. Once other theories are expressed in functional terms, then useful comparisons could be made by considering which functional theory provides the model that most closely simulates the phenomenon under investigation.

Also, because the important terms in the PCT model are defined precisely and quantitatively, there is the opportunity to be very clear when communicating. The '*r*' in the diagram is the 'should be' that we described by various terms. In a sense, it does not matter whether someone uses the word 'goal' or 'objective' or 'dream' or 'plan' or 'hope' or 'expectation', as long as what they mean when they use the word is the '*r*' in $e = r - p$. In PCT, it is important to understand the relationships between variables; the particular word terms that are used to label the variables are not of fundamental importance.

The equations in this model describe the process of negative feedback. In this context, 'negative feedback' does not mean critical opinions or harsh judgement. The 'negative' refers to the process of acting in the world to *reduce* the error or the difference between *should be* and *is*, so that goals are achieved, needs met, and ideals realised. It is also important to note that Figure 2.1 describes the working of a basic building block in the nervous system. A mature human may have billions of these neuronal control systems arranged hierarchically and in parallel, rather like the branching, entwined roots of the trees in a forest. The '*should be*s' at the trunk of the trees are deeper and more fundamental (e.g. to be a kind person) whereas the '*should be*s' at the fine root tips are those that apply to the current moment (e.g. to hold a child's hand to cross the road). They are interrelated, and the way we control experiences in the present moment are guided by the longer-term ways we want ourselves and the world to be. This dynamic, layered process is control in action.

The other benefit of paying attention to a functional model rather than a conceptual or statistical one is that the results can be surprising and illuminating. It turns out that, in order to make a model function in a way that controls like a living creature controls, it is the input that must be controlled, *not* the output. In practical terms, this means that when we control (which is all the time), what we control is what we sense or experience, and not the way we act. Our actions are the variable means by which we keep our experiences in their *should be* states. This principle might seem counterintuitive at first, but is easily demonstrated by an example. When you are driving your car, the actions could be thought of as the way you move the steering wheel and the way you apply pressure to the accelerator, brake, and clutch pedals. Your experiences or senses would include what you see as you look through the windscreen and look down at the speedometer and fuel gauge, and also what you hear and what you feel as you travel along. Clearly, when you set out in your motor car, you do not have strong preferences about how much pressure to apply to the accelerator or where your hands should be on the steering wheel. You do have strong preferences, however, for where your car is on the road, how far behind the car in front it is, what the colour of the traffic lights are, how fast your car is travelling, and so on. Driving could be summarised as a process of making your car travel at the speed you want it to and in the direction you want it to. Certainly, what your hands and feet are doing will influence this, but so will the conditions of the road on which you find yourself. On a busy road, you will produce different actions than on a quiet road. In fact, if you drive to work, you will produce different actions every day you drive *exactly the same route* because the route is never exactly the same. It was, apparently, Heraclitus who first put forward the idea that 'You never step into the same stream twice', and this sentiment captures well the nature of the variable environments we inhabit. We are, in fact, so good at controlling that we do not notice the amount of variability there actually is. It turns out that our actions are in a very precise and intricate relationship with the environment so that the way we act at any point in time is *jointly determined* by both the difference between *should be* and *is* and the current circumstances in the environment. These are the types of learnings that are possible from a functional model developed from a robust theory, and it is the implications of learnings such as these that have informed the therapy described in this book.

A model of normal functioning

So, control is the natural state of play for living things. It is the standard of 'normal functioning', if you like to think of it that way, from which models and explanations of disrupted functioning can be developed. This highlights another advantage of the PCT model. Most current models in mental health are models of disorder or dysfunction, but the model of normal functioning that people might return to after engaging in some effective psychological treatment is not specified. When therapy is effective, does it mean that people will never have any more negative automatic thoughts or dysfunctional assumptions? Will they constantly be mindful and 'in the present moment'? Will all of their doubts and worries be forever removed and will they always be motivated to achieve their goals? These questions are difficult to answer without a benchmark of routine functioning to refer to.

From a PCT perspective, normal functioning occurs when people are able to control the things that are important to them about as well as they would like to.

Control is not always perfect and life is never problem-free, but we would consider routine day-to-day living to be a process of creating and maintaining desired experiential states. People who function 'normally' experience hassles and, sometimes, even serious problems from time to time. Normal people get anxious and worried and frightened and despondent and forlorn, as well as exhilarated and playful and chirpy.

We find this perspective helpful in approaching the provision of psychological treatment because we are not trying to turn people into superheroes. Neither are we saying that there is a set 'prototype' specifying exactly how people should function. Successful therapy does not mean a problem-free life. It also does not necessarily mean people will 'self-actualise' and never think another bad thought or that they will score zero or in the 'normal' range on some symptom measure of depression or anxiety or some other problem. We think therapy is successful when people are able to resolve their psychological distress and re-engage in the life they are creating for themselves. More than anything, we think that the people who are accessing the treatment are the best judges of when treatment has been effective and when they have had enough. So, from the principle of control, implications for how therapy is applied and delivered begin to emerge. We will elaborate on these important aspects of therapy throughout the book.

Disruptions to normal functioning

There is no doubt that life has more downs than ups for some people some of the time. Because we understand life to be a process of control, we conceptualise problems from that perspective too. An event or experience, therefore, will be a problem to the extent that it interferes with someone's ability to control. There are a limited number of ways that this can happen. One obvious way is through physical damage to the system. If control systems are damaged or destroyed, such as by accident or disease, a person can lose the ability to control things that are important to them. Paraplegia and multiple sclerosis would be examples here. Apart from physical damage, there are three other general ways in which control can be compromised. Figure 2.1 provides some clues. Satisfactory control will be prevented if there is an absence of r or if d becomes too great. Having no r would mean not having a standard or goal or expectation of what should occur. If you are invited to a traditional wedding by a friend from another culture, you might be unsure about the correct procedures to follow. What should you wear? Should you take a gift? What do you do when you arrive at the ceremony? All of these queries relate to not being able to set standards or goals for yourself. If you are not able to set a *should be*, you will not be able to reduce the difference between *should be* and *is*. On the other hand, if you are driving to the wedding and you suddenly encounter some black ice on the road and your car starts moving independently of your efforts with the steering wheel, this is an example of a situation where the forces of d (environmental influences) can be overwhelming. Both absent rs and insuperable ds will interfere with control.

These effects, however, tend to be rather transitory. Once you arrive at the wedding, you might ask people what you need to do, or you might ask your friend before the wedding for a 'briefing' on the correct procedures, or you might have even done some reading on the Internet to find out what might be expected. Similarly, when you realise you are driving on ice, you might employ different driving strategies, and once you get to a safer stretch of road you might choose a different route or apply some other action. This may mean that some inabilities of control never reach clinical proportions. In terms of *r*, most people become able to hold conversations, requiring all kinds of references in the social world (language, rules, etiquette) despite there being a time in childhood when this was impossible for them. In terms of *d*, the majority of people recover from acute traumas over time. We would propose that when recovery does not occur, this is either because the environment continues to be overwhelming (e.g. hostage situations) or that the next principle plays a pivotal role.

The second important principle is conflict. Conflict can retard control processes far more chronically, pervasively, and debilitatingly than the problems we have described so far. Control will be impaired when two interconnected control systems attempt to create two incompatible experiences (i.e. two opposing *should be*s are specified) simultaneously. This type of conflict can have devastating consequences.

Conflict

Conflict is the main psychological problem for control systems (Carey, 2006a, 2008c; Mansell *et al.*, 2012; Powers, 1973, 2005; Powers *et al.*, 1960a, 1960b). Conflict occurs when, as one control system decreases the difference between *should be* and *is*, this has the effect of *increasing* the *should be*/*is* discrepancy for another control system. As the other control system responds to reduce its *should be*/*is* separation, it inadvertently pushes apart the *should be* and *is* of the first control system. Figure 2.2 (Carey, 2008b) provides an illustration of this arrangement.

An important point to notice about Figure 2.2 is the hierarchical arrangement that is necessary for the creation of intrapersonal conflict. We mentioned earlier that the single control system is regarded as a building block. These building blocks are organised in parallel and hierarchically to form the neural network of individuals. Any control system in the network receives its reference signal from one or more systems at the level above and it control its own perceptual signal by varying the references of systems at the next lower level. In Figure 2.2, it is clear that a system at the highest level is sending signals to two systems at the next lower level and these systems are sending signals to a still lower level. Thus, from a PCT perspective, conflict is considered to occur across at least three levels of the hierarchy: the lowest level is where erratic and unstable behaviour manifests; the middle level is the level of the incompatible goals; and the highest level is the level that is actually establishing the context for the conflict by generating the incompatible references.

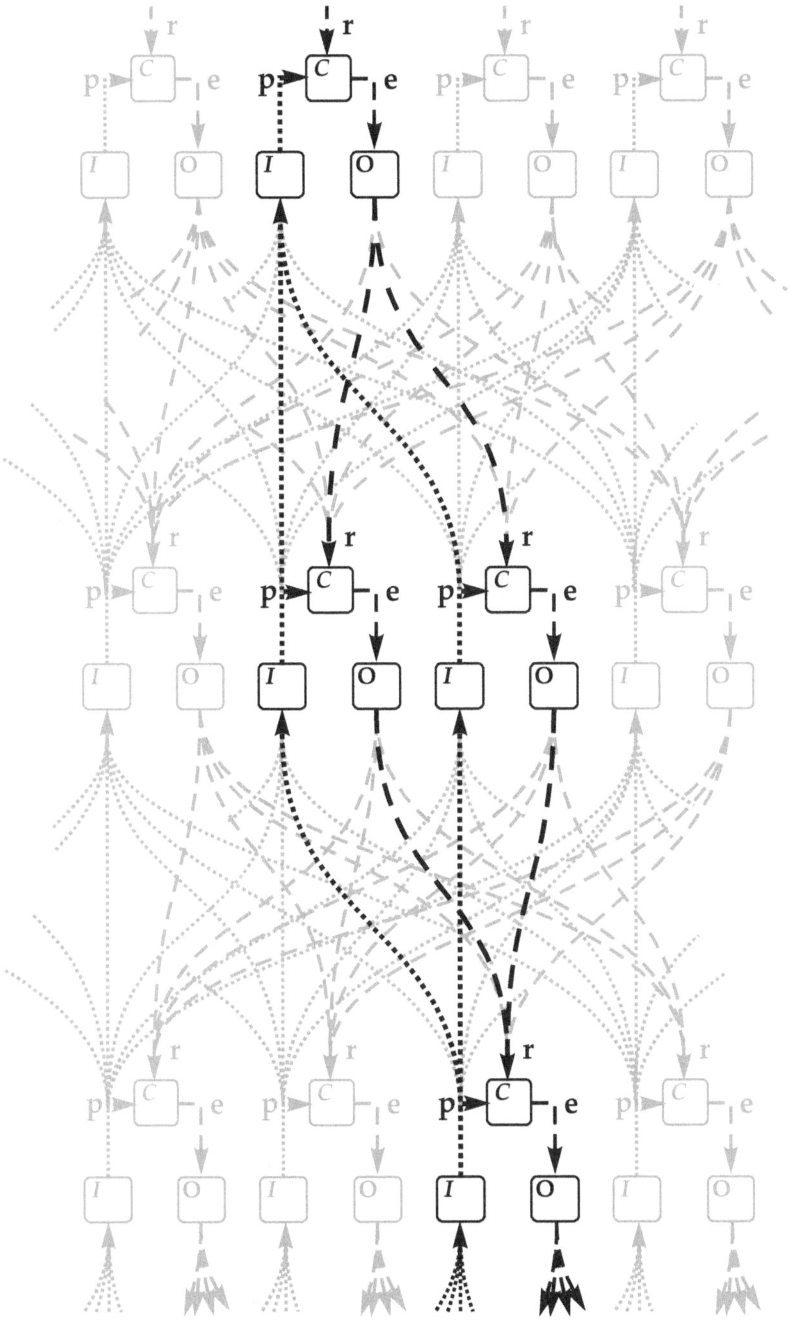

Figure 2.2 A PCT model of conflict

Source: Copyright © *International Journal of Cognitive Therapy*, 2008, reproduced with permission

Despite the devastating effects it can have, conflict is actually an extremely common occurrence. In fact, from a PCT perspective, any choice situation is, by definition, a conflict. If you have the option of holidaying in an apartment by the beach in Dubrovnik or a summer alpine holiday in a chalet in La Clusaz, it might be difficult to choose between the two. You might think about the advantages of both and spend time weighing up the pros and cons. For as long as the holiday destination remains undecided, these two options will be on your mind. You might find holiday thoughts 'popping' into your mind at different times throughout the day. Sometimes, it could seem like you cannot stop thinking about it. Your friends might even complain that all you seem to talk about these days is your holiday. As the period of indecision draws out, other considerations might come into play, such as missing the best deal if you do not book the holiday soon.

Some people would easily be able to choose between a holiday at the beach or one in the mountains. In fact, for some, it might not even be a choice at all because the options are so unevenly weighted. For others, though, having these two options before them presents a period of indecision and quivering inactivity. From a conflict perspective, it is easy to understand why people who have trouble making decisions are sometimes described as 'dithering'. The immobility of conflict produces exactly that state of oscillating within the confines of the two choice options.

If this conflict scenario concerns not a holiday, but issues such as the sort of life that should be lived, then it might be easy to appreciate how much more devastating the consequences can be. For example, if a person stays at home away from people to feel safe, but also wants to leave home to experience the acceptance and affirmation of social relationships, this significant conflict would be likely to generate distress on a daily basis. One client described having a 'thirst for life' and a 'desire for oblivion'. It might be easy to appreciate how completely the battle between these two states would usurp the ability to live a life of meaning and value.

There is a psychotherapy based on the principles of PCT, known as the Method of Levels (MOL), which targets conflict directly. The importance of the word 'levels' in this therapy can be appreciated by examining Figure 2.2. It is understood from a PCT perspective that, despite the different manifestations that psychological distress can have, it has a common basis – chronic internal perceptual conflict. Conflict is the ultimate 'wanting to eat your cake and have it too', 'being caught between a rock and a hard place', and 'biting the hand that feeds you' with regard to important values and life goals:

'I want to achieve great things and be better than other people but I also want to just let things happen and go with the flow.'

'I want to forget the past and move on, but the past was important in making me who I am and I want to make sure I never forget where I came from.'

'I want people to like me and think I'm fun to be around but I also want people to take me seriously and agree with my opinions.'

'I know there's no point but I still want to know what the point is.'

'I want to let go and move on but what we had was really special and I don't want to let go of it.'

Conflict is the 'double-edged sword' that so often confronts us in daily life. From the conflict perspective of psychological distress, there are always two sides requiring attention. One gloomy thought will not lead to despair on its own. We think there is a *relativity* to psychological distress that is often not fully appreciated (Carey, 2006a, 2009). The concept of relativity is discussed further in Chapters 3 and 8. A thought that 'life is meaningless' is itself meaningless on its own. If the thinker of this thought belonged to a spiritual or religious group that emphasised the power of an interconnected universe and the insignificance of humans, then a thought that life was meaningless might be entirely appropriate and bring solace and comfort. If, on the other hand, the thinker had been pursuing an existence of purpose and worth, then a thought that life was meaningless could be a shattering experience. The point here is that it is not the thought on its own that produces particular feelings. It is the thought *in the context of other thoughts* that will be associated with contentment or despair.

A person who had an uncomplicated 'thirst for life' might be passionate about what they do and involved in a variety of activities. They might have a fulfilling career, participate in community activities, and enjoy engaging and challenging hobbies. Similarly, a person with a 'desire for oblivion' would take the necessary steps to end their life successfully and completely. It is when both these specifications exist in the same head at the same time that neither one is able to be satisfactorily achieved.

It is, therefore, the juxtaposition of dichotomous yet equally important beliefs, attitudes, and values that sows the seeds of psychological distress. It is having a thirst for life *relative to* a desire for oblivion that generates despair. When this configuration remains in place chronically, mental health disorders in their myriad of manifestations can flourish. Hating your parents for the abuse you suffered at their hands when you were a child but also believing that it is a sin to hate your parents will produce despair and discontent until these opposing mind states can be reconciled.

Far from being a model of 'dysfunction', however, the conflict formulation of psychological distress requires robust, well-functioning control systems to achieve its most debilitating effects. Powers (2005, p. 266) points out that the 'worst aspect of conflict between control systems is that the higher the quality of the control systems, the more violent and disabling the result of the conflict'. For example, people describing themselves as perfectionists are often highly skilled at noticing the mistakes in their own and other people's work because they believe this is important for self-improvement. Couple this perfectionistic tendency with a natural desire to be unconditionally accepted by others, and there is a potential for conflict to occur within the individual as they apply their own stringent standards of perfectionism to an unrelenting desire to be accepted by others at all times.

Given how common conflict situations are – for the most part, benignly disguised as daily choices – there is every reason to conclude that we are normally very adept at resolving conflict. We do not stand jittering in front of the fridge deciding between the Chardonnay or the Sauvignon Blanc. Nor do we fail to turn up for work because we are immobilised in the bathroom unable to choose L'eau D'issey over Coco Mademoiselle or the other way around. We do not even delay our children's entry to school because we are unable to decide between a private or a public education. Fortunately, we have a range of well-learned and well-used strategies that enable us to prioritise and sort choices into satisfactory results. Even when conflict seems intractable, however, according to PCT, we have an inbuilt learning mechanism that restores order to the system. So, how exactly is order restored?

Reorganisation: the change that occurs when you do not know what change to make

Clearly, mature humans are not born with their repertoire of values, beliefs, and attitudes already established and intact. While the propensity to build neuronal control systems might be part of our genetic inheritance, the specifics of what precisely these control systems control is added in as we grow and develop. A learning mechanism, therefore, must also be part of what we inherit. It is self-evident through observing newborn and very young children that humans know *how* to learn long before they know *that* they are learning – or even *what* they are learning. That is, they learn before they know they know how to learn. In fact, some of the most important skills they will ever learn – locomotion and language – are learned before any formal teaching or learning programmes are provided.

The learning mechanism offered by PCT is called reorganisation (Marken & Powers, 1989; Powers, 1973, 2005, 2008). It has particular features that make it unique from the learning processes with which you may already be familiar (such as conditioning). Reorganisation involves random change and reduction of error (the difference between the *should be* and *is*) that remains unresolved within conflicted control systems. Although error reduction is business as usual for control systems, sometimes, particularly in conflict scenarios, error persists. When error is not reduced by the routine operation of the control system, reorganisation activity begins to increase. Reorganisation introduces random changes to the control system and monitors the changes. If the change has the effect of reducing error, then that change stays in place until error once again increases, at which time another random change is made. So reorganisation is not switched on and off, but is always active in the sense of monitoring error in the system. If error can be minimised by the routine operation of the control system, then the reorganising system delays making any further changes. If a situation arises where error persists, then the activity of reorganisation increases and alterations begin to be generated.

Reorganisation, therefore, is value-neutral with respect to the types of changes that are introduced and the decision as to which changes linger. The only criterion is error reduction. We think a lot of the seemingly 'crazy' ideas that occur to people when they are extremely distressed, including ideas of suicide, could be the effects of reorganisation generating random changes to be considered. If a change occurs and error is not reduced, another change will be generated. If a particular change does reduce error, that change is retained. Timing, therefore, is very important when reorganising. If reorganisation is too slow, changes will not be generated in enough time to restore effective functioning to the control system. Reorganisation that is too rapid, however, will have a similarly impotent effect. If reorganisation occurs too swiftly, then a new change will be introduced before the error reducing effects of the previous change can be properly assessed.

Obviously, different parts of the control system hierarchy will need to be reorganised at different times, so mobility must be a feature of the reorganising system. There must also be a way of safeguarding effective functioning control systems so that reorganisation does not introduce changes where they are not needed. A creature would not survive very long if it possessed a reorganising system that changed control systems arbitrarily and haphazardly. As early as the end of the 1950s, Powers considered that what we call 'awareness' or 'consciousness' could be closely related to the location at which reorganisation occurs (Powers *et al.*, 1960b); reorganisation and awareness are linked such that it is the systems in awareness that are reorganised. From this perspective, it makes sense that our attention is naturally drawn to the things that are a problem in our lives more so than the things that feel OK. Being aware of those areas where sustained error is occurring means that reorganisation will follow.

The process of reorganisation seems to match well with what we now know about change in psychotherapy. We know, for example, that change is a non-linear process where, sometimes, things can seem to get worse before they get better (Carey, 2011a). The time needed for effective change to occur varies from individual to individual with some people changing quite quickly and other people taking much longer. Even the timing of reorganisation might have clinical implications. Could the manifestation of some of the experiences currently labelled 'psychosis' be the effects of a reorganising system that is operating too rapidly? Similarly, might severe inactivity and catatonia be the consequences of a reorganising system that has drastically slowed?

Building a therapy

Our contention is that an effective psychotherapy can be built on the three foundational principles of control, conflict, and reorganisation. Control is the process of living. Control is what people do all day every day. Control for humans is hierarchical and multilayered. It ranges from experiences we control in the moment, to a concept of ourselves and the world that we may strive for over a lifetime. Control occurs whether our attention is focused on it or not. Dropping the kids off at school is a control process, getting to work on time is a control process, putting a stamp in the right place on the envelope is a control process, digestion is a control process, checking on the daily news headlines is a control process, and visiting Grandma for Christmas is also a control process. We are so good at controlling, we rarely realise that all of our activity is designed to make the world as we are currently experiencing it match the way we have specified it *should be*.

The main psychological problem for controllers is enduring conflict. Conflict occurs when two equally weighted, highly valued, but incompatible *should be*s are pitted against each other. The longer the conflict exists, the more devastating and pervasive the consequences can be. From a PCT perspective, there is nothing wrong or 'dysfunctional' with control systems in conflict. Actually, it is exactly the reverse. As mentioned earlier, Powers (e.g. Powers, 1973, 2005; Powers *et al.*, 1960b) suggests there is a positive relationship between the quality of the control systems and the viciousness of the conflict. When people are in conflict, we should expect erratic, sometimes contradictory, behaviour. They might seem to be trying very hard to behave in a particular way or to keep themselves in check or to control some aspect of their behaviour. At times, they might seem to do exactly the opposite of what they were saying just a few minutes before. Such is the experience of a conflicted mind. Relapse, irritability, and unpredictability may all be indicators that a conflict still lurks within a person's neural network.

Reorganisation is an innate and powerful learning mechanism that can resolve conflict. If reorganisation occurs in those places on which a person's awareness is focused and their problem is still present, then logically, awareness is not illuminating the precise place in which reorganisation can have its best effects. Thus, reorganisation needs to happen in a different place to produce a more effective result. Therapy, then, has the purpose of helping people who are distressed shift their awareness – and thereby their reorganising system – to new places in the hierarchy where reorganisation might have some ultimately satisfactory impact on the conflict. The configuration in Figure 2.2 suggests that the conflict is being generated from a system above the two opposing systems within the branching hierarchy we described. So, the suggestion in therapy is that people need to become aware of a higher order *should be*, so that reorganisation can make changes at these superordinate levels and, thus, alter the conflict that is occurring.

A therapy based on these ideas has important implications for the roles of the therapist and the client, as well as aspects of therapy such as how appointments are scheduled and for how long therapy should last. Important areas such as the therapeutic relationship are also able to be usefully understood from a PCT perspective. PCT even provides a framework for reconsidering well-worn psychotherapeutic problems such as co-morbidity, complexity, non-compliance, and treatment resistance. After discussing the implications of these principles in the next chapter, we will elaborate on the information we have provided here about these principles and demonstrate their therapeutic application throughout the rest of the book. Some aspects of the therapy informed by these principles might fit with insights you have already developed from your own therapeutic practice but there might be some surprises as well.

Summary of main points

- *Control is what we do.* It is a process common to all living things and cleverly mimicked by some non-living ones. Routine and satisfactory daily functioning is a process of control.
- *Conflict is an extremely common occurrence.* Essentially, any choice situation is a conflict in terms of having to select one option from a range of two or more similarly desirable alternatives. People are usually pretty adept at resolving conflicts but, when conflicts endure, mental health is compromised. Rather than mental health problems being generated from *dis*ability or *dys*function, however, chronic conflict often occurs between well-functioning, 'high gain' control systems.
- *Reorganisation is the natural learning you have when you do not know how to learn.* It is the learning mechanism we were born with that helped us walk and talk before we knew of any other learning strategies such as brainstorming, rehearsal, or cost-benefit analysis. Reorganisation is based on random change and error reduction.

Topics for discussion

1. Every choice is really a conflict. Discuss.
2. Control is a paradox because, for the most part, we never notice the controlling we are doing. Ironically, we mostly only notice control when it is compromised and we have to try extra hard or do something different. Are you comfortable thinking of yourself as a controlling person? Why or why not?

Activities for learning, consolidation, and fun!

1. Write down a recent choice you made. What were the two alternatives? How did you decide on one of them?
2. Can you find references to control and conflict in other therapies? How are they discussed and how do you compare them to the concepts presented here?
3. How would you sum up the principle of control in a sentence? Can you do the same for conflict and reorganisation?

Chapter 3

The clinical implications

A summary

By reading this chapter, you will learn:

1 how understanding control can influence the conceptualisation and delivery of counselling and psychotherapy;
2 what the formulation of conflict means in practice; and
3 the significance of recognising change as reorganisation.

Considering counselling and psychotherapy from the perspective of perceptual control has major implications for practice. In this chapter, we will provide a sketch of what some of those implications are and then we will elaborate on these points in subsequent chapters. This chapter, then, is a kind of 'so what?' for using the three principles we described in the last chapter in the understanding and provision of counselling and psychotherapy.

PCT provides an explanation of behaviour from the perspective of the person doing the behaving rather than the point of view of an observer, which means the PCT version of counselling and psychotherapy is inherently client-centred. In fact, more than client-*centred*, therapists whose work is informed by PCT principles describe their practice as client-*led* therapy, or client-*perspective* therapy. Distinguishing between being client-*centred* and being client-*led* is important because therapists can conduct therapy in a manner that indicates clients are at the centre of their decision-making processes; however, the decisions can still be based on the principle that 'the therapist knows best'. Making judgements about the amount of treatment a client should receive, how much improvement is appropriate or possible, and describing clients as 'treatment dropouts' if they do not make this amount of improvement is a good example of well-intentioned therapy that is delivered from the point of view of the therapist. The principles-based approach informed by PCT, however, suggests that it is the client's perspective that is paramount when considering, among other things, the gains that can be made in therapy. That is not to say that therapists cannot have opinions about important elements of psychological treatment. We have very strong views about the formulation of psychological distress and how change occurs, for example. We have equally strong views, however, that counselling and psychotherapy is fundamentally about helping people resolve the psychological impediments that are preventing them from living the sort of life they want to live. If we conceptualise therapy in this way, it becomes essential to take the client's perspective as the starting point.

PCT affects all aspects of counselling and psychotherapy, including the way in which psychological disorders are understood and formulated, the roles of the therapist and client, how we understand concepts such as 'empathy', the change process, the way in which appointments are scheduled, and how much therapy is delivered. From this perspective, the client is very much considered to be the change agent. Actually, even this understanding is not strictly accurate. When we discuss the process of change in greater detail, we will provide a more nuanced account that suggests that, from a change-as-reorganisation perspective, the client could be considered the *locus* of change rather than the *agent* of change. Change by reorganisation is not something you can *make* happen in the same way you might make yourself hit a two-handed backhand topspin lob in tennis or make yourself have that difficult conversation with a colleague. This will become clearer later in the chapter.

Principles-based PCT therapy centres around the way in which the client's own strengths and self-correcting propensities can be nurtured, promoted, and enhanced. As hinted at above, the focus in therapy is helping the client live the life they want to live outside therapy, and so every effort is made to acknowledge and respect their independence and self-determining inclinations. Thus, therapy is an optimistic activity where the therapist persistently believes that clients can learn to live satisfying and meaningful lives regardless of how chronic or complex their problems might seem, and the therapist is a resource that clients can access whenever they want to spend time and effort engaging in this learning.

The Method of Levels (MOL) is a therapy based on the three PCT principles we have described. In MOL, *dis*covery is emphasised rather than *re*covery. The therapist's role is to optimise their therapeutic usefulness by compassionately and doggedly encouraging clients to explore and review their inner worlds so that more effective ways of living and relating might germinate. The client's role is to determine how often and how frequently they access the resource of therapy and to engage in uncensored communication of their difficulties, so that different perspectives and understandings of their situation can develop. The way this occurs within an effective and efficient form of counselling and psychotherapy is outlined in detail in the remaining chapters.

Before we describe some of the ramifications for counselling and psychotherapy from a PCT perspective, it might be useful to add a proviso. In some ways, the *appearance* of therapy from the backyard of PCT might not be that different from the way other therapies currently appear. For example, we could still expect to see therapists and clients meeting for allotted times and we will still observe therapists asking questions of clients. There may be some changes in the structure of therapy and the activities that are used, but the biggest changes to occur are likely to be the internal changes a therapist makes in terms of why they ask the questions they do and how they arrange to see clients. That is, it is the 'why' of therapy provision rather than the 'what' that is possibly the biggest change to occur by switching to a PCT point of view.

It might help to draw an analogy with other areas to show that a major shift in understanding does not necessarily change one's current view of a situation. The historic example of the shift in understanding from the view that the world is flat to the discovery that the world is round illustrates the point we are making here. Regardless of whether you believe the world is flat or round, you will see ships sail out to sea and disappear slowly over the horizon. Even though the observation is the same regardless of the presumed context, your understanding about what is happening will be very different depending on the type of planet you believe you are standing on. In the same way, whether you believe environments control behaviour, or behaviour is used to control the environment, you can observe a teacher give a student a sticker and the student do more of whatever it was they were doing before they got the sticker. Whether you regard this as an example of the reinforcing properties of the sticker, or the ability of the student to get more of what it is they want, will very much depend on your frame of reference. Finally, whether you believe the sun is a golden orb that travels across the sky of a stationary earth each day or whether you believe that day and night are created by the rotation of the earth as it orbits the sun, you will still see the sun appear in the east and disappear in the west each day. You may even refer to 'sunrise' and 'sunset'. Somehow, it just does not sound the same to say, 'Hey, honey! How about we grab a bottle of wine, some nice cheese, and head down to the point to watch the earth rotate a little?' Even with completely different understandings of a phenomenon, people can still observe the same event occurring. Despite the unchanging appearance, people will have different appreciations for how and why that appearance appears as it does.

PCT provides a significantly different framework for counselling and psychotherapy, so it is our understanding of what we are doing and our goals for what we want to achieve in therapy that will change much more dramatically than many of our observable practices. Yet, the principles in this book should help these practices to be more consistently applied, more efficient, and better integrated with other interventions that share the same guiding principles. In turn, we believe this can have a lasting and fruitful impact on mental health services.

Why does control matter in counselling and psychotherapy?

As we explained when introducing the principle of control, it is discovering *how* control works that is even more important than recognising *that* control occurs. PCT explains how it is that people (and all other living things) go about making their worlds be the way they want them to be. In the last chapter, we introduced the idea that one of the most surprising results of studies based on PCT is in the specification of what is controlled. By conducting research that uses simulation models to test basic principles, it has been demonstrated that living things control what they sense (perceive), not how they act (Marken & Mansell, 2013; Powers, 2008). That is, we control *p* or *is* in Figure 2.1, not *a* or *actions*.

Some simple examples might help to clarify the distinction between controlling actions and controlling perceptions. Although this idea seems strange at first, when some time is devoted to thinking carefully about our own experiences, it is actually the idea that we control actions that turns out to be more puzzling than the idea that we control perceptions. We introduced the activity of manoeuvring a car in Chapter 2 as a clear illustration of the control of perception principle. Driving a car safely from A to B involves making sure you keep the car a certain distance behind the car in front, and in a certain position in the lane, and travelling at a certain speed. To do all of this, you have to see particular things, such as where the other cars are and what the speed is, and you have to act in various ways, such as changing the angle of your foot on the accelerator pedal, applying pressure to the brake pedal, and moving the steering wheel. There is no doubt that you *use* actions to make the car journey proceed as you want it to, but you do not *control* your actions; you *vary* your actions so that what you see *is* controlled. You cannot specify ahead of time how you will change the angle of your foot on the accelerator pedal as you drive from your house to Aunt May's for Sunday afternoon high tea. You can describe in advance, however, where the final destination of your car will be and the speed you would like to drive at to get there.

Stretching muscles before or after exercise is another useful way of understanding the concept. Stretching your right quadricep or left calf, for example, requires that you position your legs in certain ways and bend or lean in particular directions. The way you know you are stretching, however, is because of the way your muscle *feels* when you configure your body, or parts of it, according to particular patterns. The process of stretching, then, is really an activity of creating a specific feeling in a localised part of your body. If you want more stretch, you create a bigger feeling. This activity can be easily traced through Figure 2.1: to stretch your quadricep, you set a *should be* (*r*) state of the muscle; a comparison of *should be* and *is* (*p*) generates an *amount of difference* (*e*); *e* produces *actions* (*a*) that lead to a change in *is*. The *environmental influences* (*d*) reflect the fact that your *actions* would be slightly different if you were wearing a thick tracksuit or running tights or if you were stretching at home in your lounge room or in a crowded gym.

This simple principle of control of perception applies to all aspects of behaviour. As you sip your skinny decaf latte, the actions that move the cup to your lips are slightly different each time. If you could somehow produce exactly the same muscle tensions to savour the very last drop as you did when the cup was at its fullest, the cup would probably end up somewhere in the vicinity of your forehead. We are so skilled at constantly varying our actions to keep our perceptions in their preferred states that we rarely even notice we are doing it. We raise or lower the volume of our voice in a bustling cafe over lunch so the conversation continues without interruption. A teacher in a classroom smiles or nods or coughs or answers questions or moves around the room to keep the busyness of the classroom at the level they think is appropriate for the students and the lesson. Kicking penalties in rugby requires constant adjustments in how the ball is struck so that, regardless of the stage of the game or the position from which the kick is taken on the field, the ball continues to sail through the uprights.

While 'control of perception' might seem like a formal, unwieldy term, it is referring to nothing more than the fact that we control the outcomes or consequences of behaviour rather than the behaviour itself. Even then, we only control some of the outcomes. For any act, there are likely to be the outcomes we intend, as well as unintended consequences of which we are not aware. Whenever we act, we act to produce particular outcomes or experiences so that some *is* stays very close to its *should be*.

Initially, it might seem odd to consider the idea that we control perceptions rather than behaviour, but thinking about simple acts might help acclimatise to the idea. Driving a car definitely involves combining both behaviour and perception, but an analysis of the activity reveals that perceptions are what we control. Cruise control systems are convenient devices that actually do some of the behaving for us. With the cruise control system in operation, the driver's foot can be removed from the accelerator pedal and the car will maintain the desired speed. On occasion, a driver might even ask their passenger to hold the steering wheel while an action that requires both hands is performed. While actions can be substituted quite simply, the same cannot be said for perceptions. If you imagine closing your eyes while you are driving, you can get a sense of how terrifying that would be beyond a second or two. Even if you had a passenger diligently telling you where you were on the road and where the other cars were, it would still be extremely disconcerting to drive for very long in this state.

Control of perception is the reason why eating is so different when we have a cold. With a congested head, a person's senses of smell and taste are muffled. People can make the same eating behaviours when they have a cold. They can order food at the restaurant in the same way, they can dip their spoon into their favourite carrot and ginger soup just the way they always do, and they can raise the spoon to their lips. Behaving in the same way, however, will not produce the same experience because sensations are altered when people have a cold. To produce a similar taste effect, different behaviours would be needed, such as adding more salt and pepper, or ordering the spicy roasted pumpkin soup instead. At all times, it is our perceptions that are paramount to us. We use our behaviours to produce the perceptions we want but we have no knowledge of our behaviours beyond the perceptual experiences they create for us. The simple principle that we control perception rather than behaviour illustrated in the driving and eating examples applies to all behaviour.

The principle of controlling perception or controlling outcomes is particularly important when considering people who come for counselling and therapy (and the people who provide counselling and psychotherapy). People seeking therapy, for example, may be desperate to avoid re-experiencing memories of a past trauma, but the way that they try to achieve this depends on the context. For example, a person who was traumatised by an assault in his local street may have taken a sedative medication in the morning to try to keep the memories at bay, and he might keep his eyes to the ground to avoid looking at people who might remind him of the attacker. Whenever something such as a loud voice reminds him of the trauma, he might try to push the memory to the back of his mind. In a therapy session, he might talk about a topic unrelated to the assault, and when the therapist mentions it he might change the subject. He may engage in numerous other behaviours during the session – shifting away from the therapist, taking deep breaths, and talking fast. Although these behaviours are widely divergent, they are simplified by the principle of control. We propose that, in some cases, it can be important for the client to understand this principle in general and, if the general principle is understood, it is not necessary to try to explain every different behaviour used to maintain control. The principle of control therefore reduces the complexity and stigma that might come from trying to find an explanation for each and every behaviour that is noticeable by other people.

As mentioned earlier, PCT is, fundamentally, an explanation of behaviour from the perspective of the person doing the behaviour and not the vantage point of an observer. All behaviour has the function, outcome, or consequence of keeping the separation between *should be* and *is* as small as possible (or '*r*' and '*p*' from the equations in the last chapter). The subtlety of this is that no one can ever directly experience another person's '*should be*s' and '*is*es'. Also, we do not act on the world *as it really is*. We can only act on the world *as we perceive it to be*. In fact, we can never know the way the world 'really' is; all we ever know is our own perception or experience of it. As banal as that may seem, you are the only person on earth who experiences all of what is happening when you move your own personal finger (Robertson & Powers, 1990).

So even though we can observe another person's actions, we can never know for certain what the other person is 'doing'. Perhaps this is the most profound implication of the 'control of perception' finding for psychotherapy and counselling. What people are 'doing' when they behave is creating certain effects or outcomes for themselves. These are the consequences of behaviour rather than the behaviour itself. Is a person who is waving at the side of the road hailing a taxi, or saying goodbye to a friend, or trying to catch the attention of the police officer on the other side of the road? Is a person who makes a psychotherapy appointment wanting to explore and resolve psychological distress, or satisfying a demanding partner, or complying with her GP, or demonstrating to family members that nothing can help his troubles? PCT teaches us that it is perilous to assume we know what someone is trying to achieve when we see them act in particular ways.

The idea that we can observe people's actions but not know what they are doing is perhaps one of the most profound implications of PCT and the control of perception principle. This foundational notion suggests that even though we can see people act in the same ways, they may very well be doing different things from their individual perspectives. It also explains why it is impossible to control another person. It can be trivially simple to control another person's actions given the right conditions; however, actions are not the person. Viktor Frankl captures this sentiment with his quote that:

> We who lived in concentration camps can remember the men who walked through the huts comforting others, giving away their last piece of bread. They may have been few in number, but they offer sufficient proof that everything can be taken from a man but one thing: the last of the human freedoms – to choose one's attitude in any given set of circumstances, to choose one's own way.
>
> (www.goodreads.com/author/quotes/2782.Viktor_E_Frankl)

If not even something as extreme as a concentration camp can control people, then the 'control of behaviour' idea has some problems with it.

Control of perception is an idea that reverberates widely. Even cherished doctrines such as the golden rule would be overhauled in the PCT workroom. The basic idea of the golden rule is: do unto others as you would have done unto yourself, or treat others the way you want to be treated. PCT, however, teaches that we need to treat people according to *their* preferences rather than ours. The PCT golden rule would be something to the effect of: do unto others as they would have done unto themselves, or treat others the way they want to be treated (Robertson & Powers, 1990). The PCT golden rule implies that we never know for certain what it is that others are seeking, so we should remain open-minded and curious with regard to the possibilities.

The fact that we can never really know the perceptions of another adds a different flavour to many time-honoured counselling and psychotherapy concepts. Even though, as therapists, we might rate highly qualities such as empathy, in the world described by PCT, we can never actually know first-hand what another person is experiencing. This simple fact turns out to be very useful. Understanding this aspect of perceptual control helps prevent therapists from making assumptions about what clients are going through. Even when clients use terms as familiar as depression, anxiety, and schizophrenia, it is still the case that we can never really know what the experience of psychological distress is for another. Upon hearing a client say, 'I've been really depressed lately', an MOL therapist might begin to wonder things such as: what they mean when they use the term 'depressed'; how they learned they were depressed; why they used the term 'depressed' rather than some other term such as 'sad' or 'forlorn'; how being depressed is interfering with their life; and how they feel about being depressed. MOL therapy, therefore, informed by the principles of PCT, is characterised by a tireless curiosity of always encouraging clients to explain, elaborate, and expand on what they are describing of their experiences.

It is sometimes suggested that to truly understand another person, it is necessary to 'walk a mile' in their shoes. In MOL, however, it is considered an impossibility to 'truly' understand another person in the sense of knowing the experience of being them, and it is also not possible to take any steps at all in another person's shoes. PCT enables therapists to commence the therapy conversation from a position of not knowing and not understanding, and to stay in that place as they encourage each client to describe to the therapist as much as possible about what it means to be the client. We can even be quite explicit about this with clients. In the first session when we are explaining to clients the way we work, we might say something such as, 'In these sessions, I'll be asking you lots and lots of questions. The purpose of the questions isn't so that I will come to understand what you're going through, although I'll certainly learn lots about you as we talk; the purpose of the questions is so that you can come to understand yourself and your situation differently from the way you do at the moment.' Not all clients require explanations of the therapeutic process but, when they do, clients seem to find this open and straightforward approach engaging.

Since all we know is the experience of our own perceptual world, we may also revise our ideas of things such as 'objectivity' from a PCT perspective. Velmans (2009) suggests that the term 'intersubjectivity' is more appropriate than 'objectivity' in many cases. Some research and therapeutic procedures can be 'objective' in the sense of being dispassionate, accurate, and truthful, or 'objective' in the sense of following well-specified, repeatable procedures, but 'objective' in the sense of being 'observer-free' is unattainable (Velmans, 2009). Even when apparently objective measures such as blood pressure or body temperature are obtained, these measures still have *meanings* for the people using the measures or from whom the readings were obtained. A blood pressure reading of 152 over 93 or a cholesterol score of 7.9 will be interpreted differently by different people. Even though the numbers could be thought of as 'observer-free', it is the meaning the numbers have that is crucial, and meanings can never be observer-free.

The scores on standardised questionnaires that are routinely used in therapeutic practice are likely to mean something different to the therapist than they do to the client. Symptom scores may or may not represent what is important to the client, and scores in the 'normal' range are no guarantee that the client is not experiencing significant distress or is functioning as they would like to (Kazdin, 1999, 2001). This does not mean that standardised questionnaires should never be used, but it does mean that they might be considered to be 'reporting devices' rather than 'objective measures' of psychological dysfunction. Again, an MOL therapist might curiously wonder what clients want to communicate by completing the form in the way that they have. The use of standardised questionnaires was brought home starkly by one client whose wife did not think he was telling the therapist everything that needed to be told. The client brought in a completed DASS-21 (Depression Anxiety Stress Scales; Lovibond & Lovibond, 1995) and, on each line, two numbers were circled; one was circled with a red pen and the other was circled with a pencil. The therapist asked the client about the double entries and the client explained that his wife wanted to let the therapist know how the client was 'really' going. Clearly, both the client and his wife wanted to communicate different things to the therapist.

Another important area that PCT overturns is that of causality. The prevailing model in the life sciences is linear causality. For example, a classic research study involves manipulating something in the environment such as the presence or absence of a threatening facial image (the independent variable) and assessing the change in a person's behaviour, such as the time it takes for them to press a button (the dependent variable). Some researchers attempt to show that there is some connection in the reverse direction – feedback, or that there is 'processing' that occurs between the input and output. Yet, the linear march from cause (stimulus) to effect (response) still persists. In PCT, however, as we alluded to in the last chapter, the prevailing principle of control dictates a continuous, circular causality (Mansell & Carey, 2009). While there is certainly a relationship between perception and action, neither one is considered to be the cause of the other (Robertson & Powers, 1990). Demarcating causes and effects, if that is what one wishes to do, often implies drawing arbitrary temporal lines to separate one part of an activity from another. It is certainly the case that some events occur before other events in time, but accurately understanding causality as it applies to creatures that live requires a consideration of the entire context. In the eye-blink example described in Chapter 2, the puff of air came before the blink but the puff–blink relationship only occurs within the context of an alive eye being maintained in a particular condition through negative feedback control.

Rather than thinking in terms of stimuli and responses or causes and effects, life from a PCT perspective is a process of creating and maintaining controlled states. These are the *should be*s in Figure 2.1. We have states that we like our worlds to be in, and we act on and alter the environment to maintain these states in the conditions we have specified for them. We have the state we prefer our house and garden to be in, the state of our appearance we like to see when we look in the mirror, the state of our bank accounts, even our state of mind. Some of these states will be more or less important to different people and there will no doubt be other preferred states in our individual and private stockpiles. Some will change over time, some will fall by the wayside, and others will be added to the collection. In this way, PCT can be thought of as the 'Goldilocks Theory of Life'. Goldilocks had expectations for how warm porridge *should be*, for how big chairs *should be*, and for how firm beds *should be*. She tested Father Bear's, Mother Bear's, and Baby Bear's porridge, chair, and bed until her *should be/is* separation was at a minimum. Goldilocks' adventure in the Bears' cottage could be considered a metaphor for successful day-to-day living from a PCT perspective.

These preferred, or *should be*, states or conditions are closely linked to goals, so it could be considered that, as individuals, all of us have goals all of the time. We will say more about this in Chapter 5, but for now it is sufficient to flag that both the therapist and the client are goal-seeking, or state-maintaining, creatures. A central premise here is that individuals are always doing something. From before they are born until the time they die, the switch is always 'on'. Catatonic patients, non-compliant students, and disengaged clients are all doing something. Adopting this stance enables us to reconsider common therapeutic problems such as non-compliance or treatment resistance. Rather than not complying with the therapist, we could consider that the clients are complying with their own internal specifications, desires, and demands, and we could sensitively and diligently enquire about what those internal prescriptions might be. We can also reconceptualise therapeutic concepts such as 'triggers'. We could understand that a trigger is not a stimulus that initiates a cascade of responses in a chain-like fashion, but rather, it is an event that disturbs an important goal-state of the individual. The individual's actions represent their efforts to nullify the effects of the disturbance and restore the state to its preferred condition. Again, assisting clients to become aware of and describe their important goal-states and the ways in which they are being ruffled might be the most therapeutically useful thing we can do.

Therapy that is underpinned by PCT, therefore, has a much greater focus on the process of the way in which the client is thinking than the content of what they might be thinking about. Wondering about the truth or accuracy of a client's descriptions is not as relevant as the therapist curiously exploring what the client is 'doing' by making an appointment, attending the therapeutic session, and discussing their difficulties. Therapists, perhaps, make implicit assumptions that clients attend therapy because they want to diligently address their psychological distress. This is likely to be the case for many clients, but not for all. Clients might attend therapy because the court has ordered them to, or because their partner has threatened to leave, or because their parents are 'making' them. One client wanted her GP to increase her medication whereas her GP wanted her to see a psychological therapist before making the adjustment. The patient would attend the session, speak without pausing for 20 or so minutes, and then look at her watch and say, 'Well, I'll see you next week.' Despite the therapist's best attempts to clarify the problem and enquire about her experiences and perspectives, the client did not change her modus operandi. She attended as many sessions as she needed to until her GP changed her medication. Such an experience was a stark reminder that clients have their own purposes for accessing counselling and psychotherapy services. Even when clients are seeking therapy in order to reduce psychological distress, if they are conflicted, they may, at times, appear ambivalent or disengaged as their competing *should be*s wrestle with each other. Focusing on processes rather than content allows the therapist to avoid becoming ensnared in contradictions and inconsistencies that can often be a feature of the dialogue of someone who is conflicted.

What is the big deal about internal conflict?

Disrupted goal-states are the *sine qua non* of psychological distress from a PCT perspective. In MOL, it is assumed that the most common reason for chronically disrupted goal-states is conflict. Even in situations that appear to be better characterised as insuperable disturbances or lack of goals, when these situations persist, it is more than likely that an opposing goal-state is lurking in the recesses of the person's mind and preventing progress. A person who is in an abusive relationship, for example, might seem like they are experiencing overwhelming forces from their scurrilous partner. A more important consideration, however, is the goal-state they are maintaining by staying in the relationship. The abuse persists partly because of the inexcusable actions of the abuser (who is also maintaining particular goal-states in reference conditions), *and partly because of* the internal conflict of the abused in terms of whether to stay or leave. Similarly, someone who enters a new community or context might express the idea that they do not know how to make friends. While this might seem like an impoverished repertoire when it comes to goals about social interactions, the real issue preventing ease in social situations could be a struggle internally between wanting to make contact with others, and also wanting to avoid the pain, humiliation, and embarrassment of possible rejection. Identifying disrupted goal-states clients are trying to control has many implications for the way in which we understand and help them to find solutions to their problems, which we will discuss more in subsequent chapters. A focus on disrupted goals states can help us to avoid common assumptions that are made about the nature of people's problems and their behaviour. For example, a client who experienced distress resulting from social isolation had received a diagnosis of Asperger's syndrome and was informed that this syndrome 'caused' social skills deficits, making it difficult for him to form relationships. He spoke about wanting meaningful friendships, and yet when encouraged to describe his experiences, he started to explain how he actively avoided making conversation and eye contact with people for fear of them negatively evaluating him. Rather than treating his 'social skills deficits', therefore, the MOL therapist helped this man focus on his conflict between wanting to develop meaningful relationships and wanting to avoid negative evaluations.

Conflict, therefore, is the working hypothesis or formulation with which any MOL therapist approaches psychological distress. For this reason, the symptoms of psychological botheration are of secondary importance to the distress itself. When someone describes feeling sad or anxious or overwhelmed or angry or paranoid, the enquiry takes the line of investigating the source of the torment rather than the symptomatic consequences of it. Often, this involves nothing more complicated than the therapist asking, 'Does it bother you to be . . .' or, 'How do you feel about . . .' For example, a client said she was having trouble controlling her anger and, when the therapist asked, 'Do these problems controlling your anger bother you?' she said, 'Definitely! My daughter isn't going to put up with it much longer. I don't want to lose her but she's already said she'll walk out if I don't change. We have a good relationship most of the time but I really want her to listen to me. She's just wasting her life.'

Often, clients are unaware of both sides of a conflict or even that they are in conflict. They might know that they want to make friends, or that they want to trust their partner, or that they want to find meaning in life, but they are not so pressingly aware of their need to feel safe, or to avoid heartbreak, or to risk failure. From a PCT perspective, however, there are always two warring parties at the source of psychological distress. Rather than helping people modify 'dysfunctional assumptions', therefore, or even helping them detach themselves from thoughts and feelings so these experiences can be viewed from a distance, the focus in MOL is about helping people discover and understand the conflict that is raging.

In the last chapter, the idea of relativity was introduced. We will expand on this idea some more in Chapter 8. One aspect to the relativity mindset is to never be satisfied with the amount of information the client has provided. Always wonder, 'what else?' Helping the client patiently explain to you how a particular thought, action, or experience generates the distress it does is essential, because as they do, it will mean they are explaining it to themselves as well. As they listen to their explanation, they will begin to resolve incongruities and make sense of the life that they are living.

What difference can reorganisation make to clinical practice?

Despite change being perhaps the fundamental purpose of all therapeutic approaches, it is remarkably difficult to find unambiguous descriptions of what change is and how it occurs. Kazdin (2009), in fact, argues that, on the whole, we do not know how or why our treatments work. As we suggested in Chapter 2, not knowing how or why something works has serious implications for people who want to make that something work better.

One of the problems in arriving at a clearer understanding of the change process might be that the *outcome* of change is often confused with the *process* of change. Also, the question of how change occurs is often conflated with the issue of how therapy works (Carey, Carey, Mullan, Murray, & Spratt, 2006). Mineka and Thomas (1999), for example, argue that with regard to exposure therapy, disconfirming a 'low sense of perceived control is one of the critical cognitive changes that occurs in exposure treatments' (p. 750). Also, Hofmann (2004) suggests that when clients are repeatedly exposed to a feared object in the absence of negative consequences, this forces them to re-evaluate their beliefs. We have no issue with these explanations, or others like them, but we are interested in a different level of explanation. We think that while it might be important to know *that* clients' sense of perceived control changes or *that* they re-evaluate their beliefs, it is far more important to know *how* these alterations occur.

Descriptions of what it is that changes in therapy are bountiful. By reading various sources, for example, you might be informed that clients learn to tolerate uncertainty, or develop a positive sense of self, or distance themselves from their problem. What you will not find is any reliable description of how these things occur. What is the process by which the experience of uncertainty is transformed from intolerable to tolerable? In an extended programme of research (first mentioned in Chapter 2), we found that clients themselves are unable to describe how change occurs (Carey *et al.*, 2007; Gianakis & Carey, 2011; Higginson & Mansell, 2008). We have more to say about this research in Chapter 9. Clients, and even people who resolve significant psychological distress without therapy, can describe how things were for them before and after change, and they can emphatically confirm *that* change occurred, but they cannot typically describe the specific change process that provided the bridge from before to after.

Discovering that both researchers and clients can describe *that* change occurs but not *how* it happens is an intriguing yet perhaps unsurprising result. It is very difficult to even think about what might occur in the space between the events before and after change. How does a dysfunctional assumption transmogrify into a functional one? How do irrational beliefs morph into rational beliefs? Also, how does the reverse situation develop? How does paranoia appear where there was none before? In fact, how does one change one's mind about anything at all? How does it occur that you set out to have a meal at the new restaurant in town but you actually end up eating at your old favourite? Or how is it that you decided not to attend the work Christmas party but found yourself going anyway? We can often suggest *reasons* for our changes but the reasons why we changed our mind are not the same as the mind changing process itself. Articulating the way in which one *should be* is replaced by another, sometimes even an opposite *should be*, seems difficult to the point of impossible.

Given the inexplicability of change, it would seem that research relying on aggregated responses from participants' questionnaire scores would be insufficient to produce an accurate and precise account of the change process. Model building research, however, is ideally suited to this task. Using this research methodology, Powers (Powers, 1973, 2005; Powers *et al.*, 1960a, 1960b) has proposed a process of reorganisation driven by random change and error reduction. Remember that we described earlier how 'error' is the gap between our goals (*r* or '*should be*') and our current perception (*p* or '*is*') of how things are. Conflict leads to error persisting and increasing. When this error does persist and increase, random changes are made and the effect on error is monitored. If that particular change reduces error, any further change is delayed and the system persists in the currently changed state. If error does not reduce, then another random change is generated. This process persists until one of the random changes achieves lasting error reduction in the system. The successful change is likely to be felt as regaining control over experiences that had been out of control, such as maintaining relationships that were faltering, or feeling emotions that had been out of reach. In reality, it can be difficult to articulate this process over and above a 'felt sense' of things having changed or feeling better.

Reorganisation is considered to be the most basic learning process. It is the process through which other forms of learning (such as brainstorming, problem-solving, rehearsal, decision-tree analysis, imagery, and so on) are acquired and developed. It is the process that enabled us to learn to walk and talk. Despite the fact that it relies on random changes, research has demonstrated that it is a remarkably efficient form of learning (Marken & Powers, 1989; Powers, 2008). Also, the process of reorganisation maps neatly on to observations of change in clinical practice, as well as the way change occurs developmentally throughout life. We know, for example, that change is a non-linear dynamical process that can be punctuated by leaps in progress, as well as periods of regression (e.g. Hayes, Laurenceau, Feldman, Strauss, & Cardaciotto, 2007; van de Rijt & Plooij, 1993).

The clinical implications for a change-by-reorganisation model of therapy are numerous. We can expect change to be unpredictable and to demonstrate an unwillingness to be constrained by structured protocols or predetermined time frames. There is no reason why change cannot happen quickly, but this will not be everyone's experience. It is interesting that we are seldom surprised when the onset of psychological distress occurs abruptly; yet, we consider it unlikely or impossible for distress to disappear just as suddenly. For example, people can become debilitatingly distressed after one traumatic event. If change in a person's psychological state can happen quickly and dramatically in one direction, is there any reason to expect that it cannot happen the same way in the other direction?

Advising people how to change or instructing them in the execution of different strategies is likely to be helpful only haphazardly and may sometimes even block the change process. The right solution will be the one that nestles snugly into the entire hierarchy of the distressed person and solutions that appear obvious from an observer's point of view may not be ideal from the inside looking out. Reorganisation is also not something that can be done consciously. Reorganisation is more likely to occur when people have greater awareness of disrupted goals (error), but they cannot just make their own reorganisation processes reorganise. Anyone who has had the experience of trying to think of a name of a movie, or a famous person, or a past colleague and, not being able to recall the name, finds that it 'pops' into their mind at a later time – sometimes when they are no longer thinking about it – will know the experience of reorganisation doing what reorganisation does. We go into more detail about the implications of reorganisation for therapeutic practice in Chapter 9.

Reorganisation just happens. And it seems plausible to suggest that reorganisation is constantly occurring, sometimes more, sometimes less, to keep the hierarchy of control systems controlling efficiently and our lives in control. From this perspective, therapy can be considered a context to provide the space and time for reorganisation to go about its business for as long as it takes to reinstate contentment and satisfaction.

Concluding comments

We regard control, conflict, and reorganisation to be three essential principles for effective and efficient counselling and psychotherapy. They help inform both the structure and delivery of therapy, as well as where it might be most helpful for therapists to focus their attention. Some conventional aspects of therapy such as standardised techniques and strategies will be de-emphasised in favour of a systematic, sustained, and searching review of what it means for the client to be the person they are. Understanding who they are more clearly will help them move towards the person they want to be with certainty, commitment, and care.

Summary of main points

- Understanding people as state-maintaining creatures allows therapists to reframe issues such as non-compliance, treatment resistance, and non-attendance, and promotes a perspective of curiosity regarding what clients might be 'doing' when we see them act in various ways.
- Even when clients use terms we are very familiar with, we can never know exactly what they are experiencing.
- Experiences and events, such as hearing voices or being dismissed from your job, are only ever distressing *relative to* other states that are personally important.
- It is the distress associated with symptoms rather than the symptoms themselves that is the focus in MOL.
- Change should be expected to occur non-linearly and unpredictably. The best solution might not be generated first, but a successful strategy will be produced if the person continues to systematically explore their difficulties.

Topics for discussion

1 Telling people what to do is rarely effective in reducing psychological distress in the long term. Discuss.
2 Severe psychological distress can be changed quickly and dramatically with enduring positive consequences. Discuss.

Activities for learning, consolidation, and fun!

1 Ask a friend or colleague to think a thought to themselves, silently in their head. It could be a statement about them, or a recent difficulty they have had, or anything at all. Ask them to think it over and over as a succinct statement. Once they have been thinking it for a little while, ask them to say it out loud but only so they hear it, then ask them to say it to you. What happens? There is usually a big difference between thinking something inside our heads and saying it out loud.
2 Choose a label, term, or phrase for this activity. It could be 'depressed', or 'anxious', or 'panic attacks', or 'I hear voices', or anything at all. For the next five clients who use this term, ask them two things. Ask them if it bothers them and, if they say 'yes', ask them what bothers them about it. So, if you choose 'depressed', for the next five clients who tell you they are depressed, you will say, 'Does it bother you to be depressed?' Then, if they say something like, 'Of course it does', you will say, 'What bothers you about it?' What did you learn from their responses?

Chapter 4

Clarifying roles

Both the therapist and the client

By reading this chapter, you will learn:

1 the goals an MOL therapist pursues during therapy;
2 how the client's role can be explained to the client; and
3 about some of the implications of therapy involving living control systems.

Since MOL is based on the principles of PCT, it takes as its starting point the notion that both the therapist and the client are living control systems. The term 'living control system' just conveys the idea that entities that are alive are control systems. That is, they are designed according to the relationships in Figure 2.1. This means, based on the principle of control, that they are goal-achieving or state-maintaining creatures. In Chapter 5, we will explore in detail some of the dynamics involved when two living control systems develop a relationship for the purpose of reducing psychological distress, but for now we will focus more specifically on each person individually.

All about the therapist

MOL therapists understand that, as living control systems, they have preferred experiences they seek to create and perpetuate in their own lives. Some of these prioritised states will be about the therapeutic encounter. Because living control systems are organised as hierarchies of control systems of increasing perceptual complexity, therapists actually have goals upon goals upon goals regarding the therapeutic encounter. We will introduce an exercise shortly to demonstrate these many levels of goals using a specific therapeutic technique as an example.

It is important to become aware of the goals, beliefs, values, expectations, and attitudes that you have as a therapist so that you can understand your reactions and interactions more accurately. Perhaps no one is ever completely aware of the entirety of the mosaic of beliefs and thoughts that make them who they are, but we can certainly develop familiarity with important attitudes and values that are instrumental to the 'I' we know so well. We can refer back to Figure 2.1 to help guide our thinking in terms of what might be individually important to us as therapists. One of the neat things about the PCT control system loop is that it helps you learn about yourself. In particular, the environmental disturbance (*d*) aspect of the loop is instructive. This is a theory that not only helps professionally, but is informative and instructive personally as well.

From a PCT perspective, any environmental event that impacts on your ability to control is either a disturbance to a state you are controlling or part of the feedback function. The 'feedback function' is just a fancy and technical term to incorporate all those things that are part of the action (*a*) arrow in Figure 2.1, which we use to control the states, conditions, and experiences that are important to us. When we use our actions to control our perception of the position of the car on the road, the feedback function includes the steering wheel and all those components of the car that are connected in such a way that when the steering wheel is turned, the car turns also. So, in other words, anything in the environment either helps or hinders our control efforts – or has no impact at all. Some environmental happenings will have no influence to what it is you control. As you wander along the aisles of the supermarket doing your weekly grocery shopping, you might notice a queue of other shoppers at the checkout. If you have just started shopping, however, and you still have a lot of items to load into your trolley, then the checkout queues probably have no impact on your current control activity. Environmental factors are only important in terms of the impact they have on the states we are trying to control (controlled variables). Once you have finished your shopping and are approaching the checkout, however, the length of the queue may well become important. Perhaps you want to finish the shopping quickly because a friend you have not seen in a long time is coming over for dinner. In this case, a long queue will be a disturbance. It may be the case instead, however, that you are enjoying this time on your own and are in no hurry for it to finish. You might even enjoy a few minutes to look through the magazines that are invariably gathered at the checkout. How the length of the queue affects you and how you act in response to it depends very much on the *should be* state you are seeking to maintain at that moment. Every action you take in any situation is to prevent environmental disturbances from shifting your '*is*es' too far away from your '*should be*' states.

You can learn, therefore, from what you react to, the things that are and the things that might not be important to you. If you find yourself spending time discussing the value of homework with clients and emphasising its importance to them, then it would be reasonable to conclude that one of your goals in therapy is to have clients complete homework. In terms of the way our goals are organised hierarchically, you could even devote a few minutes to exploring what other therapeutic goals might be related to your goal of homework completion. One way of discovering goals in the hierarchical network of who we are is to think about 'how' and 'why' questions. The general idea is that 'why' questions shift attention up the hierarchy to higher-level, more abstract, and perhaps more preciously valued goals, whereas 'how' questions move attention down the hierarchy to more concrete, specific, and procedural types of goals.

So, in terms of the homework example, a 'why' activity might go something like this:

> *Why do you want clients to complete homework?*
> To consolidate the learning that occurred in the session.
>
> *Why do you want to consolidate the learning that occurred in the session?*
> So clients will improve more quickly and have longer-lasting outcomes.
>
> *Why do you want clients to improve quicker with longer-lasting outcomes?*
> Because then I will be doing my job well.
>
> *Why do you want to do your job well?*
> So I can think of myself as a good therapist.
>
> *Why do you want to think of yourself as a good therapist?*
> It is important to me to be good at what I do.
>
> *Why is it important to you to be good at what you do?*
> That is just the way I am.

And a 'how' activity might be:

> *How do you get clients to complete homework?*
> I make sure they know it is important.
>
> *How do you make sure they know it is important?*
> I spend time explaining how it helps.
>
> *How do you spend time explaining how it helps?*
> I leave enough time at the end of the session so I can explain it in detail.
>
> *How do you leave enough time at the end of the session?*
> I plan the session carefully and have a clock where I can see it so I can keep track of time.
>
> *How do you plan the session carefully and make sure you keep track of time?*
> I spend time before each session writing down what we will cover and I mentally track the pace of the session as it proceeds.
>
> *How do you spend time before each session writing down what will be covered?*
> I make sure I space appointments so that I have enough time beforehand to jot down some brief notes about what to cover.

As you read through those examples, you might have had the sense that you would have answered the questions differently. That is entirely appropriate. There are no right or wrong answers in this activity. In fact, it might be useful to consider how the hierarchy might have looked if your initial answer to why homework is important was, 'Because that is a technique I have been taught to use with this particular therapy.' This might, for example, lead you to realise it is important for you to follow procedures and instructions. The purpose is individual discovery rather than finding what is true or correct in an absolute sense. You might have also noticed that answers to 'how' questions often have several different options. It is one of the features of the hierarchy that branching or spreading seems to occur as attention drifts down the hierarchy. This may indicate the structure behind popular sayings such as 'There is more than one way to skin a cat' or 'Many roads lead to Rome'. In a more technical summary, William James, the pioneer of early psychology, coined the principle that living organisms show 'the pursuit of fixed ends by varying means'.

Using the 'why and how' activity can be helpful in finding out what is important to you as a therapist and why those things are important. The places where you find yourself directing most of your attention or noticing the things in therapy that you react to can be instructive in terms of areas to conduct a 'why and how' activity. Do you spend time questioning clients about childhood trauma and making connections between those distant events and their current difficulties? Perhaps a 'why' activity here would reveal what beliefs you have about trauma and psychological distress. Do you spend time redirecting clients in therapy to keep them focused on the topics you have identified as important? Again, a 'why' activity here will help you understand some more about yourself as a therapist and your understandings of your role. Do you spend a considerable amount of time at the beginning of therapy conducting a thorough assessment with the client? Is your decision-making guided by diagnostic systems such as the DSM (*The Diagnostic and Statistical Manual of Mental Disorders*; American Psychiatric Association, 2013)? Conducting 'why' activities with questions such as these will help you learn more about your motivations as a therapist.

Any time you feel yourself getting irritated or bothered about something that is happening in a counselling or psychotherapy session, you could identify the source of the irritation or botheration as a disturbance (*d*) to something you are controlling. Identifying what that something is and conducting a 'how and why' activity will help you understand why it is important to you and how you might be able to achieve the same result in different ways if you need to. For example, a therapist struggled with a client who was hard to interrupt with questions. A 'why?' questioning process revealed the answer that it bothered the therapist because he wanted to ask questions to help the client question the negative thinking being conveyed by what she was saying, and in turn a further 'why?' question revealed that the therapist's higher-level goal was to get the client to think more positively, and in turn (going up further levels) to cope better and recover. When discussing these goals in supervision, it became apparent that there would be other ways to help the client recover from her problems, and that there might be reasons why the client persists with negative thinking and is hard to interrupt. Rather than simply trying to interrupt with questions and getting frustrated, the therapist experimented with other methods – waiting until the client had stopped talking to ask the client how it had felt to talk without interruption; asking whether the client had noticed the negative tone in what she was saying; asking directly what the client thought would help her to cope better. The client revealed that she benefited from talking freely about all her problems because she felt it 'got them off my chest'. Yet, at the same time, she admitted that she could get stuck in talking too much about her problems and wanted ways to slow down her thoughts and relax. This proved to be an important turning point that might not have been discovered if the therapist had continued to focus on getting the client to answer his questions. Prior to conducting the 'why' activity, it might have been the case that the client had a *should be* state of getting things off her chest and the therapist had a *should be* state of helping the client question her negative thoughts. As each person pursued the realisation of their own *should be*, they disturbed the *should be* state of the other. We will explore more of these dynamics in Chapter 5, but it is important to highlight how the therapist was able to be more helpful to the client by increasing his own awareness of what he was doing in therapy.

Goals for an MOL therapist

It is difficult, and perhaps impossible, to outline all of the goals that MOL therapists will have regarding their therapeutic practice. However, there are two fundamental goals that flavour all of the other goals a therapist might establish. These two goals will be explained here, with further details provided in Chapter 10. Even though these goals remain consistent among MOL therapists, it is important to appreciate that, as individual living control systems, each therapist will have their own style of delivery and of doing what they do. If you observed us (TAC, WM, and SJT) doing MOL, you would no doubt see differences in the way therapy unfolds. We believe, however, that you would also be able to discern similarities in our approaches that are important and fundamental to MOL. Perhaps it is a bit like serving up a pizza. Pizzas can have lots of different toppings but there are some essential characteristics that have to be in place for pizza to be pizza rather than lasagne or fettuccine carbonara. We like to think that we each serve up MOL even though the flavour might be subtly different from time to time and from therapist to therapist.

Goal number one

The first fundamental goal for MOL therapists is to encourage clients to talk. Most often, what clients will begin talking about will be the problem for which they are seeking assistance but it might not always be that. In fact, it is surprising how frequently a client might say, 'I don't know' when asked, 'What would you like to talk about today?' or, 'What should we work on today?' or some other opening question. Even a response as simple as 'I don't know' gives the therapist a chance to wonder what the client might be 'doing' by attending an appointment and responding in that way. From this wondering perspective, a useful conversation can begin.

Often, though, clients will begin talking about their problem, and the problem, from an MOL perspective, would be conceptualised as some aspect of a client's living that is not occurring as the client would like it to. In other words, there is a gap between a '*should be*' and an '*is*' that the client is not able to reduce. The most plausible hypothesis for this sustained inability to satisfactorily reduce the '*should be*/*is*' gap brings in the second of our three fundamental principles – an unresolved conflict that is bubbling away outside the client's awareness. If a conflict is behind the source of clients' distress, then this means that there are, in fact, two sets of '*should be*s' and '*is*es' that are each opposing the gap-reducing efforts of the other. Importantly, the problem is the problem from the client's perspective, not the problem according to how well the client measures up to diagnostic criteria, not how they score on a standardised questionnaire, and not even the problem formulated from the therapist's perspective.

In MOL, there is no need to identify beliefs as being delusional, distorted, or accurate and not even really any need to make judgements about a client's level of 'insight'. The focus is simply on discovering those aspects of the client's experiential world that are not as they should be – from the client's perspective. The priority is to establish what the problem is and, in turn, why it is a problem for that individual. Establishing the problem does not necessarily mean you need to hear the client state explicitly, 'My problem is . . .' With an understanding of PCT, you can be alert to any indication that there is a *should be*/*is* separation that the client is not able to reduce satisfactorily. Statements such as: 'I'm just not the person I used to be'; 'I thought my internal scars had healed but they haven't'; 'I can't stop thinking about it'; 'I just don't feel an emotional connection to anyone'; 'Whenever I see someone thinner than me I get really jealous and think I'll never be good at anything'; and 'There doesn't seem to be a point to anything anymore' all provide openings to begin to enquire inquisitively about the difference between the way things are (*is*) and the way the client would like them to be (*should be*). In the previous chapter, we mentioned the activity of asking people if a particular event or experience bothered them and then asking what bothered them about that. These simple questions can be very efficient ways of exploring 'the problem with the problem'. Asking clients how they feel about the discontent they are describing can also have the same effect. Questions such as: 'Does it bother you that you're not the person you used to be?' or 'How do you feel about discovering your inner scars haven't healed?' will begin to illuminate those areas that may lead to the source of the distress.

The first goal in MOL, then, from a therapist's point of view, is initially to help clients talk with a view to identifying and maintaining a focus on some problematic area of their life. That is, some area of their life that is not as they would like it to be despite their efforts to make it conform to their wishes. This might sound rather obvious; after all, is getting people to talk and discuss problems not what counsellors and psychotherapists do regardless of which therapeutic modality they are working within? Yes, of course. The hair we are splitting here is that it is not necessarily *what* clients talk about that is important, but *how* they talk about it. There are two key considerations. First, in MOL, therapists are aiming to help clients to communicate openly about whatever comes into their mind without filtering what they say or how they say it, because they might, for example, feel concerned about how it might sound, or believe it to be too shaming to say out loud, or anticipate the therapist will judge them negatively, and so on. Even when clients are focusing on and talking about a problematic area of their life (goal disruption), they will also be controlling for a number of other goals simultaneously (e.g. for the therapist to like them), which might impact on the way in which they speak about the problem upon which they are trying to focus. This will be discussed in more detail in Chapter 5. Second, the therapist facilitates the client talking about a range of thoughts and feelings experienced in relation to a specific problem. It is, therefore, necessary to keep a client's attention focused on the problem long enough to process a range of associated perceptual experiences. Thus, achieving the first goal of MOL, from a therapist's stance, involves balancing both facilitating the client talking openly, and maintaining the client's attention on the problem in focus.

How the first goal is realised in practice will vary depending on the client and the therapist. The specific techniques and strategies used by the therapist are far less important than the principle of helping a client to talk openly with sustained attention on a relevant problem. The personal styles of therapists will vary but their main task is to maintain a curious attitude with regard to clients and their problems. One of the biggest threats to curious questioning is assuming that you, as the therapist, know what clients mean or you know what they are going through or you know how things are for them. The accuracy of these convictions is not in question here. Whether they are accurate or not, they will have the effect of reducing the extent to which you question in a particular area. If you assume you know what clients mean when they say they are worried about what others think of them – perhaps you have some of those worries yourself – then you will be less likely to scrutinise the details of these worries. Curious questioning will come much more easily if you are able to convince yourself that you have absolutely no idea what this person sitting in front of you is going through. And after all, you really do not!

On a practical level, at the start of MOL therapy, discussion as to what problem the client wishes to focus on is the place to start. Similarly, at the start of every subsequent meeting, the therapist asks the client to establish what is to be discussed in the session. Sometimes, clients will have a clear understanding of the problem they want to talk about and, at other times, they will be less certain but they will be aware of what is not right. As we have already mentioned, on some occasions clients might even say something such as 'I'm not really sure' in response to the therapist's initial question of:

What's on your mind today?

or:

What problem should we focus on today?

or:

What do you want to get out of the session today?

or:

What did you have in mind by coming to the appointment today?

or:

What would you like help with today?

or some other question that seeks to encourage the client to talk and establish a focus for the session. Even clients who say 'I don't know' provide MOL therapists with an area they can question curiously about. Does the client not know what the problem is? Is the client reluctant to discuss the problem? Is the client unsure about participating in the session? Can the client not see a clear place to start? Or is it something else entirely? This attitude is an important component of the first goal, which is to always ask more about whatever is being discussed at the time. The reason (or higher-level goal) for asking curiously about the current topic of conversation is to simply find a hint or clue as to the next direction to take. The principle for the MOL therapist here is not to ask questions to understand clients more clearly, or to achieve a richer formulation, or a more accurate diagnosis. Instead, MOL therapists ask questions about specific and intricate details so that clients have the opportunity to explore their experiences in a way that is unfamiliar to them and, during this unaccustomed searching of their inner world, learn new things about themselves.

Disruptions

A curious thing can be observed to happen as people generate dialogue. When people talk, from time to time their flow of dialogue is punctuated by brief interruptions. As they are talking, they might smile wryly to themselves, or shake their head, or look away, or pause, or their eyes might mist over with tears, or something else will occur that disrupts the stream of words they are producing. Sometimes, they might even keep talking but make a kind of meta or evaluative comment such as, 'Does this make any sense at all?' or, 'That sounds stupid when I say it like that' or, 'I'm feeling really confused' or, 'That doesn't sound right', or something else that indicates that, in some way, they have been listening to what they have been saying and now they are commenting on that.

Often, people do not even seem to notice that their dialogue has been disrupted and, in the blink of an eye, they resume the story from where their attention had been a moment before. In MOL, we explain these observable disruptions by assuming that, for a brief 'blip', people become aware of some other thought or image or feeling they were experiencing in the background while they were talking. A lot of the time, it seems, it is a higher level in the hierarchy that has popped into awareness and disrupted the stream of dialogue. For example, when talking about the need to check all the plug sockets several times before leaving the house, a client laughed briefly. When asked about what happened during the laugh, the client said that she was thinking how silly it must look to other people. When asked, 'What do you mean by silly?' she said that she just wanted to be normal, like everyone else. Thus, a deeper-level goal was revealed.

Goal number two

Disruptions are extremely important in MOL because the second goal of the MOL conversation is to help clients shift their awareness to higher levels in their hierarchy (Carey, 2006a, 2008a, 2009; Mansell *et al.*, 2012), and disruptions become the vehicle to facilitate this. When a disruption occurs, it is important to ask about the disruption at the same time that it is observed. While this often involves interrupting clients, if therapists wait until clients finish what they are saying, they will most likely be unable to recall the disruption. The client's attention needs to be drawn to the disruption 'in the moment' so it can be actively processed while it is occurring.

So, an MOL therapist engages a client in conversation and asks curious and detailed questions about the current topic until a disruption emerges. When the client's awareness briefly flits away from the current topic, the MOL therapist is intrigued about what might have momentarily interrupted the client's attention. At the time the disruption occurs, the MOL therapist might ask:

> *What made you look away just then?*

or:

> *What's going through your mind as you shake your head just now?*

or:

> *What's making you smile?*

or:

> *What occurred to you when you paused then?*

or something else that has the function of keeping the client's attention lingering in the area it visited only fleetingly.

At this point, we can distil the two fundamental goals of MOL. The first, as mentioned above, is to engage clients in conversation about an area of their life that is not as they would wish it to be, and the second is to ask about disruptions when they occur. Once the second goal has been achieved and you have asked about a disruption, the place they briefly visited during the disruption becomes the new topic of conversation and the first goal becomes relevant again (Carey, 2009). MOL, therefore, is an iterative process of asking in detail about whatever is at the front of a person's mind and then, when a disruption occurs, asking about the disruption, which provides new material to ask in detail about until another disruption occurs, and so on. Sometimes, clients will experience a disruption that is unrelated to the problem being discussed, in which case the therapist would help them return their attention to the problem at hand so the focus is not lost.

That is really MOL in a nutshell. Each of the three principles we have described previously are important to MOL. People who are distressed need to regain *control* over their lives, and it is *conflict* that generates distress by undermining control. A technique is needed that will help clients shift their awareness to the part of themselves that is driving this conflict and will allow their attention to persist in this place long enough for it to *reorganise* successfully. The necessary change may not happen in the session itself, but the time spent focusing on the higher-level goal generating the conflict is proposed to increase the tendency for successful change to occur. How high in the hierarchy is high enough? That is like asking about the length of a piece of string. The only proviso in MOL is that if the problem is still there, awareness needs to go higher. Of course, the only people able to say whether the problem is still there are the clients themselves.

At this point, it might also be useful to mention some of the goals an MOL therapist does *not* have during the provision of principles-based counselling and psychotherapy from a PCT perspective. An MOL therapist does not have goals about solving clients' problems for them, or providing advice and suggestions to clients, or teaching them new skills to function more successfully. MOL therapists are definitely focused on solutions, but their interest is in the novel solutions the clients have not yet generated that will resolve the conflict they are experiencing and establish a greater sense of control for them. It is not evil, nasty, or mean to make suggestions or give advice, but it is recognised that this advice can only ever be given from the therapist's perspective, and so may be just as likely to prevent successful reorganisation as to promote it. Even when solutions seem completely obvious to the therapist, the focus of curious enquiry is to wonder why this obvious solution does not yet seem so obvious to the client.

Thinking about the client

MOL can be a very different experience for clients. First, they are asked to suggest how the conversation for the session should begin. Some clients come to therapy expecting the therapist to set the agenda and decide what to talk about. Asking clients to nominate what is discussed, therefore, will be a disturbance (*d*) to some of them. They might attempt to counteract the effects of the disturbance by asking the therapist to decide or saying they do not know what to talk about. Explaining a little bit about what happens in MOL can often help to prepare clients for the work that is to come. Even saying something such as: 'When someone like you comes to see someone like me, I assume it is because some aspect of your world out there is not the way you would like it to be and, for some reason, you can't make it be right. So these sessions are all about helping you explore and understand the problem you are dealing with at the moment so that you will be able to develop solutions to what you are facing. At the beginning of every session, I will ask you where we should start or what we should focus on and we will begin the conversation at that place' can help to orient clients to what they can expect with MOL.

MOL can also be surprising for clients because it is a very different kind of conversation from what they might typically be used to. As they describe their experiences, the therapist interrupts at unexpected times to ask about something that just happened of which the client may not even have been fully aware. On occasion, clients can find it hard to answer these questions and, at times, it almost seems as though clients think they are not answering the therapist's questions 'correctly.' This can be the case particularly when the therapist might continue to ask questions about the same topic. The client, for example, might tell the therapist that they have been depressed. It is reasonable for clients to expect that discussing something such as depression would be a very familiar activity in a counselling and psychotherapy environment. Clients, therefore, might be surprised to be asked what depression means to them or if it bothers them to be depressed (and what bothers them about it), or how they know they are depressed rather than some other state such as gloomy, despondent, or miserable.

The MOL conversation can be unpredictable and even unsettling. Because the MOL therapist is following the path illuminated by disruptions in the client's dialogue, it is never known ahead of time where the trail will lead. MOL clients can be surprised at the memories and ideas that occur to them as they discuss their problems, and sometimes they can arrive in places they had not anticipated or even thought about in a long time. For a variety of reasons, the MOL conversation can, on occasion, be upsetting for the client. A degree of emotional angst can be a good sign that what is being discussed is important, and also that awareness, and therefore reorganisation, might now be in a different and more productive place.

While some amount of emotional turmoil can be an indication to the therapist that solution generation might be imminent, it is often uncomfortable for the client. Since clients are living control systems too, they are designed to oppose disturbances. There might be a strong urge from the client to minimise or remove the discomfort. The talent of the MOL therapist, therefore, is to ask questions in a sustained and systematic way, so that the client's attention stays focused in areas where reorganisation might be able to effect positive changes, but also being sensitive to the experience of the client so that the conversation does not become overwhelmingly objectionable. As we have stated in the first principle, it is important to respect and facilitate the client's need for control. We will have more to say about this in the next chapter.

At the end of an MOL session, clients have sometimes come to a different point of view or had some realisation or insight that they did not have before. On other occasions, there might be a sense of confusion in which they are questioning their previous ways of approaching things. They might also have reached a place of 'blankness' in their minds. Sometimes, they might be upset. The experience is different for different clients, but MOL takes energy and effort for both the client and the therapist. Clients have sometimes told us that, after an MOL session, they have gone home and had a nap or gone for a long walk. The active processing that is promoted in MOL sessions can continue to absorb the client's attention even after the session has finished.

During MOL, MOL therapists need to be able to track the conversation in order to be able to ask curious questions to keep clients describing their experiences. The therapists also need to be able to identify disruptions when they occur, so they must avoid becoming so engrossed in the content of the conversation that they miss important opportunities to direct clients' awareness to someplace else. Finally, therapists strive to keep their role as MOL therapists in mind and avoid assuming they know what their clients are going through or making suggestions to their clients about how they should solve their problems. The MOL session evaluation form (Carey & Tai, 2012) highlights the essentials of good MOL practice and is a useful way for therapists to reflect on their conduct in an MOL session. In Chapter 10, we will talk more about the use of this form.

An MOL client needs to identify and discuss aspects of their life that are not proceeding satisfactorily. Engaging in an MOL conversation can lead to areas of clients' worlds that they would rather not dwell on. Some people spend a lot of time and energy in *not* thinking about things or pushing things to the back of their minds. MOL requires them to do just the opposite of that. This can happen quite quickly for some clients, but other clients may prefer to adopt a gentler pace. Either is fine, as again, it is important to respect the individual preferences of clients and the specific things, such as the pace of disclosure, they might want to control. Because asking about the disruptions that occur within sessions is a fundamental goal for the MOL therapist, tracking the experiences of the client throughout the session will be a continuous process. The skill of MOL therapists is in being flexible enough in their approach to facilitate clients being able to acquire a level of control within the session in order for the session to be as helpful as possible. For example, some clients who find the experience of negative emotions threatening might require a much slower pace than others who regulate emotions much more comfortably. As mentioned earlier, clients' experience in MOL can sometimes be enhanced by preparing them for what is to come by some short explanations at the beginning.

Getting the MOL experience started

The amount of explaining that needs to be done before an MOL session starts will depend on each client, and the best way to find out how much different clients would like to know is to ask them. We have experienced many clients who do not want to know anything at all and just want to get started, and other clients who are very interested in the approach, as well as the theory behind it, and will even read more on the Internet after a session. If clients do want to know a little about what is involved, a good place to start is to explain to them that the focus of each session will be on some aspect of their life that is not the way they would like it to be and, despite their best efforts, they cannot make it be right. We generally let clients know that, at the beginning of each session, we will be asking them such questions as the ones we mentioned earlier, such as, 'What problem would you like to spend time working on today?' In the 'Thinking about the client' section above, we provided a short example of some of the things we might say to clients in the first session to help them understand what is expected of them.

It can also be useful to let clients know that you, as the therapist, will not be telling them what to do or giving them advice or suggestions or strategies to try. We let clients know that our whole focus in the sessions we have with them is about finding solutions to their problems, but we are interested in helping clients spawn their own solution rather than convincing or persuading clients to adopt the solution that we think is right. Sometimes, during this conversation, clients might get the idea that we think that they know what to do and they are just not doing it. On occasions, this might be correct, but mostly it is not. One of the very treacherous things about conflicts is that there are no existing solutions that can achieve two incompatible states simultaneously. We let clients know, therefore, that we do not expect that they already have the solution, but we do believe that they have all the resources they need to create a one-off, custom-built, made-to-order, snugly fitting resolution that will be just right for them.

It can often be helpful to also alert clients ahead of time to the vagaries of reorganisation. We tend not to go into technical details, but we do talk with clients about the learning mechanism they inherited as a birthright. It can be useful to know that the best solution might not come along first and that, sometimes, things can seem worse before they get better. Clients might also find it reassuring to know that during those times when they are really stressed and they have seemingly 'crazy' ideas running through their mind, this could be reorganisation doing what reorganisation does – generating alternatives to consider. Reorganisation does not know how to give up. So, for as long as people persist, and are given help when needed to move their awareness from place to place in their hierarchy, ideal solutions will be generated. Reorganisation is the ultimate light at the end of the tunnel, and also the means for bringing the light closer. Such is the indefatigable optimism with which MOL therapists are encouraged to approach their sessions.

From time to time, clients might be sceptical about whether or not 'just talking' about their problems will help. For these clients, having a discussion about the benefits of talking can be valuable. Clients seem to readily engage with the idea that there is something very different between having a thought inside your head and saying it out loud. It is more different still if, when you say it out loud, you say it to someone else. We do not shy away from letting clients know that we do not understand the reasons for this difference very well yet, but the difference is there nevertheless. Even when thoughts seem jumbled or racing or hard to pin down, by engaging in a conversation and answering the questions of another, some kind of change seems to occur. People cannot talk out loud the same way that thoughts seem to be able to race on the inside, so being asked to talk about the thoughts may introduce some order and organisation without even knowing how this has occurred.

Other topics may also be useful to discuss depending on the clients, their interests, and their previous experiences with therapy. It might be useful, for example, to talk about disruptions and the mobility of awareness. Most clients will agree that when they think about problems within their own minds, or talk to friends about their problems, they do not do so in a way where they sustain awareness on the problem for any length of time, or direct their attention to other background thoughts that occur as they are talking. MOL is an open and transparent process where nothing is 'done' to clients without them being able to know about it and question it. It is always best to be guided by clients about how much to tell them when they first encounter MOL but, ultimately, the ideal way of explaining MOL to clients is to give them an experience of it so, even in the first session, we try to do only as much talking about MOL as is necessary and then, with the clients' permission, we move straight into an MOL conversation.

A final word

It is important to remember that both the therapist and the client are controlling agents. As such, they can both become conflicted and they both have reorganising systems. Noticing the things that bother you as a therapist and thinking about these botherations as disturbances to your controlled processes can be a useful way of understanding more clearly the things that are important to you. Sometimes, as therapists, we discover that something that is important to us might not, in some therapy situations, be compatible with our goal of providing what is helpful to the client in that moment. This is discussed more in Chapter 5. Although this is a normal challenge for any therapist, in MOL we would encourage the use of supervision to consider how the very principles of PCT also apply to our own work and ourselves. MOL is, fundamentally, an optimistic and respectful approach in which MOL therapists offer themselves to clients for clients to use at their discretion to help them make their worlds more like the way they would wish them to be.

Summary of main points

- The two chief goals for an MOL therapist are: (1) to ask curious, detailed, and specific questions about the current topic of conversation; and (2) to ask about disruptions.

- The MOL conversation can be an unusual experience for clients where they talk, for sustained periods of time, about topics they might not ordinarily want to talk about.
- It can be useful to explain some things to clients at the beginning of an MOL encounter, but the best way of explaining MOL may be to provide clients with an experience of it.

Topics for discussion

1 Sometimes, therapists have a better understanding of the clients' problem than the clients do. Discuss.
2 Having clients become upset in therapy can be useful and important in terms of their eventual reorganisation of their problem. How can you support them while they are upset without minimising or solving their 'upsetness' for them?

Activities for learning, consolidation, and fun!

1 Identify an aspect of your therapeutic practice you would like to know more about. Ask five 'why' and five 'how' questions about the area you have identified. What did you learn? For extra fun and discovery, try the 'why and how' activity in other areas of your life. Is it important to you to stay in touch with family and friends – why and how? What are you finding out about yourself during these activities?
2 Make some notes about the things you would like to say to clients in the first session. Try these out and reflect on them. How did the clients respond? Do you need to say more or less or rephrase what you had prepared?
3 Generate question lists of how to ask about disruptions. When you notice someone smile to him or herself, what are five different ways you could ask about that?

Chapter 5

The therapeutic relationship

By reading this chapter, you will learn:

1 what the essential ingredient of an effective therapeutic relationship might be;
2 to prioritise assisting clients to review their thoughts *after* they say them rather than before; and
3 to think about the therapeutic relationship in terms of two people both seeking to achieve goals.

The importance of the therapeutic relationship is well accepted in counselling and psychotherapy. A voluminous body of literature, including therapies of many different persuasions, attests to the valuable role of the therapeutic relationship in helping people reduce psychological distress (e.g. Martin, Garske, & Davis, 2000). Sometimes, distinctions are made between the therapeutic *relationship* and the therapeutic *alliance*, although the extent to which these two things may be similar or different is not a central concern from the principles-based approach to counselling and psychotherapy that we are presenting here. In this chapter, we are discussing the situation where two people agree to meet for the purpose of reducing the psychological distress of one of those people. Furthermore, we are assuming that the person who is not distressed has some level of formal training in counselling and psychotherapy. The person who is distressed may or may not have formal training.

Like other therapeutic approaches, MOL also endorses the emphasis on the therapeutic relationship. From a principles-based perspective, however, the focus is not just *what* is effective about the therapeutic relationship, but also *how* the relationship is effective. 'Effective' in this context refers to the extent to which the therapeutic relationship can be used by the client to reduce psychological distress. If we understand what is useful about the relationship in promoting the reduction of psychological distress, we might be able to focus our efforts more precisely and be more effective more of the time. Importantly, we will also know what to adapt or modify if the relationship is not helping in the way that it can. In particular, in MOL we are interested in understanding the dynamics of the therapeutic relationship from a characterisation of the relationship as the interaction of two living control systems.

Applying the principles to the therapeutic relationship

The three principles of control, conflict, and reorganisation provide a focus for understanding how the therapeutic relationship works to enable the reduction in psychological distress. First, the principle of control emphasises that, whether the level of distress experienced by the client is low or high, it is important that they feel in control of the process. Crucial here is the understanding that clients will be controlling certain experiences while they are in the company of the therapist just as much as they are in their everyday life when they are not meeting with the therapist. Equally vital is the continual awareness that, like the client, the therapist is a living control system and will be controlling valued experiences while they interact with the client. Second, the principle of conflict implies that there is a conflict at the heart of the problem the client is experiencing. Recognising that conflict is underlying the client's psychological distress helps to guide the therapist's questioning interventions, and also helps the therapist consider possible explanations for ambivalent, contradictory, or erratic behaviour by the client. Third, the principle of reorganisation indicates that clients will need to spend some time shifting their awareness towards the system governing this conflict and sustain their awareness at this place for a sufficient amount of time for change to occur. As awareness moves from place to place in a client's neural network, there may be changes in the client's emotional state. Negative emotion is frequently but not always characteristic of reorganisation – sometimes intense positive emotions can be experienced as well. It is the case that, on occasion, a client might become more upset than they were before as their reorganising system generates random error reducing possibilities. Understanding the operation of the reorganising system and its inexhaustible nature can help the therapist help the client persist in the face of adversity and uncomfortable distress.

The subtleties of the MOL therapeutic relationship entail finding ways to balance the client's understandable, natural, and enduring need for control with the process of accessing and 'sitting with' experiences and processes related to the problem for long enough to make a difference. It is entirely reasonable that a person would seek to reduce or move away from images, feelings, and ideas that distress them. In MOL, however, the therapist constantly encourages the client to look more closely and more deeply at these areas so that they can notice things they might not have detected previously, and experience the operations of the reorganising system as it generates the changes that are necessary to realise a greater sense of contentment and satisfaction. For some clients, this occurs smoothly while for others there is an ebb and flow of attention that needs careful management. It may help at this stage to describe aspects of the general therapeutic milieu that provide some justification for why a PCT approach that uses the principles of control, conflict, and reorganisation might be important in understanding the role of the therapeutic relationship.

The role of talking

We know that a wide range of interventions help people in psychological distress. These interventions can be informed by vastly different philosophical and theoretical backgrounds and may use very different techniques in their practice. Typically, the range of available interventions involves the distressed person talking about their problem in some way. Talking about topics that are unrelated to the problem for a majority of the therapeutic time is not likely to achieve reductions in psychological distress. Yet, there are also interventions that do not involve talking, or do not even involve another person.

An area of helping known as 'expressive therapies' in which people paint or draw or dance about their difficulties can be effective for some people some of the time. Also, many people find online programmes helpful in which they access and spend time with Web-based resources. In some of these programmes, they have no contact at all with a therapist. The common element to all of these approaches, however, seems to be a sustained focus, in some form, by the distressed person, on details of their psychological distress. It is the focus on the experience, therefore, rather than the talking per se, which is important.

In talking therapies, the real value in the conversation might not be so much in what is said but the fact that the discourse from the client allows the therapist, from the outside, to gain some sense of where the client's attention might be focused at any particular point in time and how this focus shifts as the conversation proceeds. The therapist assumes that changes in the content of the client's dialogue or disruptions to that dialogue may reflect commensurate internal changes in the client's focus of awareness. It would be extremely interesting and valuable if future research could clarify the extent to which effective therapy is, essentially, a process of tracking and redirecting awareness.

For some people with some problems, the usefulness of the therapeutic relationship might be the arrangement of a face-to-face conversation with another person. Features of this type of interaction, in which the client articulates ideas and attitudes that they do not normally share with others, might raise issues, for example, of social judgement, which could have important therapeutic implications when these concerns are highlighted by awareness for an extended period of time. Future research might enhance the effectiveness of psychotherapy and counselling by investigating in detail the differential effects of talking out loud versus talking out loud *to another person.*

Rumination: an unhelpful type of focusing

Sometimes, people seem to have the experience of focusing on their problem in an unhelpful way. Rumination is a term used to describe thinking something over and over again in a way that feels uncontrollable. Rumination is generally unpleasant and people tend to do what they can to stop it or avoid it. They might develop distraction techniques to block their thoughts or bump their mind to a different topic. Also, when people ruminate, they tend to maintain a fixed focus on a particular stream of thought and ignore other thoughts that might be briefly illuminated by awareness during the period of rumination. It is almost as though awareness becomes 'locked in' on the ruminative content. Understanding people as living control systems and the fact that they are always 'on' and always doing something helps with ruminative problems. An MOL therapist helping someone who describes ruminating might curiously wonder if the rumination bothers the person and, if it does, what bothers them about it. The MOL therapist might also consider rumination to be an active process and they might be intrigued at what the person is 'doing' by devoting their attention so exclusively to this aspect of their experience. Through this inquiring perspective, the MOL therapist can help clients explore the pattern of the rumination, as well as other areas of their experiential world that might be connected in some way.

A ruminative focus is quite different from the kind of focus developed in MOL that assists people in reducing their psychological distress. In MOL sessions, people are encouraged to attend to, and explore, other thoughts that occur to them as they are focusing on their problem. Through this sustained, systematic, and structured focus on their problems, people process things differently, and they develop new perspectives and insights about that which they had found troubling. Indeed, this may very well represent the difference between the brooding and reflection components of rumination (Treynor, Gonzalez, & Nolen-Hoeksema, 2003).

The minimum that is required

At a minimum, therefore, a sustained focus on the area of distress being experienced by the person must be established. As mentioned in the last chapter, it can take skill and ingenuity on the part of the therapist to encourage people to talk in detail about those topics that they would rather push to the back of their mind or to some other place that is away from their direct attention. From this perspective, all therapy could be seen as a type of exposure situation in which people attend to difficult thoughts, feelings, images, and behaviours when they would rather try to ignore them (Carey, 2011a).

Even though talking is the main vehicle through which MOL is conducted, sometimes even the absence of talking does not preclude MOL working helpfully. One client was involved in a minor traffic accident and could clearly remember seeing the expression on the face of the young girl who was a passenger in the other car. The client accessed therapy to help her deal with the trauma she was experiencing subsequent to the car accident. After a few sessions of therapy, a pattern emerged in which the client would engage in conversation for about 15 to 20 minutes and would then become silent. She would sit quietly for extended periods of time and, eventually, the session would end without her having made any further comments. During the silences, the MOL therapist would wonder what the client was 'doing' and would ask questions from time to time about where the client's attention might be focused or what might be going through her mind. Although there was no verbal assistance from the client to indicate where her focus might be, the therapist assumed it might be helpful to continue to ask questions intermittently to draw the client's attention to the thinking in which she seemed to be engaged.

Despite the client's silences, she continued to make and attend appointments. After several more appointments, it was revealed that the car accident had triggered memories of the client's own childhood abuse, of which she had never told anyone. During the MOL sessions, she wanted to discuss this abuse with the therapist but was ashamed and embarrassed about it and could not bring herself to mention it. So the silences were manifestations of a conflict she was experiencing between wanting to talk about her abuse and also not wanting to talk about it. By continuing to make appointments and the therapist continuing to respect her silences, while also using the silences to ask questions that might help the client keep her awareness focused in a particular, yet unknown (to the therapist) area, the client was, ultimately, able to discuss her abuse, explore her memories, and achieve a satisfying outcome from therapy. The client commented that being able to figure out a way to talk to her male therapist about the abuse was important to her because she thought if she could do this that would enable her to talk to her husband about the abuse as well. Even when clients are not able to talk for some of the time in therapy, therefore, using the principles of PCT, it can still be possible to help them usefully process problematic experiences.

Why should the client regulate the focusing process?

Directing attention to difficult areas for sustained periods of time can be arduous and emotional. Some people, in fact, seem to prefer to muddle through life doing the best they can without addressing the underlying source of their distress – or their 'muddlesomeness'. We believe that it is their right to do so. Ethical codes and professional standards support this position. For example, the *Code of Ethics and Conduct* of the British Psychological Society (British Psychological Society, 2009) explicitly states that '*Psychologists should*: . . . (ii) Ensure from the first contact that clients are aware of their right to withdraw at any time from the receipt of professional services or from research participation' (p. 14). Also, the *Code of Ethics* of the Australian Psychological Society (Australian Psychological Society, 2007) states that '*Psychologists* ensure consent is informed by: . . . (e) advising *clients* that they may participate, may decline to participate, or may withdraw from methods or procedures proposed to them' (p. 13). Finally, the Australian *National Practice Standards for the Mental Health Workforce* (Commonwealth of Australia,

2002) states that 'Mental health professionals demonstrate an understanding of . . . legislation related to the application of informed consent for treatment and the consumer's right to refuse treatment' (p. 8), and 'Mental health professionals demonstrate an ability to . . . inform consumers of their right to informed consent for treatment and of their right to refuse treatment' (p. 9). Of course, issues of risk must always be taken seriously, but the way in which risk is addressed does not alter the fact that, while psychological therapy can be tremendously helpful for people who want to engage with it, the decision about whether or not to engage is ultimately one that only the individual can make. People can be detained against their will in extreme circumstances, but they cannot be 'therapised' against their will – ever.

Ultimately, what to do about the distress a person experiences is a decision that can only be made by that person. It is possible that researchers and clinicians who develop and deliver programmes of counselling and psychotherapy have a skewed perspective regarding psychological unease because, by and large, the only people they have experience of are those people who access, at some point, psychological or mental health services. Many people experiencing psychological torment, however, never access mental health services. Kessler and his colleagues (Kessler *et al.*, 1994), for example, found in a national survey in the United States that 48 per cent of participants reported a lifetime history of at least one mental health disorder. Of those people endorsing symptoms of at least one mental health disorder, only 40 per cent 'ever obtained professional help for their disorders' (p. 12). Even though this study was published in 1994, the same finding of only a proportion of those people endorsing symptoms of a mental health disorder accessing mental health services still seems to apply. Merikangas and her colleagues (Merikangas *et al.*, 2011) published results of an international study on the prevalence and correlates of bipolar spectrum disorder. They reported that 'Less than half of those with lifetime BPS received mental health treatment' (p. 241). These research findings could certainly be used to suggest that access to mental health services is less than ideal but, even if problems of access were eliminated, it would still be the case that some individuals would choose alternative means of managing their mental health. And that is their right. Psychological treatments are an invaluable resource for many, but not all, people who experience psychological distress.

Sometimes, people attend counselling and psychotherapy through the prompting of others. Even when clients attend therapy at the urging of others, therapy will only be effective if the client makes the personal decision to participate in whatever routines and activities this particular therapy has to offer – again, the principle of control is pivotal. In MOL, the basic activity is creating a sustained conversation about an area of difficulty, as well as other aspects of a client's life that may be connected to the difficulty in some way and are, ideally, the origin of the difficulty. Therefore, MOL will only be effective if the person who is accessing therapy makes a commitment to engage in the MOL conversation.

Clarifying the therapeutic relationship in terms of what is minimally required

In MOL, therefore, the therapeutic relationship is not important per se. The value of the therapeutic relationship is that it allows the liberated, uncensored expression of the client's problem specifically, and their experiential world more generally. Often, qualities such as warmth, trust, rapport, and unconditional positive regard are described as important aspects of the therapeutic relationship. The only value in these characteristics from an MOL perspective, however, is if they facilitate the open and frank discussion by the client of their problem. We emphasise the importance of considering the experience of the therapeutic relationship from the client's perspective. For some clients, for example, unconditional positive regard might elicit feelings of shame and unworthiness. Similarly, a therapist who regards their actions as emanating empathy might lead to some clients feeling misunderstood or perceiving the therapist's behaviour as patronising. Keijsers, Schaap, and Hoogduin (2000) suggest that it is the extent to which therapist and client expectations match that is important with regard to the therapeutic relationship. That is, the degree to which a therapist is warm or controlling is only important *relative to* the expectations of the client. Problems will be encountered in the therapeutic relationship, for example, if the client expects the therapist to be directive but the therapist prefers to be collaborative. In this instance, it is not a desire for direction or a desire for collaboration that is the problem. The problem arises through the juxtaposition of the two opposing preferences (direction and collaboration) being sought simultaneously in the same relationship.

While some people have no one in their social sphere to talk to about problems, it is likely to be the case that many clients who seek the assistance of counsellors and psychotherapists already have at least one other relationship in their life that is characterised by warmth, trust, and other positive qualities. Clearly, for a client to be seeking therapy, these other relationships were not sufficient to help the client solve their problem. We are suggesting, therefore, that although aspects of the relationship such as warmth, trust, and positive regard promote therapy effectiveness, they are not themselves therapeutic. We are also proposing that, for the conversation with the therapist to be more effective than their other conversations in assisting the reduction of psychological distress, then it must be a qualitatively different conversation from any they have had previously.

The feature of a therapeutic relationship that distinguishes this relationship from other warm and trusting relationships in the client's life is that in the therapeutic relationship, the client is able to express their thoughts and feelings freely and openly. In other relationships, a certain level of 'filtering' or 'censoring' occurs as the client modifies what they are saying because of their regard for the other person. Even when clients have people with whom they can talk openly and frankly, it is likely to be the case that they do not reveal to these other people all that they think to themselves. One young woman who hears voices explained to her therapist that she was very close to her parents and could talk to them about anything. Then, as the conversation proceeded, she said that she would not tell her parents all of the things that the nasty voice said because it swore at her and told her to harm herself. She would not go into details with her parents about this voice because she did not want to worry them. Clearly, then, even in the context of close family relationships, this young woman was filtering the contents of her mind before sharing them with her parents. In a principles-based MOL therapeutic relationship, however, the therapist aims to enable the client to minimise this filtering so that a candid exploration and expression of their troubles is promoted. So, when there are difficulties in the therapeutic relationship, rather than engaging in rapport-building exercises or trying to create a greater sense of trust and warmth, an MOL therapist directly addresses the client's willingness to express themselves freely.

Sometimes, a simple explanation can be helpful in letting clients know what is expected from an MOL perspective. Here is one example of what could be said to a client:

> *In the work that I do, I assume that the most important part of our discussion is that you feel comfortable to say whatever is going through your mind without filtering it, or censoring it in some way, or somehow modifying it before you say it. Often, in relationships outside therapy, we don't just say whatever comes into our mind. If we're talking to a friend, or colleague, or partner, or child, or parent, we might phrase things in a certain way because we don't want to worry them, or we don't want them to think poorly of us, or for some other reason that is connected to the relationship we have with them. While thinking about the way we say things before we say them can be important from a social relationship perspective, it can actually get in the way of being able to review and reorganise attitudes, ideas, and beliefs. From my perspective, being able to hear with your own ears what you* ***really*** *think about your troubles is one of the most therapeutic things that will happen in the work we do together, so I'll be encouraging you to speak first and to think about what you say afterwards rather than the other way around. Does that make sense to you?*

Beginning a discussion in this way can be very helpful therapeutically. One client, for example, explained that she had 'no-go zones' in her mind. These were areas that she did not want to spend time explaining or exploring because they contained difficult material. Even without this client needing to share the content of these no-go zones, a conversation *about* the no-go zones was very useful. Talking about how many no-go zones there were, how something became a no-go zone, if no-go zones ever changed to go zones, how long they lasted, and so on helped the client consider these no-go zones in ways she had not thought of before. Another example is a client who at the start of sessions would say that she did not know what to talk about and would ask the therapist what the therapist thought was important to discuss. With sensitive questioning, the client was able to reflect that she thought it was important for her to please others, although this resulted in her subjugating her own needs. These conversations were all carried out in a way that the client was able to control the extent to which these areas were explored, with the goal of the therapist being to promote an environment in which the client felt safe to freely express the ideas that occurred to her as they occurred.

After a brief explanation such as the one provided above, one client said, 'There's no way I'd be able to tell you what was going on in my head.' This led to a very useful discussion about what this young man's experience had been as he listened to the explanation, what thoughts he had become aware of, and what would stop him talking about the original contents of his mind without filtering them first. After a few sessions, the young man gradually began to filter less and less for a helpful therapeutic outcome.

Carey, Kelly, Mansell, and Tai (2012) reported one client who clearly depicted the MOL sentiment being explained here. The client said:

> Even though I know that words are never sufficient, the effort I put into putting my experiences into words seems to make them clearer, and then they make sense. I could only risk doing that in these sessions at the start, but now it's easier to put my feelings into words, and it makes them all seem so much more . . . normal!
>
> (p. 12)

Clients will often remark that their ideas sound silly, absurd, or even crazy as they say them out loud, and it is precisely this type of evaluation (of silly, absurd, or crazy) that can be very useful therapeutically.

How to talk about something without talking about it

When clients find it difficult to talk about a topic but still want to find a way of exploring their distress, it is also a possibility that they can use another name for what it is that they do not wish to talk about – maybe 'the problem', 'stuff', or even 'thunder clouds'! One young man who had experienced serious childhood trauma came for therapy after a suicide attempt. At first, the young fellow seemed ambivalent about being in therapy and then he revealed that he did not want to talk about the things that were on his mind. The therapist explained that because of the way the MOL process worked, the content of the man's troubles were not of critical importance to the conduct of the conversation. The therapist suggested to this client that he could call his problem 'falling snow' or 'green apples' or any other term he was comfortable with and the conversation could still proceed satisfactorily. The client said, 'Well, I've gone to the trouble of coming here. I might as well give it a go', and a 45-minute conversation about 'green apples' unfolded. The therapist never did learn what the source of the problem was, but the young man only attended two more sessions and appeared to benefit from the sessions. He subsequently developed plans to travel abroad and go to university.

Using a neutral term for the problem might allow clients to still talk about how they manage the problem and why it might be difficult for them, without any disclosure of the actual problem, event, or fact itself. For some people, the use of a metaphor or image is an easier way of talking about their problem. For example, one client described her experience in terms of an image of her being stuck in a box, which prevented her from being able to be seen by others and also for her to move towards others. In time, she was able to speak more freely about her difficulties in developing trusting relationships with people. These are examples of how the flexibility of MOL can help enable the client's control. Because MOL is patient-led, it uses the images and the metaphors generated by the client as vehicles for exploration. A young woman who hears voices described her voices sitting around a table in a boardroom without her present. Another client described a large Amazonian figure and a small cowering schoolgirl as images that came to her as she discussed her conflict while another client felt controlled by a troll with a whip. All of these images are valuable resources for the MOL therapist to harness in the context of the therapeutic relationship to encourage clients' unfiltered and sustained expression of different aspects of their problem.

Keeping the relationship therapeutic

The gauge of effective MOL therapeutic relationships, therefore, is the extent to which you sense that clients are talking freely about the contents of their mind during therapy. Of course, this is something that we can never know with absolute certainty, but by asking, and with careful observation – particularly of disruptions – you will get a sense of the extent to which the window they are offering you into their life has plane or frosted glass in it. A client who answers a therapist's questions spontaneously might be filtering less than another client who pauses before answering. If the therapist does sense that there may be some filtering occurring, then this can even become the focus of conversation. Questions such as:

What's going through your mind as you pause before answering?

Are you thinking about how to say what's coming into your mind?

How are you deciding what the best way is to say something?

How are you wanting things to sound as you explain them to me?

can often help to make the filtering a topic of conversation. As clients discuss their filtering, it seems to become less important for them to engage in it. Perhaps it is difficult to filter and to talk about filtering at the same time. So, in terms of the therapeutic relationship from an MOL point of view, striving to help clients feel comfortable enough to talk about the things they do not want to admit, even to themselves, and encouraging them to reflect on these things once they have expressed them, is the most MOL-effective thing a therapist can do.

While we concentrate mostly on talking as the medium through which therapy proceeds, we have also provided examples to demonstrate that therapy can still be applied with good effect even when talking about the topic is problematic. The highest priority is helping clients maintain their focus on the distress they are experiencing, as well as searching for the area that is generating the distress. Mostly, talking is the tool that is used by the therapist to keep track of where the client's attention might be focused, but even when talking is difficult, helping clients explore their distress can still occur. If the therapist's chief goal is to help their clients explore the distress the clients are experiencing, as well as exploring the higher-level source of the distress, then since the therapist is a living control system, they will find ways of realising that goal even if the talking option is unavailable or less than ideal.

Acknowledging the state-maintaining nature of interactions in the therapeutic relationship

While encouraging the client to talk freely about their problems, it is critical to keep in mind the 'state-maintaining' nature of both you and the client. As a therapist, you will have particular ideas about the way you like therapy to proceed, and the client will have expectations as well. The client may have been to see other counsellors, therapists, psychologists, or mental health practitioners, and, if so, will have developed particular ideas from these experiences. Even when clients have not experienced therapy for themselves, they might know of people who have accessed therapy or they might have formed views from television or movies. Sometimes, people might even be a completely 'blank slate' in terms of what to expect.

The main point here is that clients will have some goals, in fact a whole network of them, when you meet them for the first time. Helping clients know what to expect will be very useful in terms of enabling them to decide if this experience will be what they need. As mentioned above, it is the alignment of client and therapist expectations that is likely to be important, rather than the expectations of either the therapist or the client considered in isolation. Therefore, spending some time enquiring about clients' expectations and thinking about relationship stumbles in the context of misaligned expectations can be very useful ways of ensuring the therapeutic relationship is maximally beneficial.

A higher-level goal for MOL therapists is to be 'therapeutically useful' to their clients. That is, the reason MOL therapists set goals to ask about the topic the client volunteers and then ask about disruptions is because we regard that as the most effective and efficient way of being therapeutically useful to clients. From the principles of PCT, the most therapeutic thing a therapist can do is to direct clients' attention to higher levels in their hierarchy, which may contain the root of their distress.

One way of addressing difficulties in the therapeutic relationship is to consider the dynamics of interacting control systems. Figure 5.1 (Carey *et al.*, 2012)

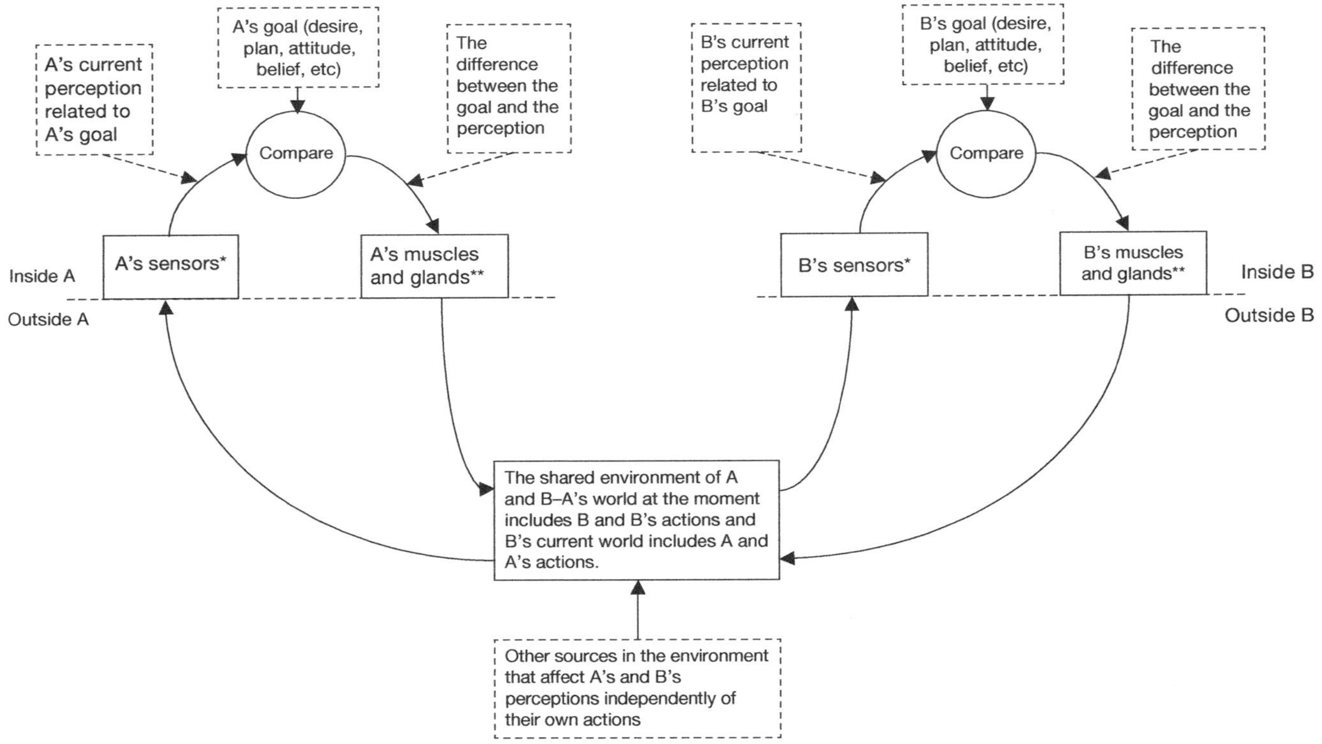

Figure 5.1 Generic model of the interaction of two people conceptualised as control systems

* Sensors can be thought of things such as eyes, ears, and skin in which environmental input is converted into neuronal signals

** Muscles and glands are those parts of the system that allow individuals to affect their environments

Source: Copyright © British Association for Behavioural and Cognitive Psychotherapies, 2012, reproduced with permission

illustrates the way in which two control systems such as the one illustrated in Figure 2.1 can be combined in order to model and understand social interactions such as a therapeutic relationship. From Figure 5.1, it can be appreciated that since the therapist and the client are in each other's environments, they can either be a disturbance to the other or part of the other's feedback function, at any one time. Disturbances act against a person's goals, whereas the feedback function enables a person to experience their goals.

Of course, it is also likely that, on some occasions in therapy, the therapist is neither a disturbance nor part of the client's feedback function as they simply observe the client listening to their own descriptions of their problem and how to manage it. The feedback of one's own speech is another important example of control in action. For the most part, however, the therapist will either be a disturbance or part of the feedback function. The times when a therapist has no influence at all on the controlling of the client are likely to be fleeting given the very intense nature of a therapeutic interaction, and we only mention those times here for the sake of completeness.

Stiles (2009) also emphasises the importance of expectations and deviations from those expectations. According to Stiles, both the therapist and client are trying to be helpful within the context of the therapeutic relationship. Stiles suggests that the therapist and the client:

> monitor expected outcome, and when they see deviations they act to make corrections [cf. Powers, 2005]. They watch what happens and use what they notice. If they discover a productive approach, they tend to continue it. If they try something that doesn't work, they tend to stop doing it or modify it.
>
> (p. 88)

This description is entirely consistent with the depiction of the therapist and the client as living control systems as in Figure 5.1.

Dealing with difficulties in the therapeutic relationship

Although, for the most part, the therapeutic relationship will be a valuable resource for clients in assisting them to reduce their psychological distress, on occasion difficulties can occur. When problems occur in the relationship, it can be useful to refer to Figure 5.1 as a way of understanding what might be happening. Rather than thinking of clients as oppositional, or non-compliant, or treatment-resistant, or even insightless, MOL therapists think of clients as living control systems, so the focus is always about trying to understand the states they are maintaining by the actions that can be observed. An MOL therapist often wonders, 'What is this person controlling by sitting here with me and talking to me about their difficulties?' Just as it is a normal feature of human beings to have their own conflicts, it is normal for conflicts to occur in relationships from time to time.

A principles-based approach informs us that the way to manage conflict is to focus awareness on the factors involved and discuss those factors rather than to ignore the fact that a conflict might be occurring. This applies to interpersonal conflict in therapy too.

On those occasions when a client does not go along with an activity, or questions something being done, or disagrees with you, you can assume that perhaps you have just disturbed one of the client's controlled states. This provides you with some good information that you can use to better understand the client and inform the areas in which you question. It is also important to maintain a tentative and hypothetical attitude towards your reasoning because the disturbance might not have occurred for the reasons you had assumed. Practising cognitive flexibility and being prepared to revise your ideas will be extremely helpful in ensuring you remain as helpful as possible to your clients. If the conflict persists, then it can be helpful to talk about what you are noticing and share your observations with the client, demonstrating genuine curiosity regarding how to understand and best proceed with the process. Of course, it may be the case that therapy will not provide some clients with what they want at a particular point in time.

Sometimes, promoting the client's control over the therapeutic relationship can even include reconsidering the extent to which therapy proceeds even for a particular session. It can occur that clients are in a different frame of mind when they attend the session compared to the frame of mind they were in when they booked the session. The entire focus of an MOL session is to help the client figure out ways to live more as they would like to outside the session. We assume that the most effective and efficient way of doing that is to spend time exploring difficult areas and, through these explorations, finding other places in a person's experiential world that might be somehow connected to the difficulty. Enabling clients to regulate this process can, from time to time, involve postponing a session when they are not entirely ready to grapple with their difficulties or when they are satisfied with their current circumstances. It would not be considered therapeutically useful to spend a session talking about topics that are unrelated to the distress, so after considering different ways of exploring clients' problems and talking to them about their hesitancy, sometimes the most respectful demonstration of promoting client control can be to end the session and assure clients that they will be able to book another appointment as soon as they want to delve into their problem.

There is definitely room to discuss adapting what occurs in therapy but, even then, the therapist might not be able to provide what the client wants. One client, for example, was frustrated at the MOL therapist not giving her strategies and telling her what to do. When discussing this client in supervision with a psychiatrist, however, the psychiatrist advised *not* to give the client any strategies and explained that she routinely offered advice and suggestions when she saw the client but the client debated every idea that was proposed and could outline in detail why the suggestion would fail. Being able to think of this client as a living control system and to raise tentative hypotheses about possible controlled states provided a useful perspective from which to consider the therapeutic encounter. Perhaps, for example, the client feels overwhelmingly burdened by her problems and wants the health professionals she visits to 'fix' the distress she experiences. She might find it painful to appreciate her own abilities or the hole she sees herself at the bottom of might seem too deep to climb out of. Directing the way her health professionals help her, by telling the health professional who does not make suggestions to make more suggestions and by telling the health professional who does make suggestions why the suggestions will not work, may be this client's way of feeling a sense of control. It could be extremely useful to discuss this pattern and explore the hypothesis with the client in terms of the processes occurring in therapy, but ultimately the client must be willing to engage in that conversation.

Do what you do do well

It might be just as important to therapists' effectiveness to know what they *do not* do as well as what they do do. MOL therapists, basing their practices on the principles of PCT, see their primary role as establishing a relationship that helps clients focus their awareness on their distress and then helps them search for the higher level source of that distress. MOL therapists have an attitude of making themselves redundant as effectively and efficiently as possible with regard to their clients living their lives according to their own design. For that reason, it is envisaged that MOL will become part of clients' lives only for as long as it takes clients to resolve their conflict and re-engage with life in the way they want to.

From the PCT-informed perspective of MOL, a therapist's primary role is to ask questions that help a client shift their awareness to higher levels in their experiential hierarchy so that they can generate solutions to their problems. There is nothing horrible or awful with suggesting strategies to a client, or advising clients on a particular course of action, but this is not considered to be part of the remit of an MOL therapist. An MOL therapist presumes that they do not know the best way for clients to live their lives and they do not know the ideal course of action for any particular client in any given situation. An MOL therapist also has immense respect for the clients' own reorganising system and understands that clients will be able to generate their own solutions to their troubles if they are helped to focus their awareness on those areas of their experiential world from which their problems are emanating.

There may also be nothing abhorrent with picking up a person's dry cleaning or their weekly grocery shopping, but these things are typically not considered part of a therapist's responsibility for their clients. A therapist provides therapy within certain professional and ethical codes, and these should always be observed. Even within those codes, therapists will provide the therapy that they think is best for their clients. MOL therapists believe MOL is the most efficiently effective way of helping, and that is what they provide. With a clear understanding of what is and is not their role, an MOL therapist might communicate, at the beginning of therapy, to the client:

We don't yet know what works for everyone, so it may be that this particular way of working is not what you need at this point in time. If you do find you're not getting the help you need, I'd certainly like to know about that so that we could discuss other options that might be available, but if this turns out to not be what you need at the moment, it doesn't mean that there is anything wrong with you or anything wrong with me. It just means that, for some reason, this way of discussing problems isn't helpful for you just now. If that does turn out to be the case, I don't want to get in the way of you finding something that will be more helpful, and you should know that you will be able to make further appointments at a later date if you think they might be helpful then.

Being open and transparent with clients will be very useful in helping them make decisions about what they need and how they can get as much of it as they require.

Final remarks

The MOL stance on the therapeutic relationship does not disagree with or contradict conventional perspectives. It just, perhaps, goes a little further in clarifying what might be therapeutic about the therapeutic relationship. By focusing directly on the extent to which clients are freely expressing their internal experiences, there is the opportunity to maximise the therapeutic value of the therapeutic relationship. Qualities such as warmth, openness, and trust are important, but they should be considered a means to an end and not as ends in themselves. With an increased refinement of the therapeutic relationship and a continued acknowledgement of the controlling nature of both the therapist and the client, it will be possible to make therapy more useful more of the time for more clients.

Summary of main points

- The main task of the therapeutic relationship is to provide an atmosphere where the client feels comfortable to talk about whatever is in, or enters, their mind.
- The most important aspect of therapy may be helping clients become aware of the higher-level systems that are the origin of their distress.
- Both the therapist and the client have goals in and out of therapy and, when problems occur, they can be understood in terms of disruptions to the realisation of important goals.

Topics for discussion

1 The idea that 'There's no such thing as a resistant client, only an inflexible therapist' has been credited to Steve de Shazer and Milton Erickson. Discuss this idea in the context of PCT and interacting control systems.

2 Is it always the case that the goals of a therapist and a client have to be similar for therapy to proceed effectively? In what situations might this not apply?

Activities for learning, consolidation, and fun!

1 Spend five minutes saying whatever is in your mind. This might be best to do on your own. Time yourself and keep talking for the whole five minutes. The idea is to adopt an observer's or reporter's perspective and just describe the things that come into your mind. What are you thinking now, and now, and now? How do those thoughts change? As you are describing that, what else is going through your mind? At the end of five minutes, reflect on your experience. What did you learn?
2 Think of a recent client you worked with. Pick one segment of your interaction and, using Figure 5.1, map out that interaction. What were your goals? Did you disturb each other at times? How were these disturbances opposed?

Chapter 6

Putting clients in charge

Client-led appointment scheduling

By reading this chapter, you will learn:

1 to think about appointment scheduling from the perspective of increasing client control;
2 that there is no empirical rationale for any particular protocol of treatment being necessary for clients to achieve effective therapeutic outcomes; and
3 that the Good Enough Level (GEL) model of treatment provision, based on the idea of responsive regulation, seems more appropriate than the dose-response model in explaining client improvement during therapy.

The way in which therapy is structured and provided to clients is often an unquestioned component of service provision, and yet it can have a significant impact on the availability of services and resources to clients. It seems to be routine practice for therapists to schedule appointments with clients in weekly or fortnightly intervals without any compelling rationale for why they do this. A lot of time and effort in training programmes is devoted to the particular types of therapy or counselling that are delivered and the skills needed to provide them effectively, but rarely is attention directed at discussing the best time frame within which therapy should be offered.

In the spirit of acknowledging the controlling nature of clients as one of our guiding principles, MOL is delivered in the time frame determined by the client. MOL therapy is considered to be a resource that is available for clients to access whenever they want to spend time making their lives conform more closely to their desires and preferences. Obviously, any service will have limits to treatment availability; very few services are available for 24 hours a day, seven days a week, 52 weeks a year. Services also do not have an unlimited supply of therapists, so therapist availability and capacity can also add to resourcing constraints. Within the temporal and resourcing limits of the service, however, MOL therapists aim to organise systems that enable clients to schedule appointments as and when they require them.

Some of the problems with treatments of predetermined lengths

It is more than a little ironic that, even though our field places a premium on 'evidence-based practice', there is actually no evidence for the necessity of regularly spaced appointments and fixed durations of treatment. This point may need some unpacking. There are certainly multitudes of studies demonstrating that manualised treatments with predetermined numbers of sessions *can* be effective in helping to reduce psychological distress (Carey, 2005; Carey, Tai, & Stiles, 2013). In fact, establishing a predetermined number of treatment sessions seems to be a standard component of developing and evaluating treatments. By browsing through the literature, for example, it is possible to find studies such as: a 12-session randomised controlled trial (RCT) of rumination-focused cognitive behavioural therapy (CBT) for residual depression (Watkins *et al.*, 2011); a 10-session RCT of acceptance and commitment therapy (ACT) for tinnitus (Westin *et al.*, 2011); and a comparison between eight and 16 sessions of CBT and psychodynamic-interpersonal psychotherapy (PI; Shapiro *et al.*, 1994). While it is relatively easy to find studies investigating the efficacy of treatments of fixed duration, it is much more difficult to find rationales for why a particular number of sessions was chosen.

There is no obvious reason to choose 8, 10, 12, 16, or any other specific number of sessions as the treatment length, and there is seldom any explanation provided by treatment designers as to why a treatment protocol was fixed at a certain number of sessions. The crucial point from our perspective, however, is that while there are stockpiles of different studies demonstrating that a particular length of treatment *can* be effective, there are *no studies* demonstrating that a particular length of treatment is *necessary* for the amelioration of psychological distress. We will say that again for emphasis: an RCT demonstrating that, on average, clients achieve effective outcomes in 12 sessions (or any other number) of a particular therapy is *not* a demonstration that 12 sessions is *necessary* or *essential* for clients to achieve effective outcomes.

This is a subtle but extremely important point. Policymakers who believe that RCTs provide evidence for the amount of therapy that individuals need may set standards and guidelines for a particular number of sessions that clients should receive. If this number is inaccurate, there can be serious implications for both the service and the individual. The service can face problems by providing either too little or too much therapy to clients. Insufficient therapy could result in dissatisfaction with the service and a loss of referrals, whereas too much therapy can produce increases in waiting times and decreases in service capacity. The service difficulties are mirrored by the problems that individuals could experience by receiving too little therapy and not having their distress adequately ameliorated, or by receiving too much therapy and becoming dependent on the service.

In Australia, uncertainty over how much therapy to provide has had important consequences for both clients and therapists. When it first began, the Australian government's Better Access initiative provided funding for a maximum of 18 sessions of psychological therapy in a calendar year (Littlefield, 2013). The scheme was introduced in 2006, but in 2013 the government reduced the maximum number of rebatable sessions from 18 to 10. Littlefield (2013) reported that, according to the government's own data, this reduction in the maximum number of funded sessions would mean that 87,000 clients per year would not have access to the amount of therapy they required. Also, a study by the Australian Psychological Society indicated that, as a result of the reduced maximum number of sessions, therapists had varied their practices, including: providing therapy at a reduced rate or free of charge, postponing treatment, referring to other service providers, or increasing the interval between appointments (Littlefield, 2013). Neither a maximum of 18 sessions nor a maximum of 10 sessions has any compelling rationale; however, reducing the maximum from 18 to 10 has tangible implications for therapists and clients.

Failing to appreciate the nuances regarding RCTs and treatment length can influence the way therapists think about service provision. It is widely regarded that RCTs provide a 'gold standard' of evidence, so for therapists seeking to base their practices on the best available evidence, they may see the number of sessions shown to achieve successful outcomes in an RCT as the benchmark they need to achieve in their practice. This could lead to them focusing on encouraging clients to attend for the number of sessions used in the RCT. Again, if a 12-session programme was shown to have efficacious outcomes in an RCT, therapists might work towards having clients attend for 12 sessions. Consequently, they may label clients who do not attend for 12 sessions as 'treatment dropouts', and may become concerned with clients who seem to need more than 12 sessions.

Actually, while RCTs are a rigorous and robust methodology, it is a mistake to consider any one methodology as a superior 'gold standard' in all circumstances (Jadad & Enkin, 2007). Methods need to be matched to research questions so the gold standard methodology is the one that is best suited to answer a particular question. Also, the outcomes for an RCT are calculated as an average, and it is almost always the case in RCTs of psychological therapy that some participants in the comparison or control group will have improved more than some participants in the treatment group. RCTs demonstrate that under certain tightly controlled conditions, the average result for the treatment group is more favourable in a statistical sense than the average result for the comparison group for a given number of therapy sessions. RCTs show what is *possible*, not what is desirable, important, or even necessary. It is possible, for example, to teach dolphins to jump through flaming hoops or to snatch a dead fish from the outstretched hands of willing volunteers, but these activities, as entertaining as they are, do not provide evidence of what is desirable or necessary to teach dolphins or what the most appropriate learnings for dolphins might be.

Rethinking treatment schedules

It is interesting to consider the way in which treatment protocols of psychotherapy have developed. Why are treatments standardised to be a particular length? Why do we think we need to schedule regular weekly or fortnightly appointments with clients? There are, perhaps, many answers to these questions. Haley (1990) raises the interesting and deliciously provocative suggestion that the course of psychotherapy was set when a decision was made to charge patients for units of time rather than for results. It is interesting to speculate where our field might be today if therapy was structured according to the achievement of particular results rather than the provision of a fixed number of sessions of equal duration. Would our programmes of research, and the subsequent interventions they inform, be very different? Given that therapy is packaged in bundles of time rather than results, a situation has been created whereby therapists in private practice do better financially by being *less* efficient and effective. A client-led protocol of therapy provision, therefore, might not be the most lucrative decision a therapist can make, but it will help to make services more efficient so that more clients can be seen at the times they need therapeutic assistance.

Even decisions regarding how long appointments should be seem to be based on factors such as logistics and finances (Perry, 1987) rather than empirical results about the nature of the change process and how best to promote it. Yet, despite the arbitrary nature of many of these decisions, they still seem to become highly valued and fiercely defended by some therapists. When therapists encounter suggestions that systems could be developed to accommodate clients' decisions about how frequently and for how long they will attend, many therapists become concerned and even suspicious about the successful provision of therapy (Carey, 2010). Therapists might be worried, for example, that people who could be described as depressed or anxious will not have the ability to schedule their own appointments. They might consider it irresponsible of therapists to leave appointment booking to the clients' discretion.

We are not aware of any compelling evidence to indicate that people who experience difficulties consistent with labels of depression and anxiety are not able to make decisions about whether they schedule and attend particular appointments. The vast majority of clients who therapists work with are voluntary clients, and problems of missed appointments are costly to services. The fact that some clients fail to attend appointments on any given day suggests that clients are making active decisions about where they will or will not place themselves at particular times throughout the day. Therapy comprises approximately one hour in the entirety of a client's week. For the rest of the time, clients are getting on with their lives as best they can. If a client misses a particular appointment or does not engage with therapy in general, is it defensible to conclude that the client has some deficiency or inability that is interfering with their capacity to attend? Would it not be just as defensible to conclude that the client had decided to do something different? Perhaps neither of these conclusions would be accurate, which illustrates our central point, and that is, that in order to know why a client is not attending or what their experience of therapy is, the client needs to be asked. An example that illustrates this point further involves a client who was diagnosed as a 'chronic schizophrenic'. After 14 years in services, this 'chronic schizophrenic' man was described as 'treatment-resistant' (Tai, 2009). He was referred for cognitive behavioural therapy but repeatedly cancelled his weekly therapy appointments. The therapist tried visiting him at home, but still he did not talk, and instead paced up and down the stairs. The therapist interpreted his behaviour as extreme anxiety. After three months of this, the therapist suggested that the client schedule his own appointments and it was agreed that other mental health workers would monitor risk in the interim. After four weeks, the client scheduled an appointment of his own accord and spoke to the therapist without pacing up and down the stairs. He disclosed that his previous experiences of services had been negative and coercive. For example, his mother and psychiatrist had colluded to crush medication in his food without his knowledge. He spoke about his anxiety over engaging with services and his need to have some sense of control in any therapy he might receive. The relatively simple process of him being able to control his own appointment scheduling was successful in helping to establish engagement, and the client was subsequently able to focus on a number of problems he felt important to address.

One study investigated alterations to the way first appointments in a service were scheduled. The standard arrangement was that when clients reached the top of the waiting list, they were sent a letter advising them of the time and date of their first appointment. Over a seven-month period, 62 first appointments were scheduled for new clients by one therapist (Carey & Kemp, 2007). Of these 62, 21 per cent failed to attend their appointment and 18 per cent cancelled their appointment. A total of 38 clients attended their appointment. Over the same seven-month period in the next year, the therapist introduced a new system whereby, once clients reached the top of the waiting list, they were sent a letter advising them of this and informing them that, if they required an appointment, they could contact the psychology department and schedule an appointment at a time that suited them. In this seven-month period, 164 clients were sent letters and 104 made contact and arranged a first appointment. Of those 104, only 2 per cent did not attend their appointment and 12 per cent cancelled their appointment. A total of 90 clients attended their first appointment.

This study is instructive with regard to a client-led approach. A therapist changed from seeing 38 clients for a first appointment over a seven-month period to seeing 90 new clients over the same time period, and the only change that was made was a different way in which appointments were scheduled. There were no costs to the service in terms of extra resources or training in new programmes. There was also no requirement for GPs to improve or otherwise alter their 'referring behaviour'.

It is interesting to note that of those 164 clients who were invited to make first appointments, 62 clients did not respond at all. What conclusions should be drawn about those clients? Should services devote additional resources to engaging with these clients or should services consider that these clients are, perhaps, making decisions that they do not want to access psychological therapy at this point in time, probably for a variety of reasons? Given that it is a person's right to withdraw from treatment, surely it is also a person's right not to engage in the first place. Acknowledging clients' rights with respect to the receipt of psychological services, however, seems to be a difficult issue for some therapists to reconcile. A large part of our rationale for emphasising an accurate understanding of the phenomenon of control is to assist in reasoning through situations such as client non-attendance at appointments.

The finding of increased service capacity through client-led appointment scheduling has been demonstrated in other studies as well. Carey and Spratt (2009), for example, reported an increase in referrals from 52 between July and December 2005 to 93 between July and December 2006, and the only difference was a change from conventional appointment booking to client-led appointment booking in June 2006. Also, in June 2006, there was a seven-month waiting list that was eliminated by December 2006. So, with nothing more than an alteration to the way appointments were scheduled, the service could accommodate almost double the number of referrals while, at the same time, removing a waiting list of seven months.

One of the obstacles to changing our current approach to the organisation of treatment is that, currently, with regard to decisions about appointment scheduling and attendance, there seems to be an implicit prejudice against people deemed to have mental health difficulties that does not apply to people with other difficulties. Generally, people experiencing other maladies are able to exercise their own discretion about the treatment they will receive. Even with illnesses as serious as cancer, people make decisions about whether or not to undergo surgery or participate in a course of chemotherapy or undertake some other course of treatment. Whether or not treatment providers and other people agree with the decision the person has made is another point entirely. The main idea we are emphasising here is the *right* of individuals to make their own decisions about the treatment they will receive. Understanding people as living control systems might help us to make better sense of people's decisions in terms of the controlled states they are creating and maintaining.

Policy support for patient control

Even though it is generally acknowledged that psychotherapy and counselling need to be provided flexibly and that clients' preferences need to be considered (Carey, 2005), it appears much harder for some therapists to relinquish control of these decisions in practice. It can be even harder for service managers and commissioners to be persuaded of the merits of a client-led approach. This is difficult to fathom given the overwhelming empirical evidence regarding the importance of personal control, as well as the professional standards and ethical codes we mentioned in the last chapter. Furthermore, national policy statements explicitly mandate for patient choice and control.

The National Health Service (NHS) in the United Kingdom (UK), for example, has a document titled *Your Choices in the NHS* (NHS, 2013). In this document, there are statements such as: 'Giving people more choice is a priority of the modern NHS. This is because research in the UK and overseas has shown that treatments are more effective if patients choose, understand and control their care'; 'NHS doctors have a duty to inform us about the options available and will advise us what they think is best. But it's you, the patient, who must decide whether a treatment is right for you'; and 'The NHS promises to involve patients in decisions about all aspects of their healthcare. Research has shown that involving patients in healthcare decisions improves the success of the treatment' (NHS, 2013). Similarly, in Scotland's *Health White Paper* published in 2003 (Scottish Executive, 2003), there are statements such as: 'Looking at services from a patient's point of view underpins everything that we are seeking to do in the health service' (p. 7); 'Understanding the wants and needs of patients whether children, adults or older people will lead to more effective and high quality healthcare, and must be a core activity of the health service. It means developing a genuinely responsive health service by seeking input and feedback from patients as a key part of developing services and improving quality' (p. 17); and 'We want to see a health service where there is . . . empowerment of individuals and communities, to enable them to increase control over and improve their health' (p. 18). Therefore, there is compelling information not only from research, but also from ethical, professional, and policy statements regarding the appropriateness of a client-led system of service provision. Moreover, there is also now a robust theoretical rationale in the form of PCT as to why therapists specifically and services generally should adopt a client-led approach.

How much treatment should be provided?

The issue of how much treatment to provide is, arguably, even more important than the particular treatment scheduling approach it is provided within. Counselling and psychotherapy approaches should be both effective and efficient. In fact, efficiency could be regarded as an inherent aspect of therapy effectiveness such that effectiveness could be considered to involve both person-effectiveness as well as cost-effectiveness (Carey, 2011b):

> Person-effectiveness ensures the amelioration of symptoms so that people do not suffer needlessly. Cost-effectiveness refers to the expeditious resolution of symptoms, which is important to ensure the responsible use of resources and the sustainability of the service.
>
> (p. 6)

As we explained in Chapter 1, our logic behind this attitude is that if two treatment approaches assist different clients to achieve similar reductions in psychological distress but require different numbers of sessions to do so, we would conclude that the approach requiring fewer sessions is ultimately more effective because it is more efficient. Indeed, maybe any two therapies could be matched on effectiveness if the number of sessions were allowed to vary rather than being constrained to set protocols, as is the case with therapies developed through RCTs.

It would be inefficient to provide more therapy and counselling than clients require, and yet this is precisely the situation confronting us today. There is, currently, an enduring and colossal disconnect between the number of sessions that therapists and counsellors want to provide or are advised to provide and the number of sessions that clients want to access (Carey, 2006b). While the treatments that are developed and evaluated in clinical trials research are often between 12 and 14 sessions, the number of treatment sessions that clients access in routine clinical practice is well below this range (Lambert, Garfield, & Bergin, 2004). If we are designing treatments to be 12, 14, or some even larger number of sessions, and clients are attending perhaps half this number of sessions and still showing improvement, this would seem to imply that not all of what we include in the design of our treatments is essential for clients to experience benefits. The converse case is just as important and persuasive – there are a minority of clients who seem to require more than the standard number of sessions and are keen to do so to maintain their long-term recovery. Yet, implementing a fixed number of sessions cannot facilitate them doing this.

An excellent example of the dramatic fracture between the amount of treatment policymakers and treatment providers think clients should have and the amount of treatment clients think clients should have comes from the UK. The recommendation from the National Institute for Health and Clinical Excellence (NICE) for people receiving CBT for depression is that 'the duration of treatment should typically be in the range of 16 to 20 sessions over three to four months' (NICE, 2009, p. 28). In the first year evaluation of the Improving Access to Psychological Therapies (IAPT), however, Glover, Webb, and Evison (2010) reported that the 'numbers of treatment sessions were surprisingly low' (p. 23). Only 1.38 per cent of the 7,825 clients for whom data were available attended 16 or more treatment sessions. The median number of appointments was less than 10.

While data such as these might seem surprising, it is generally the case that there is a discrepancy between the number of sessions clients access and the number of sessions therapists plan to provide, with most clients attending far fewer sessions than therapists expect (Boisvert & Faust, 2002; Carey, 2011b; Pekarik & Wierzbicki, 1986). In fact, Talmon (1990) reported that the modal number of sessions people attend for is *one*. Studies reporting attendance data in routine clinical practice often report between four and six sessions as the average number of appointments attended (Carey, 2011b). The results of studies such as these can be juxtaposed against other studies that suggest, for example, that 50 per cent of clients require between 13 and 18 appointments to improve (Hansen, Lambert, & Forman, 2002), or that 75 per cent of clients show measurable improvement after 26 sessions and 85 per cent after 52 sessions (Howard, Kopta, Krause, & Orlinsky, 1986). Taking these findings at face value makes it seem as though 'the more sessions the better', but this again misses the point that individual differences in the number of sessions required is huge. It would not make sense to give everyone

52 sessions to raise the rates of measurable improvement to 85 per cent when we know that the majority of people who will show measurable improvement do so with a fraction of this number of sessions.

Part of the difficulty in determining the correct number of sessions for treatment might arise from a lack of clarity about how to decide when enough treatment is enough *for the individual* and who should make that decision. That is, when statements regarding percentages of client improvement are made, it is important to ask 'improvement according to what standard' or 'improvement from whose point of view'. Typically, client improvement is assessed according to the client's scores on standardised outcome questionnaires that generally report the frequency or intensity of certain symptoms. The extent to which changes in these scores reflect important and meaningful changes in a client's life is rarely considered. Kazdin (1999) makes the point that the perspective of the client has not been well attended to in evaluating clinical significance, and that changes in symptoms may not necessarily correspond with changes that are important to the client from the client's perspective.

Whose life is it anyway?

In MOL therapy, it is accepted that a therapist can never really know the experiences of a client, and so because MOL is focused on helping clients experience greater control in their lives, the clients are regarded as the best judges of when they have had enough treatment. Sometimes, it might appear to the therapist that the client has not solved all their problems and could benefit from further sessions. Nevertheless, it may be the case from the client's perspective that they have achieved what they wanted and can engage in life again in the way that they wish to without the support of regular therapy sessions. In MOL, therapists need to be able to reconcile the fact that clients will not always make the choices in life that therapists think they should make.

Perhaps a gauge for how well you appreciate the importance of the principle of autonomous control is the way you respond when your clients make decisions that you disagree with. We are not including issues of risk here, but simply differences in the way therapy should be provided or even what occurs in therapy. When there is a divergence of opinion, do you make efforts to persuade the clients to come around to your way of thinking or do you respect the client's decision even though you might acknowledge that you disagree with it? Understanding differences of opinion between you and your clients by working through Figures 2.1 and 5.1 could be helpful. When a client expresses an opinion that is different to your opinion on the subject, is this a disturbance to you? What goal of yours might this have disturbed? Possibly, for some therapists, hearing their clients express different views could actually be part of their feedback function if they have goals of promoting client independence and assertiveness. We are not suggesting that therapists should not be able to express themselves in therapy and counselling, but we are introducing the idea that it is, perhaps, acceptable for clients to come to their own conclusions, even if they are different conclusions from the ones that the therapist wants them to arrive at.

Therapists can have immense hope, as well as optimism, for what clients can achieve in therapy, and this can be important for the resilience of therapists in the work that they do. Where this hope and optimism can become problematic is when the therapist makes persistent efforts for the client to adopt the same level of optimism and hope. Some clients will find this helpful and others will find it intrusive and coercive. One client had had a period in his life where he travelled, was fit and healthy, and felt confident and happy. Then, some years later, after a serious and traumatic event, he began to experience self-doubt, worries and concerns, and thoughts of suicide. He commenced therapy and continued to attend even though he found it difficult to focus on and explore the issues he could identify. At one point, he explained to the therapist that he had come to accept that he would always have these ups and downs now for the rest of his life. The therapist explained that she did not share this view and that she had an unshakable faith that the client could achieve whatever he wanted in life, including overcoming his current mental health turmoil. The therapist also let the client know, however, that she would make no efforts to persuade the client to come around to her way of thinking and that she would work with the client on what it was that he wanted to achieve. The client suggested he would formulate a list of the goals he had and come to therapy to find ways to realise these goals. Whether or not the client and therapist ever agree on the long-term state of the client's mental health, the therapist can still be a valuable resource to the client, providing sessions of MOL when the client requires them to achieve the things that are important to him or her.

The Good Enough Level model of service delivery

The Good Enough Level (GEL) model of counselling and psychotherapy service provision was developed by Stiles and his colleagues, and is based on the idea of responsive regulation (Stiles, Barkham, Connell, & Mellor-Clark, 2008). This model suggests that people attend different numbers of sessions until they have made a 'good enough' change in their lives. In one large study of over 9,000 clients attending between 0 and 20 sessions, it was found that the amount of pre-post therapy change on a standardised questionnaire was approximately the same regardless of whether clients attended zero sessions, 20 sessions, or any number of sessions in between (Stiles *et al.*, 2008). Some clients changed quickly and others changed more gradually, but the amount that each of them changed was not related to the number of sessions.

The GEL model challenges our assumptions that the therapist is in the best position to know for how long a client should attend therapy. This model has implicit support from the sources we have mentioned above, such as professional standards, ethical codes, and policy documents. This information reminds us that only the client knows when the world is right or in balance from their unique perspective. MOL recognises this, and organises treatment to respect and promote this point of view. This attitude does not mean at all that therapists should accept substandard outcomes. MOL therapists constantly strive to help clients produce the best possible outcomes. From an MOL perspective, the principle here is in defining 'best' from the client's point of view rather than the therapist's.

Making it work in practice

Organising treatment so that clients, rather than therapists, make decisions about the duration and frequency of therapy involves nothing more complex than developing facilities so that clients can book their own appointments as and when they require them. Some of our work has occurred in GP practices (Carey, 2010; Carey & Mullan, 2007; Carey & Spratt, 2009), and in these settings, clients arrange appointments with the practice receptionists in the same way they would make an appointment to see a GP. Even in settings where receptionists are not immediately available, such as hospital outpatient clinics, secretarial support may still be available at an off-campus site. In these situations, depending on computing resourcing and capabilities, secretaries can be given access to the therapist's Microsoft Outlook calendar (or something similar) and clients can book appointments that way.

Prior to commencing a system such as this, receptionists and secretaries might need training to be able to use the approach efficiently and effectively. Some receptionists, for example, may feel that regular appointments are best and might 'encourage' clients to book regular appointments or to book a number of appointments at the one time. While there are no absolute rules about this, we cannot see any convincing rationale for a client pre-booking multiple appointments. One of the main problems with this is a conceptual one. MOL very much conveys the message that change can occur at any time. Important and lasting change can occur just as easily after the first session as it can after the seventeenth session. Each MOL session is provided as a discrete problem-solving experience. Essentially, MOL therapists approach every MOL session as though it could be the last one with this client. If clients return for subsequent MOL sessions, there is no requirement to build on past sessions. The same conversation, based on the same two MOL therapy goals, is initiated. Even with the same process being followed, however, every conversation is unique because clients are in a different place in their mind each time they engage in therapy. Multiple bookings, however, can set up an expectation that the client might still need to see the therapist in five or six or some other number of weeks into the future. It may transpire that this is exactly what does happen, but we see no reason to pre-empt this occurrence or even to set this as an expectation. MOL is an optimistic therapy that acknowledges that lasting change can happen suddenly and unexpectedly.

Within the constraint of booking one appointment at a time, most other variations are encouraged. Clients can book more than one appointment a week if they want to spend more time working through their problem. In one practice, for example, two MOL therapists each had two clinics a week there, making a total of four MOL clinics each week. Clients were informed they could book appointments as often as they liked for as long as they liked, and they were also told that they could see one or both therapists if they wanted to (Carey & Mullan, 2007). Despite this invitation, very few people attended more than once a week, and very few people booked appointments with both therapists.

Sometimes, after experiencing MOL, clients might decide that they want to spend longer than the standard therapeutic hour working on their problem. In this situation, clients could book two appointments together to allow double the normal time to address their difficulties. As with multiple bookings in the one week, we have found that clients rarely exercise this option, but it is available nevertheless. More often, clients choose to have sessions that are shorter than the standard 'hour'. However, this is another component of treatment flexibility that provides clients with more control over their therapeutic experience.

Apart from booking multiple appointments, there might be other considerations that need to be discussed. For example, we have found it advisable to only accept bookings or cancellations from the client who will be attending therapy. Sometimes, it can be more convenient for the client to have their partner or child or parent or friend telephone to arrange the appointment, but the difficulty with this is that, as a therapist, you can never be sure under what conditions the client agreed to the appointment. In fact, you cannot even really know if the client did agree. Perhaps the parent, partner, child, or friend has concerns about the client and thinks the client would benefit from further appointments. Their concerns may be well founded, but unless the client also thinks they could benefit from attending, the session will be of limited value.

When this approach is explained to clients, some clients might ask the therapist to tell them when they should come back for their next appointment. Of course, there is nothing in the client-led approach that prevents a therapist from advising a client when to book a subsequent appointment if there are sound clinical reasons for doing so; however, in our experience, the clearest answer is to suggest that clients should come back as soon as they want to spend more time working through their dilemmas and distress. It can require an adjustment for some clients (although most clients seem to enthusiastically embrace the opportunity to take control in this way), particularly if the clients have had previous experiences of therapists advising them when to return. Encouraging clients to take control of appointment booking, however, can be an important component of their progress towards greater control in their life generally. We have encountered examples of clients where colleagues have reported them to be difficult to engage and not attending appointments, and yet, when given control over their own appointment scheduling, they have attended consistently and routinely without cancelling or not attending any of the sessions they made themselves.

There are other adaptations that may be suitable for individual clients. The principle of control tells us that everyone can, in principle, control their own access to treatment. However, it is also the case that people who are organised as living control systems can experience significant conflict, our second principle. Some people might want to seek help from another person but also not want to meet a therapist face-to-face because they do not want to feel judged and scrutinised. There can be clients who want to come to therapy to tell someone about the trauma they have experienced, but, at the same time, they might not want to come to therapy because they are afraid that they will be forced to disclose the events that distress them and experience the overwhelming emotions that are associated with this disclosure. In fact, it is likely that some of these conflicts around attending therapy are the very ones that clients would need to work on in therapy (Schauman & Mansell, 2012), so as to ultimately reorganise the systems governing the conflict (our third principle).

Often, these conflicts can be managed in a relatively straightforward way by giving people more accurate information about the therapy, such as the fact that they will not be asked to disclose information that they do not want to. When it was explained to one young client that the therapist would not tell her what to do or give her advice, but would ask questions about the client's perspective, she said, 'Really?! That is so cool. Everyone else I've spoken to tells me what to do or what I should be thinking. You mean you'll really just listen to what I think?' Another client came to a session and said she wanted the therapist to give her some tools to help her deal with her voices and feelings on anxiety. As the therapist and client discussed the client's experience of her unwanted feelings, voices, thoughts, and images, the client explained that she could make things 'quiet' when she was running by repeating a 'mantra' over and over, and also through the use of some metaphors she had developed. It had never occurred to the client, however, that she could use the same strategies at times when she was not running.

Other variations that might be helpful could include MOL delivered by telephone or videophone, or some discussion with the client around convenient locations, especially if they already struggle to see their own GP. Indeed, recent developments have included providing MOL in secondary care and inpatient hospital settings (Carey *et al.*, 2013; Tai, 2009). We are also developing self-help materials, such as group courses, mobile applications, and computerised interventions, that are designed to help raise awareness of problems and how to manage them through the principles of PCT (e.g. Gaffney, Mansell, Edwards, & Wright, 2014). Many of these adaptations will not have the flexibility and depth of MOL itself, and so for some people there will be a transition from these to one-to-one therapy. Others may find that they get 'just enough' from these adapted forms.

None of the problems mentioned throughout this section are insurmountable, but they do take some thought and preparation to ensure that the provision of therapy and counselling proceeds smoothly. At all times, understanding ourselves and our clients as living control systems provides the framework for clarifying and resolving difficulties. The ultimate goal is always to arrive at solutions where therapists and clients are enabled to control the things that are important to them within the environmental constraints that are operating at any point in time.

A final word

Based on the principles of PCT, it is accepted in MOL that only the clients know how they are living and how they would like to live. Even if they cannot articulate this easily, it is the role of therapy to allow this intrinsic aspect of being human to develop and flourish. It is important to assess client progress, and resources such as standardised questionnaires can be very helpful in this regard. Yet, it is also important to keep in mind that clients do not attend therapy because they have high scores on a questionnaire (Kazdin, 2001), and having clients' questionnaire scores change in a favourable direction may or may not mean their life has changed agreeably from their perspective.

Enabling clients to determine how much treatment they receive and how long they receive it for is a tangible acknowledgement of the importance of control in a person's life. It also communicates respect for the client in being able to make important decisions, and it is optimistic in encompassing the fact that change can happen anywhere, anytime. There are practical considerations that require some attention for a system such as this to work efficiently, but they are not insoluble problems. Improvements in such areas as access to services by clients, as well as the enhanced capacity of services, more than compensates for the time required in adopting and establishing this system.

Summary of main points

- Therapy can proceed effectively and efficiently when clients, rather than therapists, control when appointments are scheduled.
- There is a striking disconnect between the number of sessions we design treatments to be and the number of sessions clients access in routine clinical practice.
- The issue of how much treatment is enough can ultimately only be answered satisfactorily by the client.

Topics for discussion

1 Therapy can be provided effectively in one session for some clients. Discuss.
2 Clients who are depressed or anxious do not have the skills to arrange their own appointments. Discuss.
3 If clients book their own appointments, they will only attend therapy when they have problems. Discuss the advantages and disadvantages of this situation.

Activities for learning, consolidation, and fun!

1 Discuss the idea of clients booking their own appointments with some of your colleagues and peers. What are their reactions?

2 Review the clients you have seen over the last 12 months. What was the average number of sessions attended? What was the average number of missed and cancelled appointments? Did some clients stop coming before you thought they should have? How do you think about that now?

Chapter 7

Making therapy sessions more therapeutic

By reading this chapter, you will learn:

1 the secret ingredients of all effective therapeutic strategies and techniques; and
2 how to increase the potency of techniques, strategies, and activities in therapy.

There is no shortage of creative and innovative strategies and techniques in psychotherapy and counselling. Many brands of therapy have their own distinctive set of techniques and some activities are shared across approaches. It is perhaps not a startling observation to suggest that all strategies, activities, and techniques are effective some of the time with some people, but none of them are effective all of the time with everyone. In this chapter, we take a principles-based attitude towards strategies and techniques to suggest what the effective elements might be whenever a technique is effective and what might be missing whenever the technique is not able to be used effectively. If the effective components of strategies can be targeted, rather than the strategy in general, it will be possible to review and modify strategies and activities where necessary to enhance their usefulness to clients.

We are assuming that therapy works when people are able to reorganise the source of internal conflict they are experiencing and achieve greater control in important areas of their lives. Any strategy or technique, therefore, will be effective to the extent that it helps people sustain their awareness at higher-level areas where they might, through reorganisation, develop new insights, perspectives, points of view, attitudes, and beliefs regarding themselves and the life they are living. When we refer to techniques being 'effective', therefore, we mean that they are able to be utilised by clients to help these clients reduce their psychological distress and achieve greater control in their lives.

Considering strategies

It would take an extremely large volume to review all of the activities, techniques, and strategies that have been devised to help reduce psychological distress. Such a review is beyond the scope of this book, and also unnecessary for the ideas we want to introduce. We will discuss a selection of some of the more common therapeutic strategies, however, to illustrate the point we are making about understanding how techniques work for increased therapeutic impact. If our discussion does not include one or more of the techniques you are familiar with, it would be a useful exercise to apply the lessons from this chapter to the activities you are familiar with that we have not mentioned to determine if the same reasoning we use in this chapter still applies.

By focusing on the effective elements of techniques, therapists might be able to be more helpful to a broader range of clients. When applying techniques and strategies, the perspective that 'the client is always right' should be adopted. If some activity does not make sense for a particular client, then it should be the activity that is changed, not the client. Strategies that are meaningful and useful for one client or group of clients will not necessarily be experienced the same way by other clients.

The idiosyncratic nature of effective strategies was illustrated through some work with a small group of behaviourally challenging adolescents in a secondary school. These five boys were all at risk of being excluded from the school, and so staff at the school were seeking assistance in helping these boys address their conduct in school. A conversation was conducted with the boys in which they could easily describe what they did that got them into trouble and they could also identify other students who never got into trouble, as well as the way these other students behaved at school. They stated that they wanted to stay in school but they did not want to act like the students who did not get into trouble because those others students, according to these boys, were 'squares'. So it seemed that the boys had a conflict between wanting to stay in school and not wanting to be 'squares'. Given that they had introduced the idea of a shape, they were asked, 'Well, if those other kids are squares, what shape are you guys?' The boys decided they were 'circles'.

The following week, the conversation continued, and this time the boys were provided with blocks and marbles to represent squares and circles. The marbles rolled around the table with a few falling to the floor but some of the boys immediately began building with the blocks. One boy said, 'Look! The squares are building a bridge to a better future.' He was booed and mocked good-naturedly by his friends for the comment, but a salient point had been made nevertheless. Despite the advantages the boys could see with the blocks compared to the marbles, they were still reluctant to become squares. A discussion unfolded about alternative shapes they could become that would not be squares but might have some of the advantages of the squares. The boys eventually decided they could become hexagons.

Later, when this activity was explained to colleagues during a professional development activity, the colleagues became interested in the 'squares and circles technique', and focused on details such as how the squares and circles idea was presented and whether squares should be introduced before circles or whether it should be the other way around. The point of this exercise, however, was *not* that a new technique had been created for working in groups with behaviourally challenging adolescents. It was not the actual activity that was important, but rather it was focusing on the individuals' experiences, linking these experiences to their goals, and targeting conflicting goals that were considered to be the 'elements of effectiveness'. Using these basic 'rules' in a different situation with different adolescents would probably result in an entirely different but equally effective conversation. Trying to apply the 'squares and circles technique' in other settings, however, would probably not have desirable results. The danger in this situation would be that squares and circles would not have the same meaning for other adolescents as it did for the boys in this group. Also, at least some of the usefulness of the squares and circles activity was the conversational process through which these concepts emerged, and it would be impossible to replicate this process to produce a 'squares and circles' outcome with other groups. Our focus, therefore, concerns understanding the important elements of effectiveness for any technique, activity, or strategy. In particular, we are interested in understanding how any technique has the effect that it does regardless of the particular procedural aspects of the activity.

Thinking about the activities of therapy

Thought diaries are commonly used in therapy and counselling to help people record and revise thoughts that are assumed to be generating the symptoms a person finds troublesome. The general idea here is that people write down a negative thought as they experience it, and then spend some time reflecting on it and revising it by writing down a more appropriate or constructive thought. While this activity has had demonstrated effectiveness with many people, it is difficult to find convincing rationales for why it is effective. If, for example, 'I'll never find a life-long partner' was one of the thoughts that was captured and recorded, the client might be encouraged to consider this idea from a more probabilistic stance and come to a conclusion such as: 'It might take time to find my perfect partner, but since most people eventually achieve a happy partnership there is no reason to suspect that it won't happen to me.' It might be recommended that this activity be repeated several times a day in between appointments with the therapist. Over time, there is every chance that the person will adopt a more measured perspective with regard to the prospect of a long-term relationship. What is not clear, however, is how this measured perspective arises. It is not obvious why the thought 'I'll never find a life-long partner' should generate misery. In fact, for people who are pursuing a life of solitude, a thought such as this would probably provide comfort and solace. It is also not clear how writing down a thought such as this, and then an opposite kind of a thought, eventually leads to contentment and satisfaction.

Activity scheduling is another technique that many people find benefit in completing. With this technique, people write down the activities they undertake in the time between appointments. Once the current level of activity is known, different and additional activities can be planned that will generate enjoyment and fulfilment for the person. Even though this activity can be effective, the reasons behind how recording activities and then generating new ones can lead to lasting change are not clear. A colleague once reported that she had asked a client to complete an activity schedule, which he did, and brought it in the following week. As they were discussing it, he sat back in his chair and said, 'Gee, I'm not doing anything with my life am I?' This kind of self-evaluation may be a significant clue as to the way in which therapeutic strategies and techniques, in general, achieve their 'therapeuticness'.

The two-chair technique was developed in gestalt therapy, and is a procedure that involves clients creating a conversation, or replaying a past conversation, by alternating between two chairs. The general idea is that a client might re-enact a conversation between themselves and a significant person in their life. The conversation could even be between the 'I' they are now and the 'I' they were at a time in the past. Instead of re-enacting the scenario exactly as it is remembered, they might alter it by saying what they would like to have said at the time or, with the benefit of hindsight, what they wished they had said. They might give the 'I' from long ago new skills and resources to deal with the overwhelming problem. This activity can be very useful for some people, although, again, plausible explanations about how and why this technique is effective are not readily available.

Formulation is an integral part of many therapies and especially those therapies of a cognitive and behavioural orientation. Some clients can experience benefits by having past events connected with current contexts and symptoms in a coherent and plausible way. Sometimes, the formulation on its own can help people see things differently and develop new ideas about how they might alter the way they live their lives for increased satisfaction. Cognitive analytic therapy (CAT) uses detailed and complex formulations to help people make sense of their world and their experiences. Again, there is no explanation provided as to why developing and reflecting on a 'map' of the manifestation and maintenance of one's psychological distress can be of therapeutic value.

Mindfulness has become a popular activity in psychotherapy and counselling. The general idea here is that people are taught to adopt a more 'distanced' stance with regard to their thoughts and emotions. Rather than thinking a thought and becoming embroiled in the content of the thought, a more 'mindful' perspective is to view the thought as just that: a thought. There is a range of novel, even quirky, ways to help people achieve this 'stepped back' attitude to their cognitive processes. One activity involves helping clients to use imagery to place their thoughts on leaves and watch them drift down an imagined stream. Some people find mindfulness techniques engaging and helpful, although how people manage to metaphorically step away from problems that had previously ensnared their attention is unspecified.

There is, in fact, a parade of different ways of describing what happens when therapy is effective. Clients might, for example, learn to: make peace with themselves; tolerate uncertainty and ambiguity; accept themselves and the events they experience; step back or get outside themselves; and they might also learn to put their problem into perspective. We take no issue with any of these descriptions and have personally had experiences that could be captured by one or more of these terms. It is one thing to know *that* people who previously could not accept themselves are now more understanding and less critical of themselves, but it is quite another thing to know *how* acceptance materialised in a place where, previously, there was none. More than knowing *what* happens when therapy is effective, therefore, we think it is important to know *how* effectiveness is achieved whenever it occurs and by whatever means it occurs.

The importance of knowing how

Knowing how therapeutic activities work is not important in an absolute sense, but it is important in relation to maximising one's effectiveness as a therapist. For therapists who are about as effective as they want to be, or therapists who are not concerned with improving their effectiveness, the 'how' of therapy will not hold much interest. A very strong interest of ours, however, is finding ways to ensure each therapeutic encounter is as efficiently effective as it can be. An important way to achieve this is to understand how the tools of therapy work. In Chapter 2, we described why understanding how control works might be important and the same reasoning applies to the use of therapeutic techniques.

We noted at the beginning of this chapter the rather mundane observation that all techniques are effective some of the time but no technique is effective all of the time. When a technique is not as effective as intended, what should you do? Some therapists might select another technique from their repertoire but, sooner or later, there may be some clients for whom nothing seems to work. Rather than sourcing new professional development activities to add to the collection of strategies at your disposal, if strategies were supplied with statements about how they work, it might be possible to tinker with them rather than constantly scouting replacement strategies. This is not to demean the value of professional development but it is to say that we advocate learning about how something works as the most professional development of all.

If the potency of thought diaries, for example, was activated by repetition then, if the technique was not achieving the desired results, the remedy would be to increase the number of times the task was completed. If clients are currently completing their diaries four times a day and their psychological distress has not abated, then an effective solution might be to increase the activity to six times a day to generate more repetition. If, however, thought diaries worked by provoking emotion that was able to be processed by constructing alternative thoughts, then increasing the amount of times the activity was repeated would be ineffective, but ensuring that each thought that is identified is one that the person feels strongly about might be the best way of enhancing the impact of the strategy. The ability to correct and improve strategies, therefore, will be directly related to the understanding of how the strategy achieves its results.

The same analysis can be applied to any particular technique. If the effectiveness of mindfulness imagery techniques relied on how vivid the images were then, when a particular image was not helping as well as it might, the therapist would know to help the client enhance the vividness of the images. Perhaps the therapist would direct the client's attention to how much colour the client had in the images, and then would ask the client to increase the brightness of the colour. Or perhaps asking the client to add sounds and smells to the image would enhance the vividness and, thereby, increase the effectiveness of the activity. If vividness, however, was an inert aspect of the effectiveness of the activity, then any focus on the intensity of the image would be wasting therapeutic time and may even be impeding progress. Directing a client's attention *towards* the creation of more vivid images may have the effect of diverting attention *away from* whatever it is that could lead to effective therapeutic change.

The secret ingredients of change

Despite the abundant variety of techniques and strategies that exist, our stance is that all activities that are therapeutic achieve their results through a common pathway. This is not to suggest that diversity and variety are unhelpful or problematic. Quite the contrary: the existence of a vast array of therapeutic strategies quite literally means that there should be 'something for everyone' in terms of the interests, styles, and preferences of both therapists and clients. We are suggesting, however, that when it comes to the contents of the therapeutic pantry, 'all roads lead to Rome' with the roads being the techniques and strategies that are available, and Rome being a satisfactory reduction in psychological distress. To be more accurate, we could say that all therapeutic roads *can* lead to a satisfying Rome but *do not inevitably* lead there. There are detours along the way that can divert an unwary traveller who does not have an up-to-date and accurate map of the terrain. Our map is PCT.

If we could extract some commonness out of the sea of diversity, there might be some clues as to the important ways to increase the therapeutic value of techniques and strategies. The first thing to notice is that techniques and strategies in psychotherapy and counselling have the effect of focusing people's attention on their problems. Often, by engaging in these activities, they focus on their problems for longer than they would otherwise. We have already mentioned that, generally, people like to try to forget about their problems, or they push them to the back of their mind, or busy themselves with distracting activities. Therapeutic techniques and strategies, however, have the opposite effect: they require people to focus on their problems. This point can be further illustrated by trying to think of the opposite: would it be possible to create an effective therapeutic technique that did not involve at least some attention to the psychological distress the person is experiencing? Paradoxically, if a therapeutic technique did avoid all possible attending to the salient distress, would this not have the effect of actually creating an indirect focus *on* the distress? Trying not to think about something requires concerted effort but also an implicit attending *to* that something: how do you know when you are not thinking about something?

The difficulty in being able to maintain a sustained focus on a problem was underscored by a client who came in to one session and gave her therapist an assessment that had been completed online. The client explained that she had found a website where questionnaires could be completed and a report provided. When the client had completed the questionnaire, a psychologist from the clinic managing the website contacted her to talk about the report. The psychologist offered the client the opportunity to participate in an eight-week online programme to help her manage her anxiety attacks. The client was told that the programme would require four hours per week of the client's time. In her session, the client explained to her therapist that there was 'no way' she would be able to sit on her own at a computer and focus for four hours a week over an eight-week programme. For people such as this client, having a therapist who can ask a series of questions provides the support they need to maintain a focus that they would otherwise struggle to achieve.

Apart from a focus on the problem, techniques and strategies also seem to universally promote the external expression of one or more aspects of the person's experience of psychological distress. Thought diaries and activity schedules require the person to write things down, journaling does the same thing. Socratic questioning and guided discovery necessitate the client talking about their problem; creating formulations and the two-chair technique have the same requirement. Expressive therapies involving dancing, drama, or painting use novel mediums and creative techniques but still provide a vehicle for the external expression of clients' problems. Even therapies that do not involve a therapist, such as online programmes, require people to answer questions, or type responses, or engage in other activities that require both a focus on the problem and the external articulation of the problem. Again, thinking of the opposite might add further clarity to this point. Would it be possible for a person to use a technique for good therapeutic effect that required them to inhibit any external statement of their problem? Perhaps it is possible to achieve a satisfactory reduction in psychological distress through internal processing of the problem entirely. It may be that people who resolve psychological distress without the assistance of a therapist are able to accomplish this. Even if this is possible, however, it is difficult to imagine what kind of a therapeutic programme would facilitate the successful resolution of a psychological problem without any external expression of the problem at all. It may be that this could be achieved with some Web-based programmes; however, the way in which it would be obtained in face-to-face therapy is not entirely clear. Perhaps, then, this common element of effectiveness is related to the interactional aspect of therapy. When clients externally express their problems, the therapist is able to respond to this expression in some way.

It could also be that there is a difference in the processing that occurs between processing that is entirely internal compared with processing that extends into the environment beyond the skin. One obvious difference is that the time required to think a thought and the time taken to express a thought and hear it back through your own ears are different. Perhaps the increased time provides an opportunity for evaluation and scrutiny that are not available with thinking alone. One client considered her own thoughts to be 'genuine' or 'good', and the voices she heard to be 'not real' or 'bad'. She discovered during therapy, however, that she only questioned the voices when she said them out loud. If the dialogue of the voices remained entirely internal, she never questioned or evaluated them. She might argue with them but she would not question the legitimacy of them. It had never occurred to this client that there were different ways of responding to the voices, and she only came to this conclusion as she described them to her therapist. Up until she had spoken with a therapist, the content of the voices had been completely internal so she had not had the opportunity to consider her voices in a different way or even to appreciate that there was more than one way to think about the voices.

In addition to targeting the problem and providing some expression of the current and ongoing experience of the problem, there also seems to be a change in emotional state whenever therapeutic strategies are effective. If people express their problem with the same level of emotionality they had before they started engaging in the activity, it is unlikely that the activity will have much therapeutic value. People, typically, become more emotionally aroused as they focus on their problem and express their acquaintance with it in some way. They might become visibly upset or angry (or perhaps more upset and angrier), they might become more animated or agitated, they might even become calmer and detached. Whatever happens, there needs to be some kind of shift in emotional arousal as the person moves the experience of the problem from only inside their head to outside it as well.

On occasion, some clients will describe the problems in what seems to be a well-rehearsed, almost third-person tone. When this occurs, persistent and curious questioning can help to break up the clients' standard scripts and draw their attention to different aspects of their account that they might not have considered at length before. By using questions sensitively and systematically, it will be possible to identify areas where clients might be less sure, more confused, and perhaps more emotional. Helping clients to sustain their attention in these areas can produce useful results in terms of finding clues to the higher levels in the hierarchy from which lasting solutions might be generated.

One component of the effectiveness of therapeutic activities, techniques, and strategies occurs when people notice their own expression of the problem or otherwise make some evaluation of that which they have been expressing. This can occur directly or indirectly, but there needs to be some shift in awareness from the experiences they have been expressing to their views *about* what they have been expressing. In the example of activity scheduling above, when the client sat back and said, 'Gee, I'm not doing anything with my life am I?' he was making an observation about the statement of his problem expressed by his completed activity schedule. Other clients might say things such as 'I never realised I was so critical of myself', or 'When I say it like that, it doesn't sound like such a huge problem', or 'It's no wonder I feel so tired all the time', or some other statement that indicates they are no longer looking out at the world from *within* their problem, but have adopted a vantage point from which they can look *at* their difficulties.

So, our contention is that for any therapeutic technique, strategy, or activity to be effective, it must:

1 maintain a sustained focus on the problem;
2 require in some form the external expression of the problem;
3 involve a change in emotional state; and
4 generate shifts in point of view to evaluative, higher-level perspectives.

MOL therapists make every effort, in every session, to ensure that these four ingredients are part of every conversation that occurs. These aspects of therapy are so important we could call them the 'fundamental four' secrets of therapeutic success. So MOL therapists question clients about particular topics as a way of keeping the clients' attention focused on that area. MOL therapists are attuned to shifts in their clients' emotional states and, if the therapist perceives a shift, they might ask more questions about the topic being discussed when the therapist noticed the shift. They will also use questions to help clients keep their attention in a particular area when they have just made an evaluative comment about whatever it is they have just been describing. MOL therapists do not insist that their clients verbalise every detail of their problematic experiences, and they appreciate that many changes and shifts in perspective will occur for clients outside therapy, sometimes when they are doing things seemingly completely unrelated to therapy or their problem. Nevertheless, MOL therapists do facilitate clients externally expressing, in some way, different aspects of their life that are related to their problem, both as a way to provide the therapist with material to ask questions about and also as a way for clients to process their problem differently from purely internal processing.

A recent study conducted by our group illustrates the importance of these principles in therapy. A total of 18 clients in primary care reviewed their own videotaped sessions of MOL using repeated measures of their experience at two-minute intervals (Cocklin, Mansell, & Tai, 2014). The study provided us with an insight into the client's perspective of what makes therapy therapeutic in a naturalistic clinical setting. The repeated measures showed the rise and fall in clients' perceived levels of therapist helpfulness and clients' ratings of various aspects of their experience during each segment of the session. Analysis of the data collected revealed that clients' ratings of their control correlated highly with their perception of how helpful the therapist was at any two-minute segment of the session. This was the case even when clients' perceptions of the therapeutic relationship were accounted for. There was also evidence that talking freely about the problem, experiencing emotion, and a shift in perspective were all related to how helpful the clients perceived therapy to be, consistent with the account we are presenting here.

Making therapy more therapeutic

When clients are unable to create the desired result with the techniques and strategies they use, we would argue that one or more of the four elements mentioned above is absent or not included to the required potency. Furthermore, our suggestion in this book is that to maximise the impact of therapy, the focus should be about ensuring these aspects are continually present. We regard these four items as necessary and sufficient for clients to be able to use psychotherapy and counselling to achieve effective outcomes. The two goals of MOL correspond neatly to these four components: the first goal of MOL covers components one, two, and three, and the second goal of MOL addresses component four.

The four aspects of therapeutic effectiveness, therefore, can be used to evaluate or review therapy sessions. If you introduced a technique that did not seem to help as you thought it might, or if a client mentions using a strategy but not deriving much benefit from it, you could consider the technique or strategy in terms of how much each of the four elements were present. Did the activity sufficiently engage the client's attention with regard to the problem being experienced or some feature of the problem? Did the activity promote the client's external expression of the problem or some part of it in some form? Did participation in the activity affect the client's emotions in any way? Did the client experience any evaluative points of view while completing the activity or just after it? Identifying which components might need targeting for particular clients and any specific activity and finding ways to enhance the extent to which these components are present whenever clients complete the tasks will help to boost therapy effectiveness.

To maintain a sustained focus on the problem, a range of conversational questions can be asked related to various details of the distress being experienced. These questions are asked in a curious way as though the therapist sincerely did not know the answer to the question. Because, after all, the therapist does not know the answer. In Chapter 4, we discussed the dangers in assuming you know what the client is experiencing. Assuming is the antithesis of curious questioning, so, for the purposes of providing MOL efficiently and effectively, it is useful to suspend, as much as possible, the assumptions you might have about how well you can appreciate the experiences of the client. With an emphasis on curiosity, the following types of questions:

How often . . .?

Where . . .?

How many . . .?

What colour . . .?

And then what . . .?

What else . . .?

What happened next . . .?

all help to keep the client talking about whatever their distressing experience is. As they answer these questions, they cannot help but focus their attention on the current difficulty. In MOL, we often prepare clients for this work by explaining that, in MOL sessions, we assume that some part of their life outside therapy is not occurring as they would like it to, and for some reason they cannot make it be right. We tell clients that MOL is about helping them find solutions to the things in their life that are not as they would like them to be, and so the focus of our conversations is on these difficult areas.

Engaging clients in a conversation using the sort of questions mentioned above necessarily requires clients to verbally express different details of the problem. It is important to stress here that the *content* of their distress and difficulty is not considered important from an MOL perspective. An MOL therapist is not asking questions to extract a sufficient amount of content to develop an accurate formulation, or to select the most appropriate strategy, or to suggest a clever solution. Nor is the MOL therapist trying to establish the truth or accuracy of the client's account. Much like a potter uses clay, an MOL therapist uses the words provided by the client to ask more questions and to generate an ongoing, detailed conversation about the person's distress. The only value in the content is that it provides a way of continuing the conversation and ensuring that the discussion stays focused on the problem. Sometimes, content can even act as a distraction from focusing on the actual problem and the process of getting the client to process emotion or shift perspective.

When clients' problems are particularly troublesome or when their experiences have been especially gruesome, it can be very difficult for a therapist not to become absorbed in the content. A focus on content, however, can often mean that the therapist misses disruptions that are occurring in the client's dialogue or evaluative statements that are made. This is a subtle point because it can look to observers who are not well versed in the theory of PCT and the practice of MOL that MOL practitioners are *very* focused on content. An observer would notice an MOL therapist asking lots of questions such as the ones mentioned above: 'what colour'; 'how many'; 'where'; 'what happened next'; and so on, which seem completely concerned with content. The nuance here relates to the PCT principle of control of perception and the fact that you can never know what someone is 'doing' by simply observing their actions. The therapist might seem to be engaged in asking content-focused questions but, from the therapist's perspective, their goal is only to keep the client talking about the topic long enough until a disruption or evaluative comment is made. MOL therapists, then, have the difficult task of balancing their attention between staying tuned in enough to the current conversation so that they can keep asking sensible questions but not becoming so engrossed that they miss disruptions when they occur.

Many MOL conversations can appear to be intensely focused on content due to the specific nature of many of the questions. One client, for example, explained that he had a heaviness in his chest that felt like someone was sitting on him, as well as a crawling sensation like caterpillars were wriggling under his skin. He also could hear a noise like dripping water and had the sense of whirring cogs turning in his mind. A variety of questions were asked about the precise nature of the wriggling, dripping, and whirring. Through systematic and sustained questioning, it was discovered that the wriggling and the dripping and the whirring all seemed to be moving at the same pace. Moreover, the client discovered that he could make things speed up – so the caterpillars wriggled more quickly and the water dripped more rapidly – and he could also make them slow down. The client had never realised that he had some element of control over these sensations, and this was a revelation to him. He remarked, 'If I can make them speed up, I must have some control over them', which is the type of evaluative statement the therapist looks for to know what to ask further questions about. Another client described seeing colours around people. Everyone he knew or met had a different colour. The members of his family had colours, his friends had colours, and people he met only briefly had colours. Even his therapist had a colour. During MOL conversations, he could describe the colours, where the colour was in relation to any particular individual, how thick the colour was, how it changed, and so on. What had never occurred to the client was that *he* did not have a colour. He only saw colours on others – he did not have a colour himself. This was a fascinating discovery for him. So, while to onlookers these conversations might have seemed steeped in content, the priority from the therapist's perspective was to sustain a focus and encourage the external expression of internal experiences so that some shift in emotionality might occur along with a change in perspective or a helpful insight.

It is essential, therefore, that, as well as monitoring the content of the conversation to keep it problem-focused, an MOL therapist also stays alert to changes or shifts in the client's emotional state and to any evaluative comments that are made. As clients talk about their problem, there will often be a point in the conversation where their emotional state changes. They might become quieter and more subdued; they might get louder and more animated; their eyes might well with tears; they might speak in a more measured, clipped sort of way; or they might become silent. Whatever the change is, this provides an important clue as to where the conversation should centre for the time being. It is at this point especially that the talent of the MOL therapist comes to the fore. It is important to keep clients talking in this area, but if it is particularly emotional for them, questioning needs to be skilful and sensitive so clients are able to continue exploring these issues at a pace that they are able to tolerate and retain a sense of control over. We provide some example questions below of how this might be achieved. We recommend asking only one question at a time. We have provided different examples to convey a sense of the variety of questions that are possible.

Sometimes, simply repeating back a key word the client has said and using intonation to indicate a questioning stance is enough to keep the conversation going:

Frightened?

You felt 'out of control'?

Ambushed?

At other times, it might be useful to check in with clients to remind them that they can regulate the tempo and depth of the conversation:

You just started crying as you spoke about that. Is it OK to continue talking about it?

How are things going for you as we explore these areas?

What is happening to your anger as you describe your problems at work?

You said your anxiety was about 6 out of 10 when you first came in. What's happened to it as we've been talking about it? What would you rate it at now? What's different now that leads you to change your rating? How did that change occur – was it a sudden jump or has it been changing gradually? Is it still changing?

It can also be useful to focus on the process of change that you, as the therapist, just observed. This can sometimes be a way of helping the client continue talking about the topic but without emphasising the content that might be distressing:

What changed for you just then when you started to talk about . . .?

Things seem different for you now than they were a minute or two ago. Can you describe the change?

When you raised your voice, were you experiencing some of the anger you're describing? Did that occur suddenly? What did you first notice?

To promote the shifts in perspective to higher levels, it is important that the MOL therapist is alert to general disruptions to the client's dialogue, as well as the more specific shifts in emotional state or evaluative comments. We mentioned in Chapter 4 that, as clients discuss their problem, they might look away, or slightly smile, or make an evaluative comment such as: *That sounds crazy when I say it like that.* When any of these things occur, the MOL therapist's job is to ask questions to keep the client's attention in this new area for as long as it seems helpful. All of the questions described in Chapter 4, as well as questions such as:

What popped into your mind as you began to smile?

What makes you call it crazy?

Can you say some more about it sounding crazy?

You're shaking your head as you're talking. What's running through your mind?

How does it sound when you hear yourself describing these events?

What's occurring to you just now as you explain this situation to me?

How are you viewing it at the moment that makes you call it 'absurd'?

help to bring to the front of clients' minds any ideas, thoughts, and impressions that they might previously have attended to only fleetingly. It is from these higher, evaluative perspectives that novel and effective solutions will be generated.

The four elements we have outlined here can be used to improve strategies that are not working as well as they could, but they can also be used to promote and highlight improvements when progress begins to be made. Sometimes, a client may be making progress but might, perhaps, not realise the extent of the breakthrough they have made. Or clients might comment that, in between sessions, they are asking themselves the same kinds of questions that the therapist asks them in sessions or they are thinking about things in the same way they view them during the therapy discussions. Questions can be useful on these occasions to focus clients' attention on the changes that have occurred and to encourage evaluative comments that indicate a higher-level consideration of the changes they have made. A client, for example, noticed that he was periodically 'stepping back' and reviewing his thought processes during the weeks in between his appointments. This comment initiated a useful discussion involving questions such as how he did this, when he noticed himself doing it, and what the effects had been. Also, when conflicts are resolved, clients' sense of trying or forcing themselves to do things can disappear so they can engage in activities they were avoiding without even being completely aware of the significant change that has occurred. One young man, for example, who had had major problems with anger control reported in a session that he had begun to have an argument with his partner but had been able to 'step back' and 'observe' what was happening and subsequently withdrew from the argument. This was a dramatic change from how he had interacted previously, but the young chap had not reflected at all on the impact of this different way of responding. Similarly, a young woman who had been isolating herself because of her worries about how other people judged her had accepted a casual invitation from work colleagues to go for a drink after work, and then had spontaneously accompanied them to a party afterwards. She had an enjoyable evening and was unconcerned about what other people might be thinking of her. As with the young man, however, she did not seem to have taken time to appreciate what a change this was for her.

With examples such as these, it can be useful to spend some time asking questions about the changes that occurred to draw clients' attention to these shifts. The therapist could ask about important processes:

How did you achieve the 'stepped back' perspective? Can you adopt the same point of view now while we're talking?

What, in particular, were you observing while you were in the 'stepped back' frame of mind?

or even just generally inviting clients to comment on what they have just revealed:

What do you make of those changes now as you think back over them?

What goes through your mind as you describe these changes to me?

can help to keep clients' attention in a helpful place and further enhance the progress that already seems to be occurring.

Wrapping up

When therapy is not proceeding as effectively as you would like it to, it might be that clients are not focusing on their difficulties in enough detail; they might not be expressing core features of their problem, there might not be any emotional change as they discuss their problem, and they might not be attending to the higher-level thoughts they are generating about their difficulties. Our contention from a PCT-informed, principles-based perspective is that therapy will be more effective the more that the four ingredients we have described are present. Addressing problems of engagement or client motivation, for example, will only be helpful to the extent that they increase the presence of the fundamental four. It might not be the case that all four elements are equally important at all times. The framework of these four factors, however, provides a way for therapists to investigate improving the therapeutic activities when clients are finding that they are not as helpful as they could be.

Seeking the resolution to psychological distress can be difficult and demanding. When clients seem recalcitrant or resistant, it could be that therapy is not as meaningful for them as they need it to be. If clients do not complete homework or seem sceptical of different routines and procedures, they might not be experiencing the benefits they require. Focusing on increasing the extent to which the fundamental four exist in any therapeutic encounter could be the most important thing a therapist can do to assist in the effective and efficient amelioration of their clients' psychological distress.

Summary of main points

- Despite the existing panoply of therapeutic techniques and strategies, there are a small number of components that are common.
- The fundamental four are necessary and sufficient components of all effective techniques and strategies in psychotherapy and counselling.

Topics for discussion

1. When any therapeutic strategy is effective, something similar has occurred in the minds of the clients. Discuss.
2. The content of clients' problems is a means to an end but is not important in and of itself. Discuss.

Activities for learning, consolidation, and fun!

1. Create a therapeutic technique that does not have the fundamental four. How would you explain it to clients? How effective do you think it would be?
2. Ask your colleagues and other therapists you know what their favourite strategies are. How do they explain their effectiveness? Are their strategies ever less than effective? What do these therapists do when this occurs?

Chapter 8

Treat the distress, not the symptoms

By reading this chapter, you will learn:

1 why focusing on categories of disorder is often unhelpful;
2 about formulation from the perspective of a principles-based approach; and
3 how to be therapeutically useful to different people with different problems.

A principles-based approach to counselling and psychotherapy has the advantage of not being constrained by the apparent boundaries imposed by diagnostic categories. Instead, a principles-based therapy such as MOL can be useful for people who might attract a variety of different diagnoses including people who could be described as having complex or co-morbid presentations. Working from a principles-based perspective can take some adjustment for therapists who have been trained to use disorder-specific treatments. However, the benefits in terms of increased flexibility and responsiveness, and subsequent efficiency and effectiveness, may be more than adequate compensation for some initial discomfort and unease.

The problems of 'presenting problems' within diagnostic categories

One of the problems with using disorder-specific approaches is that only for a minority of people who access services in routine clinical practice do the problems that they want to address in therapy fit disorder-specific categories. For example, a client with a diagnosis of major depression may want to discuss her bouts of anger towards her partner, and a client who has attracted a label of bipolar disorder may want to work on problems that might be labelled 'social anxiety'. This means that therapists are left in the position of having to decide which aspect of which disorder to address first and how to disentangle presentations that do not fit neatly into any particular diagnostic category. Far from being a rare occurrence in therapeutic practice, co-morbidity is common (e.g. Andrews, Henderson, & Hall, 2001). In the study reported by Andrews *et al.* (2001), 21.4 per cent of participants met criteria for at least one of 14 different disorders in the previous 12 months, and, of these, 38.3 per cent met criteria for two or more disorders. For therapists interested in providing disorder-specific therapies, therefore, there can be delays in treatment as assessment processes are extended to try to gain a clearer picture of the most appropriate treatment to apply.

Descriptions provided in referral information are often not helpful either. This is not to say that referrers are incompetent or are misled by clients, but the information a client provides to a GP (for example) in order to access counselling and psychotherapy might be different from the information a client provides to a therapist once they have gained access to the service (Spratt & Carey, 2009). The tendency to provide different information to different people is easily understood from a PCT perspective in terms of a client controlling for different things, or maintaining different states, or pursuing different goals in different situations. Actually, PCT explains that even pursuing the same goal in different contexts will require different actions. Fortunately, encountering disparities between the referral information and the client's verbal reports is not disruptive to the provision of principles-based MOL therapy.

The limitations of classification

Many domains of science use a classification system. These include the classification of different species of animals and plants within biology and the periodic table of elements within chemistry. These systems help people to identify instances of a particular category when this is important – for example, to examine whether a particular species of animal is becoming extinct and requires protection. What is fascinating about classification systems, however, is that underlying the categories are more fundamental components and principles. For example, quantum physics has indicated that all elements are made from neutrons, protons, and electrons that differ in number across elements. Charles Darwin found that species are related to one another over thousands of generations and that a theory – evolution by natural selection – could account for this change. So, while classification has a role in any science, it should not be assumed that its categories are truly distinct, that change cannot occur, or that separate theories or models should be applied to each category. We shall see that this is particularly the case for the classification system used for psychiatric disorders.

The Diagnostic and Statistical Manual of Mental Disorders (DSM-5; American Psychiatric Association, 2013), for example, is now in its fifth edition despite the DSM nosology being described as a major obstacle to progress (Insel, 2012) for the mental health field. The DSM approach is simply the wrong tool to understand psychological distress (Carey, 2013). Fundamental principles underlying the categories are necessary for this type of understanding. Grouping checklists of symptoms into different diagnostic categories without any attention to the meaning of the symptoms for the clients, or to the way in which distress might emerge from these symptoms, does little to advance our understanding of psychological distress or the most effective ways to assist with its dissipation.

Timimi (2011) has provided an excellent critique of our two current classification systems for psychological difficulties, the DSM and the *International Classification of Diseases* (ICD-10; World Health Organization, 1992), which is in its tenth iteration. Timimi concludes that both the DSM and the ICD should be abolished. Neither of these systems has linked their diagnostic categories with aetiological processes such that there are no physical tests that can be used to determine the existence of any of the disorders created by the DSM and the ICD. Likewise, Insel (2012) claims that 'We still lack a fundamental understanding of pathophysiology' (p. 2) for any of the so-called mental illnesses. Timimi also argues that treatment specificity is an elusive goal, with positive outcomes being associated much more frequently with common factors such as the therapeutic alliance than with specific treatments matched to specific disorders. So even if therapists do like to use treatments designed to be disorder-specific, it is unlikely that the disorder-specific elements of the treatment they are using are the crucial components in terms of therapeutic effectiveness.

Furthermore, the problem of reliability has plagued the DSM from the beginning of the introduction of the multiaxial format (Kirk & Kutchins, 1994). Kirk and Kutchins meticulously analysed the way in which data have been manipulated to convey the impression that reliability has been satisfactorily addressed when, in actual fact, the problem of poor reliability has never gone away. Even if the reliability problem could be overcome, however, this would still not solve the problems of the DSM and the ICD (Pilgrim & Carey, 2010). Reliability coefficients tell us the extent to which two people agree on the identification or existence of a particular 'thing'. These coefficients, however, are silent with regard to the nature of the 'thing' that people can agreeably identify or even whether or not it is useful to be able to identify such a thing.

The typical way of assessing reliability for the DSM is to provide two experts in the field with case material indicating various symptoms of mental health difficulties. The experts assign a diagnosis based on their critique of the information and the extent to which the diagnostic conclusions of these experts agree is quantified as a measure of reliability. Even if these reliability statistics were routinely very high (which they are not), discovering the extent to which two people agree on the existence of a phenomenon tells us nothing about the *actual* existence of the phenomenon or even whether the alleged phenomenon is indeed a phenomenon at all. There would be quite high reliability, for example, when determining which star sign someone belonged to. Based on nothing more than a date of birth, two people could find that they agree practically all of the time regarding the star sign (Sagittarius, Scorpio, Gemini, and so on) to which someone else should be assigned. Similarly, there would probably be a very high level of agreement (reliability) at identifying Santa Claus, the Easter Bunny, and the Tooth Fairy from a line-up of different characters. We would almost certainly find that many people in the Western world agree very frequently on the identities of these three icons.

While it might be extremely pleasant to find that one agrees with a colleague a lot of the time, the frequency of this agreement does not provide any verification as to the legitimacy of what it is that is being agreed to, and the delectability of collegial consensus should not be confused with scientific rigour. If people who put faith in their horoscopes used a reliability argument to claim greater credibility for the star sign system, it is unlikely their assertions, based only on evidence of high reliability, would be taken seriously by the scientific community. Similarly, finding that some of the current mental health disorders have legitimately high reliability should provide us with little comfort that the prevailing nosological system is an appropriate way of understanding psychological distress.

Another field of work has cast further doubt on the relevance of current methods of classification. After an extensive review of the literature, Harvey, Watkins, Mansell, and Shafran (2004) found evidence of the existence of core maintenance processes across a range of mental health problems, suggesting these processes are *transdiagnostic* rather than being isolated to separate diagnostic categories. This review was a classic example of how classification has been used in the sciences of biology and chemistry – to elucidate common components – rather than trying to develop theories (of evolution in biology and of atomic structure in chemistry) for each separate category. This work is relevant to both research and practice, and is highly compatible with a principles-based approach to psychotherapy and counselling because it suggests that we need to shift the focus away from specific diagnostic understandings to consider a broader, more fluid way of conceptualising psychological distress.

Much of the evidence in the literature suggesting that a disorder-specific approach to treatment is not a sensible way to provide therapy efficiently and effectively focuses on empirical, pragmatic, and statistical issues. From our perspective, however, there are also important *theoretical* reasons for discarding existing classification systems. When day-to-day functioning is viewed through the lens of PCT, it can be appreciated that people's behaviour varies according to ongoing environmental circumstances in order to ensure that their experiences stay in their specified states. People control perceptual input, *not* behavioural output. Another way to say this is that we control the sensory consequences of behaviour, not the behaviour itself.

The discovery that we control perceptual input, not behavioural output, is remarkable and profound for the life sciences. It suggests that the behavioural patterns we identify and classify from an observer's perspective might not be experienced as patterns from an inside looking out point of view. It also suggests that, because the function of behaviour is to counteract environmental contingencies that would otherwise change perceptions in undesired ways, when we are trying to make sense of a person's behaviour, we should pay close attention to the current environment the person inhabits.

If you were observing someone's 'driving behaviour', for example, and you saw them quickly start moving the steering wheel from side to side, what would you conclude? The most obvious conclusion would be that something about the environment had suddenly changed. Perhaps they had entered a hilly area with lots of sharp bends or perhaps they had came upon a section of the road with scattered debris on it. Likewise, if you were driving with someone and, even though you could not see through the windscreen, you suddenly saw the driver withdraw her foot from the accelerator pedal, move it a little to the left, and then extend her leg forcefully towards the brake pedal, what would you conclude? Again, the simplest explanation would be that something on the road ahead had suddenly changed. Perhaps a deer leaped out of the underbrush in front of the car and bounded across the road. Or perhaps the car in front suddenly braked heavily. The point in both these examples is that the most likely reason for the change in the driver's behaviour is a variation in the environmental conditions the driver is negotiating. We would not typically conclude that some state inside the driver's head had changed and that had led to the alteration in driving action. In fact, it is because the driver is maintaining the *same* goals of, for instance, driving safely, that her behaviour *has to* change quickly and decisively in concert with variations in environmental conditions. Behavioural output, therefore, typically provides more information about the state of the environment than it does about the internal state of the behaving individual.

Diagnostic systems, however, by relying on symptom checklists, typically classify behavioural output. Even though some of the symptoms are based on what the client reports perceiving (e.g. hearing voices, unwanted impulses, intrusive memories), it is our premise that these perceptions are the *consequence* rather than the *cause* of their problems; the cause relates to deeper conflicts. The deeper conflicts tend to persist over time, but the symptoms are varied and typically change over time. Basing diagnostic criteria on these variations in the expression of a core problem is akin to grouping automobile drivers based on the way they hold the steering wheel. Those who hold the steering wheel with two hands at the top of the wheel would be assigned to one category, those who hold the steering wheel with their left hand at the bottom would be assigned to another category, and so on. Classifying people's behaviour will, from a PCT perspective, necessarily be arbitrary and inexact. More importantly, it will not tell you what a person is *doing* from that person's perspective; it will not help you understand the person.

Consider four different scenarios: someone who is miserable after his long-term relationship ended; someone who is despondent and withdrawn after losing her job because of bullying and harassment; someone who is sad and preoccupied with thoughts of how others are judging her after she was retrenched from her job; and someone who is despairing and sad and withdraws from social situations because he thinks his life is pointless and that his social presence does not matter to anyone so he should stay away. How should these people be 'sorted' diagnostically? Should they be sorted diagnostically at all? Would their outcomes in therapy be significantly improved if it could be somehow determined which diagnosis best summarised their presentation? The focus from an MOL, principles-based position is on understanding the problem from the perspective of the person experiencing it and using questioning to deepen and broaden their awareness of what is at the root of their problems, again from the client's own perspective. The person who is miserable after his relationship ended, for example, might be unhappy because his ex-partner has moved to another city with their child and he now sees his son only on school holidays. Knowing that the person met the diagnostic criteria for 'major depressive disorder' would not help a therapist understand the nature of this person's misery or how best to help him resolve it. Often during MOL, the job of the therapist is to help the client get past the diagnostic label and medical explanation for their problems (e.g. depression as an imbalance of brain chemicals) to explore deeper perspectives on what may be troubling them.

Where is the distress?

Appreciating symptoms from a PCT perspective helps explain the otherwise puzzling situation that alleged symptoms of mental health problems are not uniformly and reliably associated with psychological distress (Tai, 2009). Many people in the general population, from time to time, experience what might be identified as symptoms of mental health disorders, and many of these people continue to function satisfactorily and do not attend psychotherapy and counselling services (Kazdin, 2001). As we mentioned in Chapter 5, many people who would meet the criteria for a mental health disorder never access mental health services. Moreover, people who do become clients of therapy services do not do so because they have high scores on symptom questionnaires (Kazdin, 2001).

Even when symptoms are considered to be related to severe mental health problems, it is not the case that identification of a symptom necessarily implies distress. Hearing voices, for example, is one of the symptoms that might be used to assign someone to a schizophrenia category. Voice hearing, however, is widely reported in the general population (Ohayon, 2000). Indeed, there are now communities of 'voice hearers' who regard very favourably their ability to hear things that other people cannot. Actually, for any collection of symptoms that a client brings to therapy, one can invariably find other people in the population with similar behaviours and thoughts who are not distressed by these experiences. There is not a direct correspondence between distress and symptoms even though treating symptoms sometimes has the effect of reducing distress.

There seems to be an implicit assumption in the mental health field, however, that symptoms themselves are inherently distressing. Many self-report questionnaires, for example, ask people about various bodily states or occurrences that are thought to be related to diagnostic categories without ever checking if these self-reported phenomena are actually distressing. The *Depression, Anxiety, and Stress Scale* (DASS; Lovibond & Lovibond, 1995) includes statements such as: 'I was aware of dryness of my mouth'; 'I found it difficult to relax'; and 'I felt that life was meaningless'. The *Hospital Anxiety and Depression Scale* (HADS; Zigmond & Snaith, 1983) includes statements such as: 'I feel tense or "wound up"'; 'Worrying thoughts go through my head'; and 'I have lost interest in my appearance'. The *Kessler Psychological Distress Scale* (K10; Kessler *et al.*, 2002) includes statements such as: 'During the last 30 days, about how often did you feel tired out for no good reason?'; 'During the last 30 days, about how often did you feel nervous?'; and 'During the last 30 days, about how often did you feel that everything was an effort?'

For both the DASS and the HADS, people completing the questionnaires indicate on a scale from 0 to 3 how frequently the various items were occurring for them. People completing the K10 are provided with a scale from 1 to 5 to indicate how frequently the listed items were occurring. The general idea is that the higher the number, the greater the quantity of depression, anxiety, stress, or whatever it is that is being assessed. Thus, it seems to be assumed that having a dry mouth, or finding it difficult to relax, or having worrying thoughts, or losing interest in your appearance, or feeling tired out or nervous are distressing in and of themselves. The K10 is explicitly named as a distress scale.

From an MOL principles-based perspective, there is no assumption that any particular symptom is *necessarily* distressing. We emphasise 'necessarily' here because we want to be very clear that we are *not* saying that the items on these questionnaires never indicate or hint at distress. It *might be* very distressing to having worrying thoughts or to be unable to relax. It might, and then again, it might not. Our point is that it cannot be assumed that these items *always and unquestionably* indicate distress. Because there is not an uncomplicated relationship between symptoms and distress, MOL targets distress directly.

In Chapter 2, we explained why even a statement such as 'I felt that life was meaningless' is, on its own, meaningless. In order to understand the impact a belief such as this has for the individual, it is necessary to enquire about the ideas, attitudes, and values that the individual has and how this belief of meaninglessness measures up to the other standards the individual has. The practical importance of this sentiment was illustrated in one session as a client was completing a questionnaire at the end of therapy. The client was happy with what he had achieved in therapy but he paused on the DASS item 'I felt that I was using a lot of nervous energy'. The client hesitated and said, 'What should I put here?' The therapist was puzzled and replied, 'What do you mean?' to which the client responded, 'Well, I feel like this a lot so I should put 3 but I actually like feeling this way. It doesn't bother me at all so should I put 0?' The discussion continued and the client explained that he did not want to get a 'high score' on the questionnaire because his emotional angst had largely disappeared and he was feeling good about himself and life in general.

While the relationship between symptoms and distress is not straightforward, it might be expected that the relationship between impairment and distress would be less ambiguous. To investigate the relationship between impairment and distress, we used the *Work and Social Adjustment Scale* (WSAS; Mundt, Marks, Shear, & Greist, 2002). The standard form of the scale has five items, which ask people to rate from 0 (no impairment at all) to 8 (very severe impairment) their level of impairment in the areas of work, home management, social leisure, private leisure, and forming and maintaining close relationships. What is more, the wording of the items directly links level of impairment and disorder. Item one, for example, is 'Because of my [disorder], my ability to work is impaired.'

We modified the WSAS by adding another sentence to each item that asked how bothered people were about their stated level of impairment. After each item, we asked, 'How bothered are you about this level of impairment?' and people could indicate their level of 'botheration' from 0 (not at all bothered) to 8 (very, very bothered). We gave this adapted form of the WSAS to 61 people to complete in routine clinical practice and we found that there were strong but not perfect correlations between impairment and botheration for each of the five items. The correlations for the five items were: item one – 0.59; item two – 0.79; item three – 0.69; item four – 0.76; and item five – 0.71. While these correlations are high by conventional psychological standards, an inspection of a scatter plot provides a more sobering perspective from a therapeutic point of view.

Figure 8.1 is a scatter plot of the relationship between level of impairment and level of botheration for the responses provided to item two. Item two was chosen as an example because it had the strongest correlation between impairment and botheration out of the five items. It can be seen in Figure 8.1 that, for a level of impairment rated at 2, the level of botheration for different people ranged from 0 to 8. A level of impairment of rating 4 had botheration ratings from 2 to 7. Finally, a level of impairment rating of 6 had botheration ratings from 4 to 8.

The variability illustrated in Figure 8.1 with regard to the level of botheration associated with a particular level of impairment provides a powerful reminder of the dangers of assuming that symptoms or impairment *necessarily* imply distress. It can also be seen from Figure 8.1 that knowing how distressed someone is about a particular area does not necessarily explain how impaired that person is in that area. People, for example, who were very, very bothered (rating of 8) about their level of impairment varied from being mildly impaired (rating of 2) to be being very severely impaired (rating of 8). It should be emphasised also that in routine practice, the WSAS does not ask people to rate how bothered they are about their impairment. The standard form only provides ratings of impairment. The MOL position, however, is that it is not impairment per se that is important from a therapeutic perspective, but rather it is the extent to which this impairment distresses or bothers the person that is paramount. Importantly, only knowing how impaired people perceive themselves to be does not provide explicit information about how distressed they are regarding this impairment.

We do not want the information we are discussing here to be interpreted as suggesting that self-report questionnaires should not be used in therapeutic practice. On the contrary, we use questionnaires in our clinical work and find them a helpful adjunct to the information clients provide in other ways. Rather than viewing the questionnaires as 'measures' of particular disorders, however, we consider them to be 'reporting devices' and we curiously surmise what clients might want us to know by completing the questionnaires in the way that they have. The implication for therapeutic practice of the WSAS exercise is that, for any

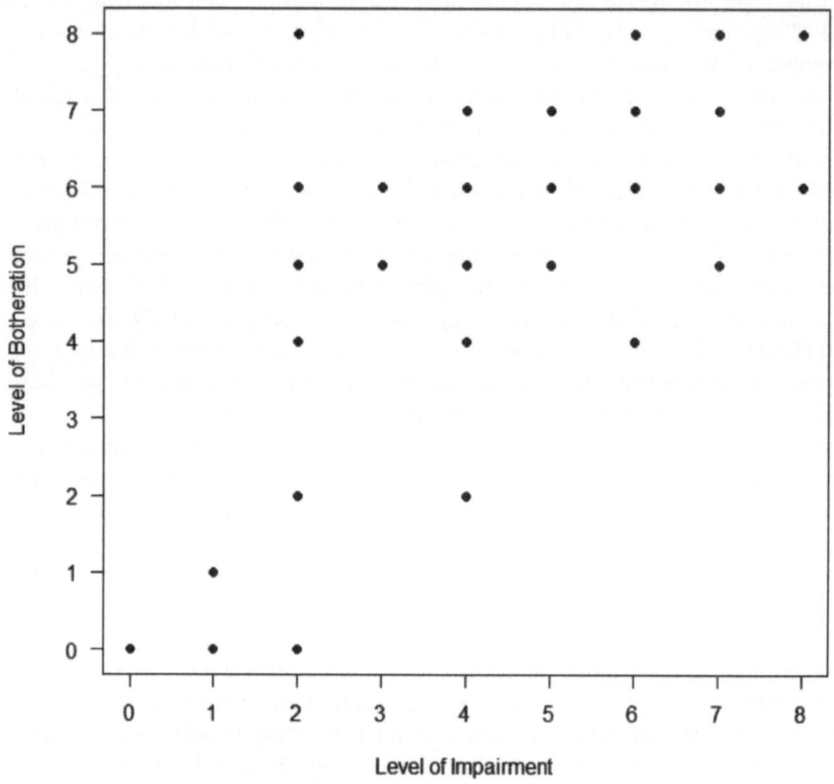

Figure 8.1 A scatter plot of the relationship between impairment and botheration for an adapted form of item two (Home Management) of the Work and Social Adjustment Scale

Source: Mundt and colleagues (2002)

questionnaire, we cannot take the scores as an unequivocal indication of the problems to which therapy should be directed. We need to always remember to verify with our clients about the extent to which the symptoms or problems they are reporting bother them or prevent them from living as they would wish to live.

The point that particular states and sensations are not inherently distressing should be an unremarkable claim for any therapist who has more than a passing understanding of the cognitive behavioural psychotherapies. This collection of therapies has as their bedrock statements such as the famous edict from Epictetus that 'Men are disturbed not by things, but by the view that they take of them.' Typically, it seems that 'things' have been assumed to be outside events and circumstances, but there is no reason why a thought – or a voice or an image or a feeling – could not also be considered a 'thing'. To take Epictetus's sentiment to its logical conclusion would seem to imply that people are not disturbed by thoughts (or voices, images, or feelings), but by the view they take of these thoughts. Contemplating thoughts in this way suggests that it would be a misnomer, for example, to isolate and identify a cognitive process as a 'dysfunctional assumption'. An assumption or belief can never be dysfunctional on its own. The dysfunctionality arises when the assumption is considered in the context of all the other attitudes, beliefs, and thoughts that currently exist in the landscape of the mind being examined. This is the concept of relativity that we introduced in Chapters 2 and 3, and will return to later in this chapter.

Formulation is not a straightforward alternative to diagnosis

Therapists who eschew diagnoses as a way of understanding mental health problems sometimes use a formulation approach as an alternative. Often, formulation is presented as a replacement to diagnosis, although there is disagreement in the literature regarding the extent to which diagnosis and formulation are incompatible or complementary (Pilgrim & Carey, 2010). The general idea with formulation is that a detailed history is obtained from the client and then this information is used to construct a plausible-sounding account of how the client's problems arose and the way in which they are being maintained. Ideally, this explanatory account is developed as a collaborative activity between the therapist and the client.

It could be expected that the approach to formulation that is adopted will be heavily influenced by the therapeutic style and theoretical predilection of the therapist. A therapist using cognitive behavioural therapy, for example, would look for remembered experiences in the client's past that might have been significant learning events in which, it is assumed, particular attitudes, belief patterns, and schemas developed. One of the goals of using formulation in the early stages of therapy is to encourage clients to 'socialise to the model' of the therapist and to foster their engagement in the activities that will be introduced in subsequent therapy sessions. It is not clear, however, the extent to which the formulation is later referred to and relied upon in subsequent sessions of therapy and it could be argued that the time spent developing a convincing formulation is time that detracts from providing the actual therapeutic elements of effective therapy.

Formulation can also be plagued by the same problems as diagnosis when the focus of the formulation is symptoms rather than distress. Formulations are often accounts of how symptom patterns develop and continue to exist rather than explaining how and why a person came to be, and continues to be, distressed. Even when a formulation targets the explanation of the manifestation of distress rather than the display of symptoms, it is still the case that a formulation is only an indirect way of assisting with the resolution of distress. In contrast, the modus operandi of the MOL principles-based approach to psychotherapy is to target the distress directly.

Formulation can also be problematic if the discrepancy between actual and intended numbers of therapy sessions is not considered. Boisvert and Faust (2002) make the point that therapists might often provide a formulation with the expectation that the problems that are highlighted in the formulation will be addressed in subsequent sessions. If the client attends only that session, or a small number of further sessions, they may be left with an overly narrow or negative view of their situation. With this in mind, therapists could approach each session as though it might be the last one with this client (Boisvert & Faust, 2002). This is very much the mindset of an MOL therapist.

In MOL, a generic formulation of psychological distress underpins all therapeutic work (Spratt & Carey, 2009). Considering that control is the first principle of our approach, it is assumed that people are distressed because they are unable to control important aspects of their life. That is, people become distressed when they experience too much or too little of a particular state and are not able to make the state be the way they want it to be. There might be too many thoughts that they cannot sort and process or there might be too little enjoyment that they cannot appreciate and increase. Thus, distress arises when people are not able to control, to their satisfaction, particular perceptual activity (Carey, 2006a). Conflict, as the second principle, is regarded as the most parsimonious reason for this disruption in control processes. In MOL, therefore, it is generally assumed that control processes become chronically interrupted because people are, inadvertently, attempting to control two equally important but incompatible experiences simultaneously. It is impossible to be hot and cold at exactly the same time, or serious and light-hearted, or relaxed and pedantic, or friendly and aloof, or negative and hopeful. When this situation of incompatibility occurs, loss of control results, and consequently the symptoms that we traditionally associate with mental health disorders arise.

Conflict, therefore, is very much on an MOL therapist's mind as they engage in conversation with the client. Although the conflict formulation has a generic structure, every conflict with every client is always different because each client has a hierarchy that is unique. In MOL conversations, clients often describe fighting or arguing with themselves or telling themselves one thing but then doing the opposite thing. MOL therapy focuses on helping clients explore this conflict so that the therapist can look for disruptions as signs to possible background thoughts, images, or feelings that might be a clue to the germination of an effective solution. It is not necessary that the client becomes aware of the conflict diagram (see Figure 2.2), although there is no imperative to keep this information a secret from them either! In MOL, the guiding principle is always do what, as a therapist, you think might help the client become aware of higher-level control systems that are related to the conflict. It is this guiding principle that shifts the emphasis to distress rather than symptoms.

As long as the two goals of MOL are being pursued, there are no hard and fast rules about what MOL therapists should or should not do. Generally, the introduction of standard techniques and activities is minimised so the conversation time can be maximised in which clients are asked to discuss whatever is on their mind and indications of awareness shifts to higher levels are monitored and explored.

Conversations would particularly home in on any mention of people disagreeing with themselves or any other hint that there is an internal tug of war playing out.

Clients, for example, might be talking about 'forcing themselves' to do various things. Logically, the only reason someone would need to force the occurrence of a particular event is if there was an equally strong desire to do the opposite of the event. One client described forcing himself to go out to a regular social club he had previously joined. The sense of force was important because it indicated that there might be a conflict occurring. This hunch was confirmed when the client explained that, even though he used to enjoy these encounters, he did not want to face people again because he imagined they were thinking negatively of him.

It is not important, therefore, that clients are presented with a diagram of Figure 2.2 that has their particular conflict mapped on it. It is also not essential for clients to articulate that they are experiencing a conflict and for them to name both sides of the conflict. It is considered vital, however, that they are engaged in a conversation about whatever fighting, arguing, criticising, trying, forcing, uncertainty, or indecision they are experiencing. Experiencing rather than naming the conflict is considered essential in MOL, and clients will experience the conflict by describing it. One client described wanting to tell her parents to 'get lost' and leave her alone because she described them as always being 'on my case'; however, she also did not want to speak badly of her parents. The conversation in this instance explored her ideas about such things as: what she wanted to tell her parents; what else she wanted to tell them; how long she had wanted to tell them this for; what she imagined happening when she thought about saying these things to her parents, and also what was important to her about not speaking badly about her parents; what did she want to say about her parents; how did she like speaking about her parents; and what did 'speaking badly' mean from her perspective. The important point here is that it is the experience of the conflict that is paramount and exploring the conflict in whatever form in which it exists for the clients you are talking to. Therapists might keep a mental map of Figure 2.2 in their minds to help their discussions of conflict with their clients, but it is not essential for clients to learn about the figure in therapy.

Maintaining a focus on conflict will help to sustain conversations that might seem to get bogged down or go off track. It is the case that clients can vary markedly in the conversational 'style' they bring to therapy. Some clients might seem unemotional, some might seem to 'intellectualise' their experiences, other clients might seem to be guarded or ruminative or to be externally focused. For each client, it is likely that MOL therapists will have to slightly vary their conversational approach to be as helpful as possible to the person sitting across from them. However, there would be many drawbacks if we were to try to 'prescribe' certain types of MOL questions for certain client presentations. First, it would take the emphasis away from the core principles that are at the foundation of MOL. Second, it would encourage the therapist to take less control and responsibility for generating questions that seem appropriate in the immediate context. Third, it would have the potential to overload the therapist with lists of questions rather like they might have been overloaded with techniques for dealing with different disorder-specific presentations. Fourth, it would discourage the requirement for therapists to remain flexible in how they achieve the two goals of MOL when seeing differences between clients or experiencing shifts in how clients present their problems from session to session. By steadfastly pursuing the two goals of MOL, and doggedly cultivating an atmosphere of curious exploration in which conflict and its source are the treasures being searched for, MOL therapists will be able to vary and adapt their approaches for the benefit of the variety of clients with whom they work.

Focusing on distress rather than symptoms

As mentioned in Chapters 2 and 3, an important but frequently ignored aspect of the symptoms of psychological distress is their 'relativity' (Carey, 2006a, 2009). Relativity is conveyed in the lesson from Epictetus mentioned earlier. It may be that relativity accounts for the fact that there is often not a direct relationship between any specific symptom and the experience of distress. The concept of relativity is elegantly accounted for by the PCT explanation of conflict. The conflict formulation of psychological distress suggests that a thought, behaviour, or feeling is only distressing *relative to* other thoughts, feelings, and behaviours the person is simultaneously experiencing. Clients are often only aware of one set of behaviours, thoughts, and feelings, and an important function of therapy can be to help clients understand the role that other feelings, thoughts, and behaviours are having *relative to* the ones they are aware of in generating their distress. Perhaps counselling and psychotherapy has an equivalent to Einstein's law of relativity.

The relative nature of the distressing component of problems is repeatedly demonstrated in therapy. One young male client, for instance, wanted to move on and forget about his father. He was teary, sad, and withdrawn, however, because *simultaneously* he also would not let himself move on and wanted to repair his relationship with his father. Thus, from an MOL principles-based perspective, the young man's distress was not generated because he wanted to forget about his father and nor was it produced because he wanted to repair his relationship with his father. The man was experiencing distress because he both wanted to forget about his father *and* repair his relationship with his father *at the same time*. Also, a young single mother who was anxious, angry, and frightened wanted to let her son do normal things and wanted to bring him up like other mothers bring up their children but she also wanted to keep her son safe and did not want to let him out of the house. Again, it is the juxtaposition of these two opposite states coexisting simultaneously within the confines of one skull that generates distress.

Carey (2009) suggests that 'the value we attribute to a particular thought is *always* determined by the way in which it measures up to other thoughts, ideas, goals, and beliefs that we have' (p. 168, emphasis in original). The thought 'I'm going to make a fool of myself and people will laugh at me' (Carey, 2009, p. 168) provides a cogent example of this point. It can easily be appreciated that if you were preparing for an important presentation that might influence decisions regarding your career progression or recruitment to a highly desired new job, then this kind of thought would probably generate anxiety and fear. If, however, you were a stand-up comedian or a circus clown and you were waiting for your cue to begin your performance, then a thought such as this would bring comfort, confidence, and encouragement. Without a conflict formulation, it is very difficult to make sense of the way in which the same thought can generate both anxiety and confidence in different circumstances. Another example of a situation often encountered within the therapeutic context is when people who have experienced being abused in their childhood have the reoccurring and distressing thought that 'I am to blame'. The distress they experience can be understood as the result of them simultaneously not wanting to take the blame. The concept of relativity easily explains these situations.

MOL therapists, therefore, work hard to minimise the extent to which they *assume* they understand what clients might be experiencing. MOL therapists are aware that they can never really walk a mile in their clients' shoes. This attitude of believing that they *do not* understand their client is very helpful for maintaining a curious questioning perspective. The focus of MOL questioning is about looking behind the scenes of the symptom presentations that are on display to enquire about the distress lurking in the background. As we indicated in Chapter 3, even when clients use well-known terms such as 'depression' or 'anxiety', MOL therapists assume they do not know what the experience of depression or anxiety might be for their clients, so they ask about it. An MOL therapist might begin the session by asking:

> *What would you like to talk about today?*

and the client might reply with:

> *Well, I've been really depressed lately so I'd like to talk about my depression.*

to which the therapist might say:

> *Tell me some more about your depression?*

or even just:

> *Depressed?*

The purpose of these questions is to encourage the client to begin focusing on the problems they want to resolve. Very quickly in the conversation, MOL therapists encourage clients to begin considering the distressing aspects of their depression (or any other problem they bring to the session) by asking:

Does it bother you to be depressed?

and:

What bothers you about it?

Although it might seem almost nonsensical to be asking depressed people if being depressed bothers them, it is surprising the answers that often follow. Clients, for example, might say:

Well of course it bothers me.

and then follow that statement with:

I don't feel motivated to see anyone anymore.

Another client might have a completely different reason for why depression bothers them and may respond with:

I just can't function like I used to.

Immediately, then, there is an area beyond depression to begin exploring. The therapist could say:

Tell me some more about the way you used to function.

What's the main difference in the way you function now compared to the way you used to function?

Is the way you used to function important to you? What are the important aspects of your functioning?

Does it bother you to not function like you used to function? What bothers you the most about that?

Perhaps, through this line of questioning, the client might explain:

I don't think my partner is going to put up with me much longer and I'm not there for my daughter when she needs me.

With further questioning, the client might elaborate that she is feeling really stretched at the moment. She has taken on a new business in a new town, which was always her dream, but it has become very difficult to retain staff, which has resulted in her working much longer hours than she had anticipated. Additionally, her daughter is having difficulty adjusting to a new school and has been bullied.

The client feels she needs to spend more time at work building the business but she also thinks that her daughter needs extra support at the moment. She has begun feeling that she is not doing anything properly and she has become irritable and snappy with her partner. The MOL conversation, therefore, focuses on the stretched feeling the client identified, as well as her dilemma about spending more time with her daughter while needing more time at her new business.

Focusing on distress rather than symptoms will often move the discussion to the source of the problem quite quickly. Shifting the emphasis in sessions from altering symptom presentations to understanding the conflict and its source often involves little more than recognising that the symptoms are not the problem and asking clients what bothers them about the problem they are thinking about rather than allowing the discussion to linger on the symptoms of the problem. A slight change of direction in questioning can yield big rewards in terms of therapy efficiency and effectiveness.

Final comments

Principles-based MOL counselling and psychotherapy identifies and explores the distress associated with any particular symptom rather than the symptoms themselves. Therapeutic change occurs most efficiently by understanding distress and reorganising it from within the source, not by overcoming symptoms. While reductions in distress can be achieved by addressing symptoms directly, this is akin to the tail wagging the dog. When the source of distress is reorganised, symptoms rapidly melt away. Principles-based MOL counselling and psychotherapy, therefore, requires an unwavering attitude of constantly searching behind the symptoms that clients are describing to reveal their distress, as well as the purposes and goals that are outside awareness but which are currently generating the distress. By helping clients become aware of their higher-level values and expectations, they will have assumed a very useful vantage point to begin plotting a more satisfying life course for themselves.

Summary of main points

- Distress and symptoms are not related in a regular, direct, or straightforward way.
- Thoughts, feelings, and behaviours are only ever distressing *relative to* other thoughts, feelings, and behaviours.
- Using a conflict formulation allows MOL therapists to work flexibly and responsively with a wide range of problems without being restricted by diagnostic categories.
- Focusing on distress rather than symptoms entails a shift in emphasis of a therapist's questioning away from the actual problem to bring into view the things that bother the client about the problem.

Topics for discussion

1 Clients' problems rarely fit neatly into diagnostic categories. Discuss.
2 Underlying all clients' problems is conflict. Discuss.

Activities for learning, consolidation, and fun!

1 Identify the last time you were feeling irritated or upset. What was the problem and what was it about the problem that bothered you? Can you identify a conflict at the bottom of your feelings of botheration?
2 Think about the last client you saw. What did they say their problem was? Summarise their problem in a sentence. What makes their problem a problem? In terms of what you have learned in this chapter, can you identify a conflict in the background of their problem? What might be some questions you could ask them in the next session?

Chapter 9

Therapeutic change

Expect it at any time

By reading this chapter, you will learn:

1 that all theories and models underpinning different forms of psychotherapy subscribe, either implicitly or explicitly, to a model of change;
2 that change is a non-linear, unpredictable process with no regard for predetermined schedules; and
3 that reorganisation is a fundamental learning mechanism incorporating random changes and error reduction.

All methods of counselling and psychotherapy reflect assumptions about change and how it happens. If the fundamental purpose of therapy is to help people move from a state of psychological distress to a state of contentment, satisfaction, or even simply less distress, then it seems reasonable to suppose that the designs of different therapies convey statements, either implicitly or explicitly, about how that movement occurs. Psychotherapies, for example, that are provided in set time frames of regularly scheduled sessions, endorse, by their structure, a model of change as a stepwise linear process. The way in which psychotherapy research is conducted also seems to assume that change occurs gradually and linearly despite the fact that prospective studies of change indicate a non-linear process (Hayes *et al.*, 2007). Furthermore, the activities conducted within therapies, as well as the role of the therapist described by the therapy, convey assumptions about the way in which change occurs. In this respect, MOL is no different. Based on the tenets of PCT, MOL incorporates reorganisation as the principle underlying the change required to resolve psychological distress (Carey, 2006a, 2008a; Mansell *et al.*, 2012).

Given that change could be regarded as the fundamental purpose of counselling and psychotherapy, a robust explanation of change would seem to be a necessary prerequisite for the development of efficient and effective therapies. Surprisingly, however, this is not the case (Carey *et al.*, 2006). Also, it might be reasonable to expect that therapies would be developed based on the state-of-the-art understanding of how change occurs and what best promotes it. Again, this does not appear to have occurred (Carey *et al.*, 2006). Our current position in psychotherapy and counselling is that we do not have a generally accepted straightforward answer to the question 'How is psychological distress ameliorated?'

Even Castonguay and Beutler's (2006b) contribution mentioned in Chapter 1 does not move us much closer to understanding the change process despite its tantalising title. The title of their work is *Principles of Therapeutic Change That Work*, and some of the principles provided in Table 1.1 are: '1.1203 If patients and therapist come from the same or similar racial/ethnic backgrounds, dropout rates are positively affected and improvement is enhanced'; '1.1204 The most effective treatments are likely to be those that do not induce patient resistance'; '1.225 Therapy outcome is likely to be enhanced if the client is willing and able to engage in the treatment process'; and '1.226 The therapist is likely to increase his/her effectiveness if he/she demonstrates attitudes of open-mindedness, flexibility, and creativity'. These principles might explain different aspects of therapy that have been associated in a general and statistical sense with positive outcomes, but they do not expose the apparent mysteries associated with the way in which psychological distress transmogrifies into contentment and satisfaction or even simply less distress. There are other principles that describe features of therapy that may compromise or interfere with change: '1.112 Clients who have been diagnosed with a personality disorder are less likely to benefit from treatment than those who are not'; '1.1202 Patients representing underserved ethnic or racial groups achieve fewer benefits from conventional psychotherapy than Anglo-American groups'; '1.211 Clients who experienced significant interpersonal problems during their early development may have difficulty responding to psychotherapy'; and '1.1209 Psychotherapy for anxiety is less likely to be successful if the client has low internal attributions of control or high negative self-attribution. Thus, rigid externalizing or internalizing coping styles are negative prognostic indicators'. Again, however, these principles provide no hints as to what the process is that is somehow interfered with, nor how these factors, such as being diagnosed with a personality disorder, create the interference.

Having a clear understanding of what the change process is and how it unfolds would enable us to be more confident about how, as therapists, we can promote change more often. We might know that people who are diagnosed with a personality disorder are less likely to benefit from treatment, but that information does not help therapists improve their usefulness to the clients they work with who have attracted a personality disorder diagnosis. If we had an accurate appreciation of the mechanics of the change process, we could figure out how a personality disorder diagnosis obstructs that process (if, in fact, it does hinder the process) and we could take steps to mitigate the impact that such a diagnosis had on the change that occurred in therapy.

Overall, it seems as though therapies have been designed and delivered based on what therapists have found to be effective in the past or according to what research indicates seems to work on average or in general. Kazdin (2009) considers the question of how therapy leads to change as one of the most urgent questions for our field. Without the answer to this question, it is remarkable that therapies are as effective as they are as often as they are. Perhaps they could be much more effective as well as more efficient if there was a robust understanding of change guiding the development of therapy. The fact that clients can improve in different therapies, with different activities, different roles for therapists, and different assumptions about the change process, is perhaps the best evidence available that the mechanism that produces change is not reliant on specific therapeutic styles. It is relevant to once again mention Voltaire's attitude (first introduced in Chapter 1) of keeping the client amused while nature cures the problem.

What we know about therapeutic change

It is increasingly acknowledged that therapeutic change does not always occur in a stepwise, linear fashion. Non-linear change, characterised by sudden and unpredictable fluctuations, is a more accurate way of describing much of the change that occurs in counselling and psychotherapy (Mansell *et al.*, 2012). Curiously, change in therapy can occur linearly and gradually on some occasions and, at other times, it can be discontinuous and non-linear (Hayes *et al.*, 2007). This feature of change, occurring in a variety of different ways, seems to mimic the way that change occurs in nature through developmental transitions and other perturbations that arise (Hayes *et al.*, 2007).

It makes sense that any model of change in therapy should be similar in important ways to the change that occurs generally in life. We know, for example, that only a proportion of people experiencing severe psychological distress access counselling and psychotherapy services, yet many people seem to find ways to reduce psychological distress satisfactorily without a therapist. In Chapter 5, we mentioned that research indicates that many people who would otherwise meet the criteria for one or more mental health disorders never access mental health services. Kazdin (1999) suggests that the number of people in the community with symptoms of mental health disorders is probably quite high. Additionally, self-help resources have been shown to be reasonably effective (Norcross, 2000). If one of the goals of psychotherapy and counselling is to help the client to learn how to get along without the therapist, it makes sense that our methods in therapy should be aimed at promoting the sort of change that might occur for people who do not access therapeutic services.

A series of studies first mentioned in Chapter 3 further emphasised the similarity of the change process regardless of whether people change with or without therapy (Buchan, Galbraith, & Carey, 2013; Carey *et al.*, 2007; Gianakis & Carey, 2011; Higginson & Mansell, 2008). These studies interviewed people who had experienced and then resolved psychological distress. The first study (Carey *et al.*, 2007) interviewed people who had received different forms of therapy, the second study (Higginson & Mansell, 2008) interviewed some people who had received therapy and others who had not, and two subsequent studies (Buchan *et al.*, 2013; Gianakis & Carey, 2011) interviewed people who had not received therapy. The studies found that the change process described by people attending therapy was similar to the change process described by people who had resolved their problems without therapy. For all people, change involved sudden and gradual components. The sudden component was often experienced as an 'Aha!' moment or a 'che-ching' (Higginson & Mansell, 2008, p. 319); 'a light going on, putting a shilling in the meter, a load being lifted' (Carey *et al.*, 2007, p. 182). The gradual aspect of change occurred both before and after the sudden aspect, with some participants having the sense that change crept up on them or happened without them realising it (Higginson & Mansell, 2008). Other participants described change as a natural progression and still others described a gradual process of dealing with one thing at a time after a sudden realisation of what needed to occur (Gianakis & Carey, 2011). No participants described change occurring in a neat series of stages or steps.

Apart from the sudden and gradual components of change, people also described a significant emotional component in which the experience before change was extremely negative and the experience after change was very positive (Carey *et al.*, 2007). There was also a sense of a threshold for participants (Buchan *et al.*, 2013; Gianakis & Carey, 2011), with many describing experiences such as hitting 'rock bottom' (Gianakis & Carey, 2011, p. 449) before the change occurred. For some participants, the threshold experience involved facing up to their problem rather than avoiding it (Higginson & Mansell, 2008). Aspects of the self also featured frequently in participants' description of change. Some participants identified features of themselves that either hindered or facilitated change (Carey *et al.*, 2007; Gianakis & Carey, 2011). Other participants talked about themselves before and after the resolution of the problem with the view that 'I'm not the same person as I was before' (Higginson & Mansell, 2008, p. 320).

One of the most interesting aspects of these studies was that participants could not identify *how* change occurred. They could identify what changed; for example, attitudes (Carey *et al.*, 2007), perspectives (Higginson, Mansell, & Wood, 2011), and thinking processes (Gianakis & Carey, 2011). They could also identify techniques or tools that they believed had facilitated the change process, such as problem-solving strategies (Buchan *et al.*, 2013), cost-benefit analyses (Gianakis & Carey, 2011; Higginson & Mansell, 2008), and various other strategies such as homework, medication, thought diaries, and relaxation techniques (Carey *et al.*, 2007).

Despite their confidence *that* change had occurred, participants were at a loss to explain *how* their distressed state transformed into a state of contentment or satisfaction. Participants could not describe the 'che-ching' process or what occurred in that moment when the light came on or the shilling dropped. In some ways, it is astonishing to discover that such an important and palpable experience would also be indescribable, yet this apparent inability to articulate the process of change is supported by everyday experience. Many people are familiar with the phenomenon described in Chapter 3 of trying hard but unsuccessfully to recall the name of an enjoyable movie or a famous actor only to have the name 'pop' into awareness at a later time. Despite the undeniable certainty of the occurrence of this experience, it is very difficult to describe how this 'popping' occurs.

Change in psychotherapy and counselling, therefore, seems to be the same change that occurs for distressed people who do not access psychotherapy and counselling. It can occur in a gradual and linear way, but can also occur unpredictably and non-linearly. In fact, it seems to be the case that change involves both sudden and gradual components; at least, people who experience change describe it this way. A range of different means can be useful in promoting change, and yet clear descriptions of the actual change process remain elusive and mysterious.

The knowledge summarised here fits quite neatly with a PCT understanding of change. In fact, PCT is able to clarify and extend this knowledge. We first began discussing the PCT approach to change in Chapter 3, and will continue that discussion here. PCT enables us to distinguish between two different kinds of change. The first type of change is very much part of the routine operation of control processes. The hierarchy of perceptual control systems maintains control by varying lower level systems so that higher-level systems can keep discrepancies between desired ('*should be*s') and perceived states ('*is*es') at a minimum. When moving a car from home to work, for example, a driver uses different actions every time the mission is accomplished. If you were somehow able to ensure you used exactly the same series of muscle tensions on Tuesday that you had successfully used on Monday, you probably would not reach much further than the end of your street, if you even got that far. This sort of change is very much the state of play for successful day-to-day living as a control system. We inhabit environments, including our bodies, which constantly change. In fact, it is precisely because of the changing nature of the environments we occupy that we need to control at all. We are so good at dealing with this kind of change that we barely notice we are doing it. We walk along busy pavements without bumping into people or falling over by constantly changing and adjusting our path. We hit tennis balls back across the net even though they never bounce in the same place at the same height and at the same speed twice and we never strike them from exactly the same position.

Powers (1992) provides a striking example of the way in which change and variability are accommodated by the routine operation of living control systems:

> I used to have a martin house . . . in my backyard. Those birds often wouldn't bother to use the perch: they'd fly up to the hole, fold their wings, and pop in without touching the sides. Consider the precision of control that's needed to do that from an infinitely variable set of starting positions and trajectories. How accurately do you think the aerodynamic forces of the wings had to be adjusted to make a twenty-foot approach curve on a breezy day go within a quarter of an inch of the center of the hole? I never saw a bird miss a try.

So it did not matter from which angle the little martins approached their house or the direction and strength of the breeze that was blowing; they made it through the hole and into the nest every time. That kind of exactitude is extraordinary but also quite commonplace for control systems. In fact, it is the way control systems are designed. The hallmark of control is stable ends by variable means. Over and over again, control systems modify and adjust their output to negate the effects of environmental activity so that what they are sensing or experiencing stays the way they want it to. Therapists vary the way they ask questions and how animated they are and the pace of their voice and the amount of eye contact they have and the angle of their body in relation to their clients and many other things in order to keep their sense of therapeutic helpfulness as they like it to be. Again, this is the way in which control systems function routinely. The type of change that occurs as control systems are doing what control systems do is the first kind of change.

The first kind of change can be indicated when tasks are able to be accomplished in one context but not in another. A client who was an inpatient in a secure forensic facility was being reintroduced into the community. To help with her adjustment, the client was spending four nights a week at supported accommodation in the community and three nights a week back in the secure facility. At a team meeting about this client, the team member responsible for helping her integrate successfully back into the community was explaining that the programme was proceeding as planned but she identified financial management and problem-solving as two priority areas to be addressed if living in the community safely and satisfactorily was ultimately to be achieved. Later in the team meeting, concerns were raised about a discovery staff had made that marijuana was being brought into the facility. The staff were baffled as to how this was occurring because stringent checks occurred with people entering or leaving the unit. Also, it was noted that the client who was spending time in the community had been making regular deposits into her bank account and her bank balance had been steadily growing. Team members 'joined the dots' and were fairly confident that it was the client on the community integration plan who was, despite the best efforts of the staff, obtaining marijuana and bringing it into the unit to sell to other clients. Given this new information, it was suggested at the team meeting that perhaps the client had adequate financial management and problem-solving skills after all. It was acknowledged that the client was currently not using these skills in ways that would contribute to safe and satisfactory community living, but the tasks one applies their skills to is quite a different matter from whether or not one has the skills in the first place. This client, then, did not need to learn new skills; she needed to change the goals she was using these skills to accomplish. This is an example of the first kind of change. When a person has learned how to sew, or cook, or trim hedges, applying these skills to make a garment or meal that one has not made before, or to trim a different kind of hedge, does not necessitate altering the existing repertoire of abilities. These tasks require employing competencies that one already possesses in novel situations.

The first kind of change does not require the control systems themselves to change. Changing various aspects of control systems, or connections between control systems, is a feature of the second kind of change. The second kind of change creates and installs capacities and capabilities that were not there before. It is this kind of change that provides us with the ability to learn to walk and talk, turns us into the people we are, and helps us keep on being who we want to be.

When a person experiences an 'epiphany' and leaves a high-powered job in the city for work in the country that allows for family time and a less harried lifestyle, major adjustments have occurred in beliefs and values so that the world and life in general are viewed differently than they were before. This kind of change involves a reorganising of existing skills and abilities so that new capabilities emerge. Change of this nature is regarded as the most fundamental type of learning.

Reorganisation as a general model of therapeutic change

When Powers (Powers 1973, 2005; Powers *et al.*, 1960a, 1960b) was developing PCT, he was faced with the formidable task of proposing a plausible account of how the hierarchy of control systems develops. How do we develop the hierarchical network of control systems that make us the adults we are? Because of the rigorous way Powers developed the basic concepts of PCT, along with the specificity and precision of the terms, and the quantifiable expression of relationships, the same standards of exactitude needed to apply to any model of hierarchical development that was suggested. Furthermore, although neural plasticity is now commonly regarded as an accepted feature of the adult brain and the tremendous capacity of the brain to modify and correct itself are well appreciated, these features were not so familiar in the 1950s, 1960s, and 1970s. Moreover, the constant, ongoing, dynamic relationship between the brain and the environment and the way in which they simultaneously influence and modify each other (Barrett, 2011) is more readily accepted now, although ironically it was this concept that Powers pioneered with PCT.

The problem to be overcome was to discover a learning process that did not, itself, need to be learned. That is, how does someone learn before they know how to learn? What mechanisms must be in place to help babies lift their arms and hit the toys dangling above them? By the time individuals reach maturity, not only have they learned many things, but they also have many useful learning strategies at their disposal. Activities such as rehearsal, force-field analysis, brainstorming, cost-benefit analysis, method of loci, decision-tree analysis, and problem-solving are extremely useful strategies in the right context, but each of these activities had to be learned (Carey, 2011a). None of these activities, therefore, could be contenders for the most fundamental learning process. Other types of learning such as observational learning, imitation, or experiential learning describe methods of learning but not the learning process itself.

Powers advanced the idea that the most basic kind of learning involves random changes and error reduction. This idea developed into the model of reorganisation, which, despite its rudimentary nature, has been shown to be a powerful and efficient learning mechanism (Marken & Powers, 1989; Powers, 2008). It is considered that reorganisation, as a process, is ubiquitous throughout the dominion of living things. The concept of reorganisation was developed and tested through building functional models that appear to simulate change as it occurs.

The general idea of reorganisation is: when there is persistent error in the system of variables that are important for our survival known as intrinsic variables, random changes are generated in the hierarchy of perceptual control systems and the effect on error is monitored. If a change in the hierarchy has the effect of reducing error for the intrinsic variables, that change persists. If error does not reduce, another random change occurs. The consequence of error reduction, therefore, is a delay in the next random change. Reorganisation is a 'dumb' system in that it does not make decisions regarding whether the change about to be introduced is good or bad, moral or immoral, or naughty or nice. It does not make judgements at all; it just makes changes. If ingesting various substances, for example, reduces error, then that might be a change that persists until error once again increases.

Reorganisation is exactly the process that is needed to resolve psychological distress resulting from internal conflict. One of the things that makes persistent conflict so insidious is that there is no logical or rational way to solve it. There is no solution from a person's existing repertoire that can create the experiences of 'laid back' and 'striving to achieve' at the same time. A person cannot 'fit in and be like everyone else' and 'be independent and be my own person' simultaneously. A novel perspective is required to alter the situation that is currently pitting these two ambitions against each other. The task of generating new insights and perspectives is one for which reorganisation is ideally suited.

When solutions or new abilities are required, it is imperative that only the control systems involved in the problem are reorganised. Reorganising control systems that are functioning efficiently and successfully would be a disastrous tactic for a creature's ongoing survival. To address this issue, Powers (1973, 2005) has suggested that reorganisation is linked to awareness such that it is the control systems in awareness that are reorganised. This seems to make intuitive sense since chronic error is something that is hard to ignore. Often, however, awareness fixates on the goals that cannot be achieved or the frenetic and chaotic symptoms that are manifesting. Figure 2.2 illustrates why reorganising at these levels would be ineffective for the ultimate resolution of the conflict. The conflict is actually being generated at a higher, third level. Focusing on changing the lower levels in the conflict is a bit like plugging the holes in the bucket while the tap supplying water to the bucket is still turned fully on. The misdirection of awareness in the conflicted control systems configuration provides a plausible hypothesis for the longevity of some conflicts – awareness has not been directed to, and maintained at, the higher level for reorganisation to make the alterations necessary to resolve the conflict.

So the suggestion from PCT is that moving awareness to this highest level in the conflict configuration is the central task that is achieved when any approach to psychotherapy and counselling effectively helps people reduce psychological distress. We are, therefore, proposing reorganisation as a generic change mechanism that has been usefully redirected whenever any therapy is effective. We also think this is the process that is occurring when people solve problems of psychological distress without the assistance of psychotherapy or counselling.

Analysing the way that mundane choices are negotiated provides support for the hypothesis that shifting awareness to higher levels is what is required to resolve conflict. We stated in Chapter 2 that, from a PCT perspective, any choice is essentially a conflict scenario. Typically, however, we are not debilitatingly immobilised by daily choices. We do not stand in front of the wardrobe unable to decide whether to wear the checked or the striped shirt. Why not? How do we come to decide? Usually, something like this happens: 'Hmmm. Checks or stripes, stripes or checks. Oh! I know. I've got that management meeting this afternoon and I want to look professional – I'll wear the stripes.' A similar process happens with other choices: 'There's a great comedy movie on tonight at the cinema. Oh, that spy thriller looks good too. I really like spy movies and I haven't seen a good Andropolous film for ages. Which one, which one. Nope, work has been hellish today – I need a good laugh. I'll go to the comedy'; and 'What should I do for my holidays? I could go to Majorca again – I always enjoy it there. What about the Pyrennes? I've been wanting to do a walking holiday for ages. Oooh. This is tough. I do love the beach. Mmmm. You know what? I'm going to the mountains. I really need to just get away from things for a while. Walking in the mountains will give me a chance to clear my head and get things back in perspective.' Whenever a choice is made, there is some appreciation or hint of a higher order goal or value. Once the 'bigger picture' comes into view, the choice element disappears from most choice situations. Having awareness illuminate the bigger picture and keep it in the spotlight may be the ultimate challenge in resolving any conflict.

Awareness is still, largely, an unfathomable aspect of our existence, yet its mobility is undeniable. In an instant, awareness can highlight the pressure of your body on the Chesterfield lounge upon which you are reclining, or it can bring into focus a moment of hilarity on your recent holiday abroad, or it can prick you with a poignant memory from your childhood, or it can remind you to pick the kids up after school. Although the experience of awareness is that it is stationary and thoughts, images, ideas, and feelings 'pop' into the spotlight or waft through under leisurely inspection, the explanation from an MOL perspective is that it is awareness, rather than its contents, that does the moving. Thoughts do not 'pop' into our mind, but awareness showcases various ideas from the network of our being. Similarly, thoughts do not race, but awareness might move from one thought to another with increased speed from time to time. And when we have the experience of thoughts 'jumping' with little apparent order, it is awareness that we assume to be flitting from one place to another.

Implications of reorganisation for therapy

Reorganisation has profound implications for counselling and psychotherapy. As a general model of change, reorganisation is regarded as being relevant to different problems and also to different therapies. This is not a model of change just for major depressive disorder, or generalised anxiety disorder, or any other discrete problem set that might be identified. Reorganisation is regarded as being important whenever a person's problems have the form of an internal conflict. Also, this model of change is not specific to cognitive behavioural therapy, or cognitive analytic therapy, or acceptance and commitment therapy, or interpersonal psychodynamic therapy, or emotion-focused therapy, or any other individual 'brand' of therapy. Reorganisation is regarded as the change process that occurs in any programme of therapy whenever that therapy is effective. Reorganisation is also considered to be the mechanism at work whenever people reduce their psychological distress by completing an online programme or reading a self-help book. Regardless of the myriad of ways people explain the experience of change, we are suggesting that the common, inbuilt process of random change and error reduction is the key.

With an understanding of reorganisation, therapists can optimistically expect clients to change in meaningful and comprehensive ways at any time. Clients who attend very few sessions can change just as thoroughly as clients who attend many more sessions. It may be reorganisation that explains the findings of the GEL model (Stiles *et al.*, 2008) discussed in Chapter 6 of different clients attending different numbers of sessions (from zero to 20) all making about the same amount of change. Some clients changed quickly and abruptly, and others changed more slowly and gradually, but they all changed by about the same amount. From a reorganisation perspective, even clients with chronic and complex conditions who may have seen a parade of counsellors, psychotherapists, and other healers can achieve contentment and satisfaction with sustained reorganisation. Reorganisation, therefore, allows therapists to adopt a positive attitude of dogged hopefulness regarding the successful resolution of every client's conflict.

Reorganisation is a creative process whose only function is to generate alternatives. Sometimes, the best alternative is not generated first and clients may feel they are getting worse rather than better. Some increased confusion, as well as a decrease in current abilities, can be associated with learning any new skill and is often a sign that reorganisation is beginning to have some effect. Explaining this to clients can help them persist until a successful resolution arrives. Sometimes, things get worse before they get better. Sometimes, too, things can seem to start getting better and then get worse before finally improving again. On occasion, a deterioration in function may indicate that a change in therapeutic strategy is warranted; however, this is not necessarily so. We would recommend a period of 'watchful waiting', which could include monitoring with outcome questionnaires, whenever clients seem to become more confused or more distressed because an effective solution and improved condition could be just around the corner. Figure 9.1 shows the outcomes scores of two different clients who completed the Outcome Rating Scale (ORS; Miller & Duncan, 2004) at every appointment. As can be seen, it is not atypical for clients to have a drop in function and well-being at some stage of their therapeutic encounter. This drop could be an indication that this type of therapy is not useful for this client at this time, but it could also indicate that reorganisation is starting to generate changes and an effective solution might not be far away.

It is also interesting to note in Figure 9.1 the different patterns of access to therapy by the clients. One client attended 14 sessions of therapy over 59 weeks and the other client attended 12 sessions over 15 weeks. Also, they both started therapy reporting different levels of distress. Nevertheless, they both eventually achieved a similar low level of distress as reported on the ORS (Miller & Duncan, 2004). These two plots of different clients' use of therapy provide excellent illustrations of why the client-led approach to treatment scheduling is so important. If these plots illustrate how different clients prefer to engage in therapy, what effect would constraining these clients to a set programme of regularly spaced appointments have had?

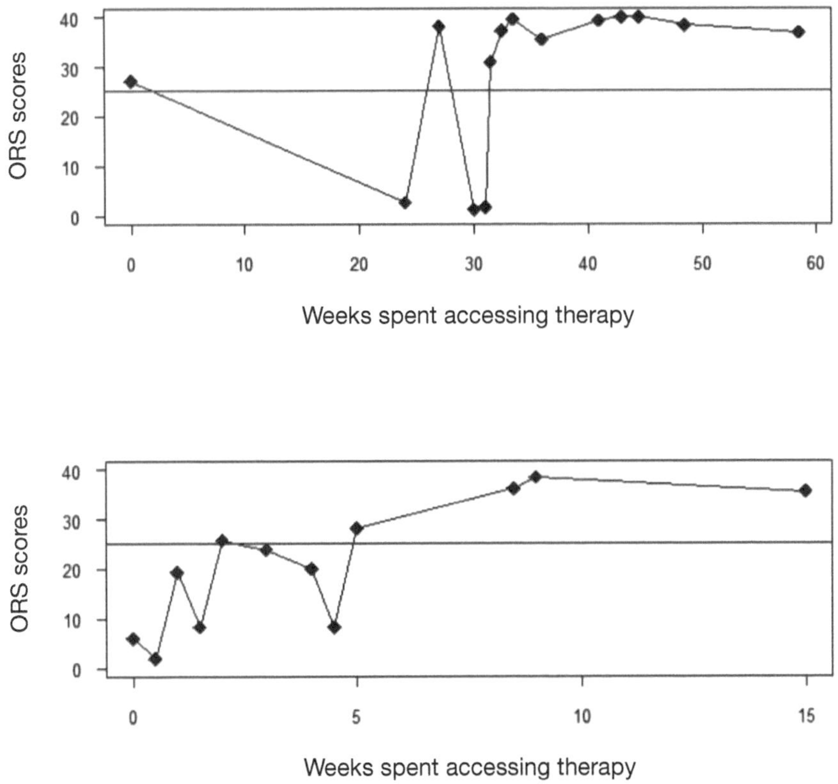

Figure 9.1 Plots of data obtained from completed Outcome Rating Scales (ORS) for two clients. The horizontal line represents the clinical cut-off with scores below the line being considered indicative of clinical levels of distress. The plots illustrate the non-linear nature of change and how decreases in ORS scores (indicating increases in distress) do not necessarily indicate that therapy is ineffective

It appears to be the case generally that some change in emotional state indicates that a fruitful area to focus attention has been found. Reorganising the distress associated with conflict is an emotional experience. Sometimes, clients can discuss their difficulties in an emotionless, detached, almost third-person tone. This is quite different from the 'stepped back' observer perspective that clients often achieve when their awareness moves above the conflict they are experiencing. If clients describe their problems as though they are reciting a well-rehearsed script, then additional questioning needs to be used to draw their attention to the details they may not be considering closely. In MOL sessions, an increase in emotionality is often regarded as a positive indicator that reorganisation may have arrived at a useful location. It can often be profitable to let the client's awareness linger in this area so that reorganisation has sufficient time to generate changes that will be useful. Asking gentle, compassionate, yet probing questions can help to keep a client's awareness fixed in an area that might yield an effective solution:

I noticed you looking more upset as you're talking just now. Can you tell me a little bit about what's happening for you as we discuss this?

What sorts of changes are you aware of while you're talking to me just now?

What do you notice occurring for you as we discuss this?

As conflicts are discussed, it can be the case that clients appear to reach an impasse. They might get to a point where they feel stuck, as though they do not know what else to say or do. It can be tempting at this point for the therapist to offer suggestions or strategies for the client to try. In MOL, it is recognised that the therapist can only ever offer solutions from their own perspective and understanding of the client's difficulties and, regardless of how carefully they have listened, the therapist can never know how it is to live the client's problem. These 'stuck' places are actually important areas to find because they indicate that the client is currently experiencing the brunt of the conflict. Continuing to question the client at this point may help to generate useful disruptions that could indicate an important higher level to draw the client's attention to. So, when clients say they feel stuck or that they just do not know what else to do, MOL therapists could say things such as:

Do you often feel stuck like this?

Tell me more about the 'stuckness'.

Is there a particular place in your body where you feel the stuckness most strongly?

Is it a completely immobilising kind of stuckness or something else?

Does it bother you to not know what else to do? What bothers you about it?

Do you have other situations where you don't know what to do?

What goes through your mind as you discuss your situation this way?

An important and obvious implication for therapy is that change can happen at any time. Therapists should be alert to implicit or explicit messages they are conveying to the client that suggest that therapy will take a particular amount of time or number of sessions. Lasting and pervasive change can occur in any time period. A person who achieves a satisfactory solution in 10 or 20 sessions has not necessarily changed more thoroughly and effectively than someone whose solution was generated in one or two sessions. Therapists should approach therapy with the expectation that lasting change might be just around the corner. It is also important to remember that reorganisation in terms of producing a successful solution might not necessarily occur during the therapy session. It often seems to be the case that, once directed to a useful place in the hierarchy, reorganisation continues to churn out and test solution possibilities even when people are occupied by other activities. Perhaps this is a bit like the common experience of trying to think of a name of a movie or famous person and, not being able to recall it, finding that it 'pops' into your mind at a later, unexpected time when you are not even thinking about it. Reorganisation explains why approaching each session as though it could be the last is such a sensible attitude to adopt. From this perspective, initiatives such as setting limits to session numbers and discussing 'brief' therapies may not be particularly helpful. Clients should be assisted to create an appropriate solution in whatever period of time is necessary. In school classrooms, it is well accepted that students learn at different rates. The same understanding should be common knowledge in the therapy clinic as well.

In some ways, it should come as no surprise that distress could be satisfactorily resolved in a small number of sessions. We know, for example, that people can become severely distressed after one traumatic event. As we alluded to in Chapter 3, if distress can appear quickly, there seems to be no reason to suppose that it cannot disappear just as quickly.

MOL is provided in a spirit of therapy being conceptualised as a resource that people can access whenever they want to spend time making their life be more like the way they want it to be. If someone returns to therapy after an absence, there is no assumption that the first therapeutic experience was somehow faulty or did not 'work'. Relapse prevention programmes, therefore, are not considered necessary in MOL.

The GEL model (Stiles *et al.*, 2008) we introduced in Chapter 6 provides striking empirical support for the temporal variability of the change process. The evidence from Stiles and colleagues (2008) supports the suggestion in MOL to not make assumptions about how much change, or the kind of change, that is right for a particular client. An MOL therapist works hard to provide the highest quality MOL they can and they leave decisions about how much is enough to the client.

MOL conversations can be unpredictable in the path they take. Neither the therapist nor the client knows the 'right' level to go to for reorganisation to have its best effects. An MOL therapist, therefore, needs to be comfortable with uncertainty and needs to be responsive and flexible to the changing topics of conversation. To reiterate, the general guideline is that if the problem still exists, look for a higher level.

As we hinted at in Chapter 2, the rate of reorganisation can be important in generating effective solutions (Carey, 2011a). If reorganisation is too slow, then error will not be reduced, and if it occurs too rapidly, then new changes will be generated before the effect on error can be adequately assessed. An important function of therapy through the use of systematic, sensitive, and sustained questioning may be to provide a structure for not only the direction, but also the rate, of reorganisation. Therapists have an important role to play by the way they ask questions in helping to modulate the rate of reorganisation. The structure of therapy sessions can help to guide the reorganisation process to the location in the client's experiential world where it will have maximum effect.

Perhaps the most fundamental implication of all, from a reorganisation perspective, is that the client does not consciously or willfully reorganise. While there is growing acknowledgement that the client is the agent of change in therapy (Bohart, 2000; Bohart & Tallman, 1996), we suggested in Chapter 3 that the PCT model of reorganisation clarifies that although the client is the *locus* of change, the client is not the *agent* of change. Reorganisation is the agent of change. In the same way that people who sustain a broken leg or a deep gash in the forearm cannot *make* their bone knit or their flesh fuse, psychologically distressed people cannot make themselves be satisfied and happy. They cannot wilfully force the right solution to materialise. The most people can do when they are experiencing conflict is to put themselves in a position where reorganisation can do what it does so well. Reorganisation does not know how to give up, so as long as the person persists in becoming aware of different aspects of their problem, reorganisation will, sooner or later, create the kind of change for which the person yearns.

A final word

Based on the principles of PCT, we are able to offer an answer to the question: 'How is distress ameliorated?' The answer is: *reorganisation*. The PCT model of reorganisation offers a powerful and optimistic change mechanism. However, it is not all plain sailing. Along with the knowledge that reorganisation will resolve the conflict that has been distressing and debilitating comes the understanding that a given time frame cannot be guaranteed and a factory-made solution cannot be applied. Solutions cannot be called forth when it is convenient, and when they arrive they may be unpredictable, surprising, or even mundane. Therapy, then, becomes a resource that the tenacious therapist continues to offer and re-offer whenever people wish to turn themselves into clients and work hard at exploring regions of their tribulations of which they are not yet fully aware.

Summary of main points

- Change is not a linear or predictable process.
- Legitimate and lasting change can occur within any time period: change in one or two sessions can be just as profound and effective as change in 10 or 20 sessions.
- Reorganisation is an innate learning process designed to reduce error and improve control.
- Reorganisation cannot be controlled in the same way that someone can start and stop a brainstorming activity. From a reorganisation perspective, the client is the locus of change, but not the agent of change.

Topics for discussion

1. Sometimes in therapy, clients can get worse before they get better. Deterioration does not necessarily mean that the therapy needs to change. Discuss.
2. People do not change according to ordered, discrete stages. Discuss.

Activities for learning, consolidation, and fun!

1. Think of something you believe strongly in. It could be: a religious belief; an attitude about honesty; a political view; opinions about discrimination and prejudice; or any other strongly held stance. Write down this view in a succinct statement. Now write down the opposite of this statement. Can you 'make' yourself believe this? Spend a day believing this idea as convincingly as you can. What happened?
2. Write down in a short paragraph how you think therapeutic change occurs. Ask some of your colleagues how they think therapeutic change occurs. How similar or different are your answers? What do you think of the ideas of you and your colleagues in the context of the information in this chapter?

Chapter 10

How it all works in practice

By reading this chapter, you will learn:

1 about the goals of MOL therapists; and
2 how MOL therapists monitor and maintain their delivery of MOL.

We believe that principles-based counselling and psychotherapy using MOL is an exciting and refreshing approach to helping people resolve psychological distress. It provides counsellors and psychotherapists with clarity about their role and confidence in the aspects of therapy that have the greatest potency in facilitating psychological change. Therapists can be liberated from prescriptive protocols and programmes, and can allow their own creativity its full expression as they focus on reflecting the application of three important principles in their therapeutic work: control, conflict, and reorganisation.

Research indicates that the most effective counsellors and psychotherapists – the 'supershrinks' – have the same habits as the most effective people in any field, such as expert chefs, professional athletes, and business leaders (Miller, Hubble, & Duncan, 2008). Supershrinks work hard at what they do; they set goals, they reflect, they routinely evaluate their performance, they seek feedback, they have a thirst for knowledge and a desire to improve, and they have regular supervision and training. An MOL supershrink is no different in developing the habits of goal setting, reflection, evaluation, and seeking feedback from their clients. With PCT as a framework, however, the goals that an MOL therapist sets, the tools they use for reflection, and the way they seek feedback might be different.

Because of the importance of PCT to the application of MOL, a sound understanding of PCT is also an essential component of using MOL effectively. Spending time exploring websites such as: www.pctweb.org; www.livingcontrolsystems.com; and www.mindreadings.com would be time well spent in terms of coming to grips with the fundamental concepts of PCT. These websites have papers on different aspects of PCT, vignettes and video clips, and interactive demos. Since PCT is a theory about a physical phenomenon, it will be a boon to your learning to undertake some of the interactive activities. It can be very different reading about a concept to feeling the phenomenon in action. The results can sometimes be surprising and are often counter-intuitive. The video segments and interactive demos, therefore, are valuable complements to the wealth of information contained in the easily accessible books and papers that are available. Powers' last book *Living Control Systems III* (LCS III; Powers, 2008) also has interactive demonstrations that are provided on a DVD that accompanies the book. LCS III provides an excellent tutorial on the basic principles of PCT that form the foundation of MOL.

Recapping on the principles of MOL: control, conflict, and reorganisation

MOL is based on the premise that people function as living control systems. That is, from before they are born until the time they expire, they control. Rich people control, poor people control, farmers control, and stockbrokers control. Clients control and therapists control. Control is a process of making things be right, or making things be the way we want them to be. It is a process of minimising the difference between our world of '*should be*s' and '*is*es'. Control includes activities as simple as straightening your tie before a meeting, or walking the dog after a day at work, or tapping the keyboard to type 'the', or stretching your muscles before your gym class, or scratching that itch behind your right eyebrow. It also includes activities as complex as organising your dad's surprise 60th birthday party, or planning your wedding and honeymoon, or buying and renovating the home to raise your family, or negotiating peace treaties between two countries, or graduating from university.

As control systems, we control our perceptions, not our actions. We vary our actions so that our perceptions do not vary, or only vary as we want them to. Our actions are indispensable to us, but only because of the perceptual effects they create. They are a behavioural means to a perceptual end. We have no knowledge of our actions apart from the changes they produce to our perceptions. The only evidence we have that signals are being sent to our muscles is because we can see and feel our muscles in action. We have no independent knowledge of those muscle-activating signals and we cannot arbitrarily direct a signal to any particular muscle. We know we are clapping hands because we can see and feel our hands moving and hear the effect of them coming together. Creating hand-clapping behaviour involves making certain feelings, sounds, and images occur. We know we are clapping hands rather than grating cheese because we can see, hear, and feel different things happening. There are undoubtedly different signals being sent to our muscles to produce these different actions but we have no privileged knowledge of those signals beyond the perceptual consequences they create for us.

All we know of other people is what we can observe from the outside and the only thing we know of ourselves is our experience of the world from the inside looking out. We can never really understand how our actions are understood by others, just as they can never really know how it is for us to act the way we do.

PCT requires that we rethink our notions of apparently commonplace concepts such as 'objectivity'. All of our actions are designed to keep the world as we experience it in the states we have specified. These states may not always make sense to other people or may not seem right to others. But they make sense to us. They are right from our perspective, which is the only perspective we have. Keeping our perceived world in the states we like to experience it in is the daily task for the entire duration of the activity we call 'living'.

The states we prefer are organised as an entire hierarchy of controlled states with states at higher levels varying the level to which lower states must be brought. Thinking of an experience and asking 'why?' and 'how?' questions about that experience can give a sense of moving up and down the hierarchy. Goals that are in the front of our minds are being established by higher-level goals and are, in turn, being achieved by setting the goals for lower levels. The only reason a pressing deadline is on your mind is because you need to meet that deadline in order to keep the *should be/is* discrepancy at a minimum for more important, higher-level states or goals. You will achieve the deadline by varying the states of lower levels such as the time you get up in the morning, or the time you leave the office, or how many emails you respond to during the day, or how many telephone calls you take, or how long you spend at lunch.

Understanding therapy as an environment of interacting control systems provides a different view of time-honoured therapeutic concepts such as transference and countertransference, resistance, collaboration, and engagement. All concepts in therapy are different aspects of control processes. Therapists are controlling to make therapy be right for themselves and, similarly, clients are controlling to make therapy be right for themselves. Generally, perhaps due to the flexibility, adaptability, and resilience of control systems, therapy proceeds satisfactorily for both the therapist and the client. Coming to understand the important states you seek to maintain during therapy and thinking of your clients as state maintaining creatures will help to enhance each of the therapeutic relationships you enter into.

The more you can recognise any action in terms of its function in keeping a *should be/is* separation as small as possible, the more you will be able to work effectively with a broad range of clients. It is likely that you will not know what the particular states are that different clients are maintaining, but you will know that there is a state there nevertheless. When clients fail to complete homework or disagree with an interpretation you have offered for their behaviour, they are not being ornery or cantankerous. They are controlling some of their *should be/is* states and counteracting the disturbing effect that your homework or analysis has created. Perhaps a client thinks that the homework you suggested, if she completed it, would reveal to the people she lives with or maybe her colleagues at work that she is seeing a therapist. Divulging to others that she is receiving psychological support may be something she is avoiding, so your homework is neglected. The homework may even inadvertently create a conflict for your client who wants to complete the homework you have assigned but also wants to keep her therapy appointments a secret. Sometimes, you might offer explanations to clients about why they act in particular ways. If they disagree, it is not necessarily because they are ungrateful of your help or unappreciative of your insights. It might be that your interpretation sounds to a client as those you are hinting that he is responsible for creating the distress he is now experiencing. Irrespective of the accuracy of that suggestion, your client might find it confronting and will, therefore, seek ways to once again think of himself as a victim of circumstances. Explaining actions in terms of their error-reducing function will not prevent disagreements from occurring, but it will give you more options in figuring out what to do whenever there is a fracture in the alignment of opinions.

Since control is everything we do, problems of living will necessarily be problems of control. The main psychological problem for control systems is conflict. Conflict blossoms when two control systems strive to simultaneously achieve two incompatible and opposing experiences. A person might want to be liked and be assertive at the same time. Or they might want to be a doting parent while also wanting to be an esteemed colleague. Not all situations where mutual goals are pursued will lead to conflict. It will not always be the case, for example, that wanting to pursue your own dreams and wanting to maintain a close relationship with your parents will be incompatible. Sometimes they will and sometimes they will not. Conflict is, however, a very common feature of our existence. Basically, any choice situation has the form of a PCT conflict. The very fact that a choice is being made means that there are at least two equally desirable options, but only one alternative can be selected. Presenting you with a menu as you are seated at the restaurant is, essentially, presenting you with a conflict scenario. If the soup of the day was the only meal on offer, there would be no conflict. There would probably, however, also be a lack of enjoyment and interest. Having choices is, for the most part, a very good thing. It is also clear that if conflict occurs as often as we make choices, we are ordinarily very efficient conflict resolvers.

Some conflicts, however, are not so readily resolved. Enduring conflict is the PCT explanation for all forms of psychological distress regardless of their symptomatic manifestations. Reformulating mental health disorders as chronic conflict between control systems is an invigorating new perspective on psychological afflictions because the most crippling conflict occurs between high functioning control systems. Debilitating psychological distress from a PCT point of view does not indicate that there is anything dysfunctional or deficient in the individual. There is nothing deficient in individuals who want to be their own person and there is nothing dysfunctional in individuals who want to be liked by others. The psychological incapacity arises from the positioning of these two desires in temporal opposition to each other. Nor does the PCT stance on conflict suggest that anything is broken. The PCT attitude towards chronic conflict is that the problem is an organisational one and these robust and high-functioning control systems, and the network they are contained within, need to be reorganised.

Reorganisation is the PCT principle of change that relies on making random alterations to the perceptual hierarchy and monitoring the effects on error in the system of intrinsic variables. Changes that reduce error persist, and changes that do not are swiftly replaced by another change. Reorganisation does not judge whether a change will help or hinder. A judgement such as that would require the reorganising mechanism to have abilities it does not possess. It is not a 'clever' system in the sense of knowing what changes should be made or what the consequence of any particular change will be. All the reorganising system does is generate a change and monitor error. The good news is that it does not know when to stop. It will keep generating changes for as long as there is error in the system, so if the first change or the first few changes are not helpful, it will continue until a satisfactory solution is hatched.

The principle of reorganisation helps explain why people in therapy take different amounts of time to discover satisfactory solutions and it also allows us to make sense of the finding that people who change in one or two sessions can change just as resolutely as people who need 20 sessions to find their tailor-made solution. Through reorganisation we can also understand why all therapies are effective some of the time with some people. To the extent that a therapeutic technique of any persuasion helps a person become more fully aware of aspects of their problem they were hitherto ignorant of, the technique will be an aid to reorganisation. By embracing reorganisation as a general principle of therapeutic change, we might be able to understand more clearly why some people adopt what appear to be risky or unsafe behaviours. The only thing reorganisation knows is error reduction, so if ingesting illicit substances happens to reduce error, then that behaviour will persist until error once again increases and further random changes are generated.

Reorganisation also provides clarity about who or what is doing the changing. Reorganisation cannot be directed in the sense of ordering particular changes. People cannot make themselves reorganise satisfactorily but they can have some influence on where reorganisation takes place. A person can influence the locality of reorganisation through the proposed link between reorganisation and awareness. It is suggested that reorganisation and awareness are intertwined such that it is the territory in awareness that is massaged by reorganisation. That is to say that we have to be aware of the important elements of a problem in order to solve the problem. It does not appear to be the case, however, that awareness needs to be kept at the source of the problem until the problem is solved.

Experientially, it seems that once a person has spent time exploring a problem, new insights and successful solutions can often materialise at unexpected times when the person is doing something else entirely. While the length of time that the core of the problem needs to be in awareness is currently not known, it is clear that awareness needs to pluck out the source of the problem for *some* time. It may be that there is no predetermined specific duration or time period in which awareness should be held at the higher level. The length of time that is needed for the effective resolution of the conflict might vary from individual to individual and might be influenced by factors such as how long the conflict has existed and the position in the hierarchy in which the conflict is placed. It might also be that the higher level that has been identified is important but not key to the conflict.

Continuing to offer MOL at the clients' discretion will ensure that they are able to obtain the 'right' amount of higher-level awareness-raising time whatever that right amount may be for different individuals.

Successful therapy, then, is fundamentally a process of enabling people to explore aspects of their dilemma and distress that they have previously not considered. The mobility of awareness is striking and is capitalised on in MOL. By continuing to expand the scope of awareness, new areas become susceptible to the machinations of reorganisation with an ever-increasing likelihood of the emergence of the right solution.

Using the principles of control, conflict, and reorganisation, MOL has developed into an effective and flexible therapy that has been used successfully in both primary care and secondary care with people experiencing a broad spectrum of problems (e.g. Carey, Carey, Mullan, Spratt, & Spratt, 2009; Carey & Mullan, 2008; Carey *et al.*, 2013). For some therapists, MOL will be very similar to the way they already practise. For others, acquiring the habits of an MOL therapist will warrant major changes. It is likely, however, that all therapists who are new to this approach will undergo some of their own reorganising, as they come to grips with the notion that they are living in a PCT world. Regularly setting goals and monitoring and evaluating them can help to make the transition as swift and smooth as possible.

Goal setting from an MOL perspective

An important feature of setting MOL goals is that the goals are about the therapist, not the client. From a PCT perspective, it is acknowledged that no one can ever know with certainty what the right course for someone else should be, so it is considered counterproductive to set goals for what others should do. MOL therapists, however, set goals for how they can maintain a high level of MOL delivery and how they can improve their performance where necessary. They set goals, for example, regarding how well they adhere to their role as an MOL therapist, how curiously they ask questions, how stringently they refrain from assuming, and so on.

As outlined in Chapter 4, the two chief goals of an MOL therapist are to use detailed questions to help a client talk and then to ask about disruptions. The MOL session evaluation form (Carey & Tai, 2012) can be very useful in helping therapists pursue these goals successfully. The form takes only a few minutes to complete but provides a useful structure within which to consider the quality of one's provision of MOL. The form unpacks the two goals of MOL by considering aspects such as the extent to which the therapist asked questions rather than advised, informed, or suggested, and the extent to which the therapist followed rather than led the client during the conversation. After completing the form, therapists have the opportunity to identify areas for improvement and specify what they will concentrate on in future sessions.

The MOL session evaluation form has 'Self' and 'Other' versions so that colleagues or supervisors can also assist therapists in their quest to achieve a high level of adherence to MOL in their therapeutic delivery. If a supervisor or colleague observes a session, and then both the therapist and the observer complete the evaluation form, a comparison of the two sets of ratings can generate useful discussions. As with other therapies, regular and ongoing supervision is an important part of MOL practice.

A note on the qualifiers that are used in the scales of the MOL session evaluation form is warranted. Item three, for example, on the session evaluation form is: 'To what extent did the therapist ask about disruptions?' The scale ranges from 1 (not at all) to 10 (constantly). In using this form, we have discovered that 'constantly' does not mean that every single disruption should be noticed and asked about. The conversation would not progress very far if each and every disruption that occurred was addressed by the therapist. The high end of this range should, perhaps, more appropriately be labelled 'constantly as appropriate'. This introduces an element of judgement on the part of the therapist, which is part of the skill in becoming an effective MOL therapist. As you work with more and more clients, you will develop a more refined ability to discern the disruptions to pay close attention to and those that are more likely to be part of a client's mannerisms or conversational style. This is not a crucial point because as long as clients keep talking about whatever is on their mind, they will keep having disruptions. If you miss one or more disruptions, there will, more than likely, be another one to catch before too long. If you ask about a disruption and it does not lead to someplace useful, then returning to the conversation of a few minutes before will provide fresh opportunities to search again. The ability to assess which disruptions to ask about and which to ignore may not be critical to the ultimate effectiveness of MOL, but it will help to provide therapy more efficiently. Scoring 10 on item three, therefore, would involve asking about disruptions constantly but appropriately to ensure the conversation continues to flow.

Use of the 'why?' and 'how?' activity can be informative for therapists to learn more about what is important to them and the way in which they go about creating the therapy they want. You could identify something you particularly like to do in therapy and then ask why and how questions about that. If, for example, you think scheduling regular appointments is important, or you like to set homework, or you feel most helpful when offering advice and suggestions, then each of these areas could be subjected to a why and how scrutiny. The information revealed through this activity can be very useful in helping therapists learn more about themselves as therapists, as well as identifying areas for further development. In MOL, none of the range of therapeutic strategies or techniques is considered necessarily bad or off limits, but the criterion for any activity in MOL is: 'Will it help clients shift their attention to the higher-level source of the conflict?'

We have found that the only 'technique' needed to effectively and efficiently shift clients' attention to higher levels is to engage them in conversation and to use these conversations as a vehicle to produce disruptions that can be asked about.

In one session, a client with a spider phobia asked if she and the therapist could find pictures of spiders on the World Wide Web for her to look at and consider. As they did this, the therapist asked the client a plethora of questions about what was happening for her as she viewed the pictures, how did some pictures generate a greater reaction for her than others, what thoughts were going through her mind as she scrolled through the images, what was the most distressing image she could look at, what made it the most distressing, what happened as she continued to look at it, and so on. Thus, through the use of the Internet, the therapist was still able to pursue the two goals of MOL and help the client explore her spider phobia experience.

Monitoring progress in MOL

Standardised questionnaires are often used in the provision of MOL to monitor clients' progress, although the limitations of such resources are also acknowledged. As well as questionnaire scores, MOL therapists pay attention to tangible changes in clients' lives that they may report during therapy sessions. As an MOL conversation proceeds, an alert MOL therapist may keep a mental note of comments the client makes about socialising more frequently, smoking fewer cigarettes, drinking less alcohol, returning to work, completing fewer rituals and routines, taking up a new hobby, or sleeping more soundly. Any of these changes could be considered to be indicators of improvements in a person's quality of life. In addition to mentally flagging these as possible markers of progress, they also provide topics for detailed and curious questioning that might lead to fertile higher ground where important reorganisations can occur.

Also of interest in terms of monitoring progress can be behavioural observations that may or may not be congruent with the client's reports of changes that are occurring. One young male client attended the first session with his mother waiting in the reception area. The therapist noted that he had a pullover with the hood pulled over his head and he kept the hood in this position throughout the interview. By session four, however, his mother no longer accompanied him to the reception area and the hood was not covering his head. At session six, he did not wear the pullover at all. The therapist also noticed in session six that the client was clean-shaven for the first time, and this corresponded with the client reporting in session six that he started shaving again once he decided that life was worth living. Another client sat at right angles to the therapist in the first session but, over the next few sessions, the angle of orientation shifted until the client was sitting facing the therapist. Possibly no piece of evidence is conclusive on its own, but when behavioural observations are considered in conjunction with scores on self-report questionnaires, and client verbal reports, a compelling picture can be constructed of the client's progress in therapy.

The Outcome Rating Scale (ORS) and Session Rating Scale (SRS; Miller & Duncan, 2004) are simple visual analogue scales that are designed to be used every session to chart client progress, as well as to assess the therapeutic alliance. These are two of a variety of resources designed to provide continual feedback to therapists regarding the client's experience in therapy. The ORS is not the only resource available for the ongoing monitoring of client progress. The Outcome Questionnaire Measures (www.oqmeasures.com; Lambert *et al.*, 1996) are a suite of measures that are also designed to monitor progress throughout a course of treatment and provide regular feedback to the therapist regarding the gains clients are making. Feedback makes profound sense from a PCT perspective, and is an essential component of keeping experiences in their preferred states. Figure 9.1 shows the ORS scores for two clients as examples of the kinds of data that are generated from the use of these questionnaires. Similar plots are also possible with the SRS; however, as might be expected, they tend to show much less variability.

As well as monitoring progress from session to session, it can also be helpful, at times, to address processes that might be occurring within sessions. This is a more fine-grained approach to monitoring progress than pre and post questionnaires or even questionnaires used every session. MOL is conducted in a spirit of openness and transparency where nothing is done *to* a client. Instead, therapists spend their time trying to be as therapeutically useful as possible to their clients from their clients' perspective. For this reason, whenever it seems appropriate to do so, we ask for feedback from clients as we go along in the session. 'Appropriate to do so' would mean that asking these questions would help to achieve the two goals of MOL. So, when it seems appropriate, we might ask:

How is it going talking about this?

Are we talking about what you want to talk about at the moment, or is there something else you want to be spending the time on?

How is it for you for me to be asking these questions?

Is this going OK, or is there anything that would be more helpful right now?

What's happening for you as you're talking about this?

Sometimes, it can be therapeutically useful to ask about the processes that may be occurring within the interaction between the therapist and the client. It is not essential that this occurs every session, but when it seems like it might be helpful, it can be a useful way of helping the MOL therapist achieve the two goals of MOL. If the therapist develops the idea that the client might be worried about what the therapist thinks or is filtering what they say before they say it to the therapist, these can be useful things to ask about:

Are you wondering what I'm thinking as you explain these things to me?

Are you deciding what to tell me or the best way to say it? How are you going about making these decisions?

What's going through your mind as you tell me about your difficulties?

Questions such as these can help to draw attention to the processes that are unfolding between therapist and the client. It may be that the anxieties and concerns that the client has in the conversation with the therapist are similar to the concerns the client has in social relationships outside therapy. Spending time discussing the dynamics of the client-therapist relationship can sometimes be a very useful way of coaxing into view the important higher-level states that are generating the source of the client's dilemmas.

Walking through a programme of MOL therapy

In closing, we thought it might be useful to provide an outline of how a programme of MOL therapy could proceed. We cannot specify all the particular things that occur on a session-by-session basis, and we are unable to predict how each conversation will unfold; however, we can provide a general framework for how MOL therapy is delivered. At all times, the professional and ethical standards that a therapist works within need to be observed but, fundamentally, MOL is a respectful way of conversing with psychologically distressed individuals to help them discover solutions to their torment. It is hard to imagine a service that could not accommodate communicating with clients in this way. We do not intend this example to be a prescription for how every MOL therapist must deliver therapy, but more as a general outline of the way we have found to provide MOL efficiently and effectively.

MOL is a therapy that was developed in clinical practice. The seeds that spawned MOL had been developed by Powers since the 1950s, but Powers, himself, was not a clinician. It was not until he began working with clinicians who were interested in understanding PCT and wanted to nurture in their therapeutic practice the MOL seeds he had sown that a working therapy was developed. The current form of MOL, therefore, has grown and flourished out of an understanding of important PCT principles, as well as the discovery of what is needed or most effective in practice. Initially, for example, a brief but detailed outline of MOL was provided to clients at the first session to help prepare them for the conversations ahead. It was learned, however, that many clients did not need nor want to have MOL explained to them. When asked, clients in general were willing to simply commence the conversation. Some clients, to be sure, do want to know something about the therapy, and for these clients information is provided. It is now no longer assumed, however, that all clients will want to know the details behind why particular questions are asked. In the interests of starting the therapeutic aspects of MOL as early as possible, only as much information as the clients require is provided. As soon as the clients are ready to engage, the conversation commences.

In outlining this MOL programme, we will, for ease of expression, describe the therapist as female and the client as male. MOL begins, therefore, once a referral has been received and actioned and the client has arrived for his first appointment. Depending on the service and the professional and ethical codes of the therapist, there may be some things that the therapist needs to explain in the first session. MOL therapists like to use questionnaires to monitor progress, so the therapist will have the questionnaires she uses ready for the client to complete. Because the MOL therapist understands that the client is a living control system, she will appreciate that the client has his own goals and expectations about the session. So, the therapist begins by describing what she has in mind for the first session and then checks with the client that this matches with his expectations. She might ask if the client had specific things he wanted to have addressed in the session as well.

After a brief introduction, the therapist will provide the client with the questionnaires she has prepared and provide some time to complete them. Some clients might want to begin telling their story straight away, so it is not terrible or dreadful to delay providing the questionnaires, but completing them at the beginning is often convenient and then allows an MOL conversation to proceed for the rest of the session. The therapist does not want to overwhelm the client with questionnaires but she does want to get some data to be able to use as part of the information she relies on to track progress. She will use the ORS (Miller & Duncan, 2004), and her service requires that she also uses the DASS (Lovibond & Lovibond, 1995) and the K10 (Kessler *et al.*, 2002).

After the questionnaires are completed, the therapist explains some standard protocols to the client such as the limits to confidentiality, how issues of risk are addressed in the service, and how further appointments can be made. The therapist uses a client-led approach to appointment scheduling so she informs the client of her availability; she works at this service on Mondays, Tuesdays, and Thursday afternoons. She explains to the client that people vary in how quickly they find solutions to their problems, as well as in the pace at which they like to address their problems. Because of this variability, the therapist lets the client know that she has organised a way for the client to make appointments when it suits him. She tells the client that he is able to make appointments to see her in the same way he would make appointments to see his GP, by phoning the receptionist and arranging a time that suits.

Prior to beginning MOL, the therapist asks the client if he has any questions he would like to ask or if there is anything he wanted to know about that has not been explained. She then asks the client about what he has in mind by coming along to see her and what outcomes he would like to achieve. Once the client starts discussing this, the MOL conversation begins and the therapist becomes alert to disruptions she might ask about. The conversation continues until the appointment duration is reached or until the client arrives at a place that suggests discontinuing the conversation might be useful. The client might get to a point where he is really confused or he might say that his mind has just gone blank and feels empty or he might say that he feels a bit detached, as though he has stepped back from his problem. The therapist concludes the session by asking the client to complete the SRS (Miller & Duncan, 2004). Scores on the SRS are usually very high, but whatever the scores are, it is useful to spend just a minute or two commenting on the client's scores and asking him about his experience. The therapist might say:

> *These scores are all pretty high, how was it for you today to have this conversation with me? Was there anything I could have done differently, or anything I could have done more of or less of to make this session better for you?*

If one score is lower than the rest, the therapist might ask about that specifically:

> *I noticed that the score about you working on and talking about what you wanted to work on and talk about is not as high as it could be. Is there something I should have done differently so this score could have been higher for you?*

The client might respond with:

> *Oh no. It wasn't you. I just didn't really feel very focused today.*

The actual response from the client is perhaps not as important as having the conversation. Even if the client says:

> *No, everything was great. I thought it was a really good session.*

The therapist might ask:

> *Would you feel OK about telling me if there was something that was happening that was not quite right or if there was something I was doing that you wanted me to change?*

The session concludes and, after the client has gone, the therapist completes the MOL session evaluation form. She spends a couple of minutes reflecting on the session and identifies that, at times, she was a little 'passive' in the session and did not ask as many questions as she could, and she let some disruptions slip by that she thought might be useful. The therapist identifies, as she is completing the form, that she felt a bit hesitant to interrupt the client, so she sets a goal for herself to ask about at least five disruptions at the time they occur in the next session.

On his way out of the clinic, the client stopped at the receptionist's desk to make another appointment. He had gotten a lot out of this session and felt a bit 'buzzy'. He wanted to keep the momentum going and, since this was Monday, he decided to make another appointment for Thursday afternoon. Unfortunately, the next available appointment was the following Tuesday morning, but the receptionist offered to put the client on a cancellation list for Thursday afternoon.

As it happened, a client who had a Thursday afternoon appointment did cancel and the client was able to attend.

The therapist begins the second session by providing the client with the ORS to complete and then asks a question to get the conversation started. The therapist might ask something such as:

> *What would you like to work on today?*
>
> *Where should we start today?*
>
> *What did you have in mind for the appointment today?*
>
> *What would you like to get out of the session today?*

or any question to invite the client to start discussing those aspects of his life that he is distressed or disgruntled about and that he would like to be different. The therapist would not typically engage in any rapport-building activities as a 'warm-up' to the session. This is not because she thinks rapport is unimportant. On the contrary, the therapist believes rapport is very conducive to the client being able to talk freely and without filtering or censoring. The therapist believes, however, that the most powerful rapport-building activity she can do is to provide effective MOL so that the client's distress will dissipate as efficiently as possible. Because of her focus on raising awareness to higher levels as the chief ingredient of therapeutic therapy, the therapist wants to maximise the amount of time in the session that she and the client spend engaged in an MOL conversation. The therapist realises that the more time she spends engaged in other activities with the client is less time that she can spend engaged in the primary therapeutic activity. Therefore, she does not engage very much in what might be described as 'small talk' for the purpose of rapport building. Nor does she ask the client to recap on what he learned in the last session, and she does not ask him to report on what he has been doing since the last session. Often, clients will volunteer this information during the therapeutic discussion, which can provide useful information for the therapist about how helpful MOL is being for the client, but the therapist does not make a point of obtaining and reviewing this information outside the context of the MOL discussion.

The second session finished after 40 minutes when the client reached a point where he said he had never considered his situation like this before. He asked the therapist if he could spend some time thinking about what he had just realised. The therapist agreed without hesitation and provided the client with an SRS form to complete. The scores on this completed SRS were slightly higher than the first session from a few days ago.

The therapist saw the client for his third appointment in a week's time, and again the conversation commenced in the same way with the therapist providing the client with the ORS to complete and then starting the MOL conversation. At the end of the session, the client said he felt like he was on the verge of a 'breakthrough' but felt like the hour session was a little short. He asked the therapist if there was any scope for longer sessions. The therapist explained that using extra time when needed was part of the client-led approach she had adopted, and she let the client know that he could book two appointments back to back if he wanted to spend up to two hours discussing his problem.

The therapist completed the MOL session evaluation form again at the end of this session, and was pleased with the way she had picked up on disruptions in this session. She identified that this particular client made quite a few meta or evaluative comments as he described his experiences. He would often punctuate his dialogue with 'You must think I'm crazy with what I'm saying', or 'I can't believe how this sounds when I say it out loud', or 'That's really ridiculous, isn't it?' The therapist reflected that she had not paid a lot of attention to these meta comments and, on a couple of occasions, she had actually answered the client's questions with 'Well it doesn't sound crazy to me', or 'I think what you're describing is really understandable'. While it is not catastrophic to respond in this way, it does detract from the amount of time spent 'MOLing', so the therapist set two goals for herself in the next session: she wants to ask two or three questions of any meta comment that are made as a way of extending the time the client's attention stays at this meta level, and she wants to respond to meta comments in the form of a question by asking about processes that might be occurring. During the session, she would count off on her fingers each time she asked a question about the meta comments so that she would know if she had met her goal. To experience the first goal, she will ask questions such as:

> *What makes you say 'crazy'?*
>
> *Can you say a bit more about the sense of disbelief you're experiencing?*
>
> *How are you looking at things just now that makes what you're saying seem ridiculous to you?*

To achieve the second goal, the therapist will, in a curious tone, ask questions such as:

> *Are you wondering what I'm thinking as you're describing this to me? Is what I might be thinking important to you? What's important about that?*
>
> *Are you wanting to know if I also think it's ridiculous? Is it just my opinion you're interested in or are other people's opinions generally important to you? How does finding out what other people think influence things for you?*

The programme of therapy continues in this way for as long as the client makes appointments or until some arbitrary session limit has been reached. The therapist provides the ORS and SRS to the client at every session, and following every session she reflects on the MOL she provided through the use of the MOL session evaluation form. The client continues to make appointments as he requires them, which includes monthly and two-monthly intervals at some points. In time, his psychological distress vanishes and he is engaged again in the meaningful and satisfying life that his conflict had locked him out of only a few months before. He experiences the ups and downs of life but no longer becomes immobilised in the quicksand of chronic psychological conflict.

The best is yet to come

MOL may well be the most exhilarating innovation in psychotherapy and counselling for a long time. Based on three principles of the robust, rigorous, and integrative theory of PCT, it offers a flexible, responsive, and unflinchingly optimistic approach to helping people resolve the psychological distress of chronic internal conflict. PCT enables us to clarify the role of both the therapist and the client so that therapists can set goals that they are able to realise, and that can help them become effective and efficient therapists who are maximally helpful to as many clients as possible. You may well be able to identify elements of your own practice that are already consistent with an MOL approach. That is as it should be. We like to think that MOL is an integral yet unrecognised component of all effective therapies. From our perspective, there is a little bit of MOL going on each time any therapy is therapeutic.

Improving the effectiveness of therapies may well be similar to the way in which a talented sculptor fashions a magnificent piece of art from a block of marble. When asked how he created David, Michelangelo is reported to have said that he could already see David within the block and he just chipped away all the bits of marble that were not part of David. For us, improving any therapy involves whittling away those bits that do not help clients reorganise their conflicts to achieve greater control and bringing to the fore anything that does enhance the reorganisation of conflicts.

For us, MOL has been, and continues to be, an exciting and rewarding journey. From the principles of PCT, there is the opportunity to reconsider the psychological distress of mental health disorders and the ways in which we address this distress more thoroughly and meticulously than ever before. We could not imagine practising psychotherapy and counselling in any other way. Yet, we are also steadfastly insistent about continuing to research, refine, and improve the therapy and the theory that underpins it. Your scrutiny, talents, and insights would be invaluable in helping our field scale new heights and, if something in these pages has piqued your interest, we would love you to join us in the adventure.

Summary of main points

- MOL therapists set goals about what they will do, and not what their clients will do.
- MOL is an open and transparent therapy where information is shared when the client requires it.

- MOL therapists routinely reflect on their practice and discuss process issues with their clients as they arise.

Topics for discussion

1 All effective therapies have a common element of effectiveness regardless of their apparent differences. Discuss.
2 A person can never really set goals appropriately and effectively for another person. Do you agree? Why or why not? How would you test this assertion?

Activities for learning, consolidation, and fun!

1 Choose three clients and use the MOL session evaluation form for three consecutive sessions for each client. What do you notice? What do you find easy and straightforward? Where do you need to improve? What is your plan for that?
2 Ask a colleague to observe a session of yours. At the end of the session, complete the MOL session evaluation form and ask your colleague to complete the supervisor version of the form. To what extent do you agree or disagree? Where you disagreed by more than one or two ratings, what were the reasons for your disagreement? How will you use this information to improve your practice of MOL?

References

Alsawy, S., & Mansell, W. (2013). How do people achieve and remain at a comfortable weight? An interpretative phenomenological analysis. *The Cognitive Behavioural Therapist*, *6*, e13.

American Psychiatric Association (2013). *The Diagnostic and Statistical Manual of Mental Disorders* (5th edn). Washington, DC: American Psychiatric Association.

Andrews, G., Henderson, S., & Hall, W. (2001). Prevalence, comorbidity, disability and service utilisation: Overview of the Australian National Mental Health Survey. *The British Journal of Psychiatry*, *178*(2), 145–153.

Andrews, G., Sanderson, K., Slade, T., Issakidis, C. (2000). Why does the burden of disease persist? Relating the burden of anxiety and depression to effectiveness of treatment. *Bulletin of the World Health Organization*, *78*, 446–454.

Asay, T. P., & Lambert, M. J. (1999). The empirical case for the common factors in therapy: Quantitative findings. In M. A. Hubble, B. L. Duncan, & S. D. Miller (eds), *The Heart and Soul of Change: What Works in Therapy* (pp. 23–55). Washington, DC: American Psychological Association.

Australian Psychological Society (2007). *Code of Ethics*. Melbourne: Australian Psychological Society.

Barrett, L. (2011). *Beyond the Brain: How Body and Environment Shape Animal and Human Minds*. Princeton, NJ: Princeton University Press.

Beutler, L. E., & Castonguay, L. G. (2006). The task force on empirically based principles of therapeutic change. In L. G. Castonguay & L. E. Beutler (eds), *Principles of Therapeutic Change that Work* (pp. 3–12). Oxford: Oxford University Press.

Bohart, A. C. (2000). The client is the most important common factor: Clients' self-healing capacities and psychotherapy. *Journal of Psychotherapy Integration*, *10*, 127–149.

Bohart, A. C., & Tallman, K. (1996). The client as active self-healer. *Journal of Humanistic Psychology*, *36*(3), 7–30.

Boisvert, C. M., & Faust, D. (2002). Iatrogenic symptoms in psychotherapy: A theoretical exploration of the potential impact of labels, language, and beliefs systems. *American Journal of Psychotherapy*, *56*, 244–259.

British Psychological Society (2009). *Code of Ethics and Conduct*. Leicester: British Psychological Society.

Buchan, C., Galbraith, V., & Carey, T. A. (2013). *An Interpretative Phenomenological Analysis Investigation into Men's Experience of Psychological Change Without*

Psychotherapy. Poster presented at the Counselling Psychology Annual Conference, 11–12 July 2013, Cardiff, UK.
Carey, T. A. (2005). Can patients specify treatment parameters? *Clinical Psychology and Psychotherapy: An International Journal of Theory and Practice, 12*(4), 326–335.
Carey, T. A. (2006a). *The Method of Levels: How to Do Psychotherapy Without Getting in the Way*. Hayward, CA: Living Control Systems.
Carey, T. A. (2006b). Estimating treatment duration in primary care. *Journal of Public Mental Health, 5*(3), 23–28.
Carey, T. A. (2008a). *Hold that Thought! Two Steps to Effective Counseling and Psychotherapy with the Method of Levels*. St Louis, MO: New View.
Carey, T. A. (2008b). Perceptual control theory and the Method of Levels: Further contributions to a transdiagnostic perspective. *International Journal of Cognitive Therapy, 1*(3), 237–255.
Carey, T. A. (2008c). Conflict, as the Achilles heel of perceptual control, offers a unifying approach to the formulation of psychological problems. *Counselling Psychology Review, 23*(4), 5–16.
Carey, T. A. (2009). Dancing with distress: Helping people transform psychological troubles with the Method of Levels two step. *The Cognitive Behaviour Therapist, 2*, 167–177.
Carey, T. A. (2010). Will you follow while they lead? Introducing a patient-led approach to low intensity CBT interventions. In J. Bennett-Levy, D. A. Richards, P. Farrand, H. Christensen, K. M. Griffiths, D. J. Kavanagh, B. Klein, M. A. Lau, J. Proudfoot, L. Ritterband, J. White, & C. Williams (eds), *Oxford Guide to Low Intensity CBT Interventions* (pp. 331–338). Oxford: Oxford University Press.
Carey, T. A. (2011a). Exposure and reorganization: The what and how of effective psychotherapy. *Clinical Psychology Review, 31*, 236–248.
Carey, T. A. (2011b). As you like it: Adopting a patient-led approach to the issue of treatment length. *Journal of Public Mental Health, 10*(1). 6–16.
Carey, T. A. (2013). The problem with the DSM-5 is the DSM not the 5. *Australasian Psychiatry, 21*, 409.
Carey, T. A., & Kemp, K. (2007). Self-selecting first appointments: A replication and consideration of the implications for patient-centred care. *Clinical Psychology Forum, 178*, 33–36.
Carey, T. A., & Mullan, R. J. (2007). Patients taking the lead: A naturalistic investigation of a patient led approach to treatment in primary care. *Counselling Psychology Quarterly, 20*(1), 27–40.
Carey, T. A., & Mullan, R. J. (2008). Evaluating the Method of Levels. *Counselling Psychology Quarterly, 21*(3), 1–10.
Carey, T. A., & Spratt, M. B. (2009). When is enough enough? Structuring the organisation of treatment to maximise patient choice and control. *The Cognitive Behaviour Therapist, 2*, 211–226.
Carey, T. A., & Tai, S. J. (2012). MOL session evaluation form – revised. In W. Mansell, T. A. Carey, & S. J. Tai (eds), *A Transdiagnostic Approach to CBT Using Method of Levels Therapy* (pp. 137–141). London: Routledge.
Carey, T. A., Tai, S. J., & Stiles, W. B. (2013). Effective and efficient: Using patient-led appointment scheduling in routine mental health practice in remote Australia. *Professional Psychology: Research and Practice, 44*, 405–414.

Carey, T. A., Kelly, R. E., Mansell, W., & Tai, S. J. (2012). What's therapeutic about the therapeutic relationship? A hypothesis for practice informed by perceptual control theory. *The Cognitive Behaviour Therapist*, *5*(2–3), 47–59.

Carey, T. A., Carey, M., Mullan, R. J., Murray, L., & Spratt, M. (2006). Psychological change: What changes and how does it occur? A critical review. *Counselling Psychology Review*, *21*(4), 28–38.

Carey, T. A., Carey, M., Mullan, R. J., Spratt, C. G., & Spratt, M. B. (2009). Assessing the statistical and personal significance of the Method of Levels. *Behavioural and Cognitive Psychotherapy*, *37*, 311–324.

Carey, T. A., Carey, M., Stalker, K., Mullan, R. J., Murray, L., & Spratt, M. (2007). Psychological change from the inside looking out: A qualitative investigation. *Counselling and Psychotherapy Research*, *7*(3), 178–185.

Castonguay, L. G., & Beutler, L. E. (2006a). Common and unique principles of therapeutic change: What do we know and what do we need to know? In L. G. Castonguay & L. E. Beutler (eds), *Principles of Therapeutic Change that Work* (pp. 353–369). Oxford: Oxford University Press.

Castonguay, L. G., & Beutler, L. E. (eds) (2006b). *Principles of Therapeutic Change that Work*. Oxford: Oxford University Press.

Cocklin, A., Mansell, W., & Tai, S. (2014). *Client Perceptions of Helpfulness: A Study of the Therapeutic Relationship*. Paper presented at the BABCP conference, Birmingham, July 2014.

Collins, M., & Carey, T. A. (2015). Identification of real and artefactual moderators of effect size in meta-analysis. *Multivariate Behavioral Research*, *50*, 109–125.

Commonwealth of Australia (2002). *National Practice Standards for the Mental Health Workforce*. Canberra: Commonwealth of Australia.

Frances, A. (2013). *Saving Normal: An Insider's Revolt Against Out-of-Control Psychiatric Diagnosis, DSM-5, Big Pharma, and the Medicalization of Ordinary Life*. New York: HarperCollins.

Gaffney, H., Mansell, W., Edwards, R., & Wright, J. (2014). Manage Your Life Online (MYLO): A pilot trial of a conversational computer-based intervention for problem solving in a student sample. *Behavioural and Cognitive Psychotherapy*, *42*, 731–746.

Gianakis, M., & Carey, T. A. (2011). An interview study investigating experiences of psychological change without psychotherapy. *Psychology and Psychotherapy: Theory, Research, and Practice*, *84*, 442–457.

Glover, G., Webb, M., & Evison, F. (2010). *Improving Access to Psychological Therapies: A Review of the Progress Made by Sites in the First Roll-Out Year*. Stockton-on-Tees: North East Public Health Observatory. Retrieved 27 November 2012 from: www.iapt.nhs.uk/silo/files/iapt-a-review-of-the-progress-made-by-sites-in-the-first-roll8208-out-year.pdf.

Haley, J. (1990). Why not long-term therapy? In J. K. Seig & S. G. Gilligan (eds), *Brief Therapy: Myths, Methods, and Metaphors* (pp. 3–17). New York: Brunner/Mazel.

Hansen, N. B., Lambert, M. J., & Forman, E. M. (2002). The psychotherapy dose-response effect and its implications for treatment delivery services. *Clinical Psychology: Science & Practice*, *9*(3), 329–343.

Harvey, A., Watkins, E. R., Mansell, W., & Shafran, R. (2004). *Cognitive Behavioural Processes Across Psychological Disorders: A Transdiagnostic Approach to Research and Treatment*. Oxford: Oxford University Press.

Hayes, A. M., Laurenceau, J-P., Feldman, G., Strauss, J. L., & Cardaciotto, L. A. (2007). Change is not always linear: The study of nonlinear and discontinuous patterns of change in psychotherapy. *Clinical Psychology Review*, *27*, 715–723.

Higginson, S., & Mansell, W. (2008). What is the mechanism of psychological change? A qualitative analysis of six individuals who experienced personal change and recovery following a significant life difficulty. *Psychology and Psychotherapy: Theory, Research and Practice*, *81*, 309–328.

Higginson, S., Mansell, W., & Wood, A. M. (2011). An integrative mechanistic account of psychological distress, therapeutic change and recovery: The perceptual control theory approach. *Clinical Psychology Review*, *31*, 249–259.

Hofmann, S. G. (2004). Cognitive processes during fear acquisition and extinction in animals and humans: Implications for exposure therapy of anxiety disorders. *Clinical Psychology Review*, *28*, 200–211.

Howard, K. I., Kopta, S. M., Krause, M. S., & Orlinsky, D. E. (1986). The dose-effect relationship in psychotherapy. *American Psychologist*, *41*(2), 159–164.

Insel, T. R. (2012). Next-generation treatments for mental disorders. *Science Translational Medicine*, *4*, 155ps19.

Jadad, A. R., & Enkin, M. W. (2007). *Randomized Controlled Trials: Questions, Answers and Musings* (2nd edn). Malden, MA: BMJ Books.

Kazdin, A. E. (1999). The meanings and measurement of clinical significance. *Journal of Consulting and Clinical Psychology*, *67*, 332–339.

Kazdin, A. E. (2001). Almost clinically significant ($p < .10$): Current measures may only approach clinical significance. *Clinical Psychology: Science and Practice*, *8*, 455–462.

Kazdin, A. E. (2009). Understanding how and why psychotherapy leads to change. *Psychotherapy Research*, *19*, 418–428.

Keijsers, G. P. J., Schaap, C. P. D. R., & Hoogduin, C. A. L. (2000). The impact of interpersonal patient and therapist behavior on outcome in cognitive-behavior therapy: A review of empirical studies. *Behavior Modification*, *24*, 264–297.

Kessler, R. C., McGonagle, K. A., Zhao, S., Helson, C. B., Hughes, M., Eshleman, S., Witchen, H-U., & Kendler, K. S. (1994). Lifetime and 12-month prevalence of DSM-III-R psychiatric disorders in the United States: Results from the National Comorbidity Survey. *Archives of General Psychiatry*, *51*, 8–19.

Kessler, R. C., Andrews, G., Colpe, L. J., Hiripi, E., Mroczek, D. K., Normand, S. L. T., Walters, E. E., & Zaslavsky, A. M. (2002). Short screening scales to monitor population prevalences and trends in non-specific psychological distress. *Psychological Medicine*, *32*, 959–976.

Kirk, S. A., & Kutchins, H. (1994). The myth of the reliability of DSM. *The Journal of Mind and Behavior*, *15*(1/2), 71–86.

Lambert, M. J., Garfield, S. L., & Bergin, A. E. (2004). Overview, trends, and future issues. In M. J. Lambert (ed.), *Bergin and Garfield's Handbook of Psychotherapy and Behavior Change* (5th edn, pp. 805–821). New York: Wiley.

Lambert, M. J., Hansen, N. B., Umpbress, V., Lunnen, K., Okiishi, J., Burlingame, G., Huefner, J. C., & Reisinger, C. W. (1996). *Administration and Scoring Manual for the Outcome Questionnaire (OQ 45.2)*. Wilmington, DE: American Professional Credentialing Services.

Littlefield, L. (2013). Executive Director's report: Seven years of Better Access. *InPsych*, *35*(6), 6–9.

London School of Economics (2006). *The Depression Report: A New Deal for Depression and Anxiety Disorders*. London: Centre for Economic Performance. Retrieved 12 October 2011 from: http://cep.lse.ac.uk/textonly/research/mentalhealth/DEPRESSION_REPORT_LAYARD.pdf.

Lovibond, S. H., & Lovibond, P. F. (1995). *Manual for the Depression Anxiety Stress Scales (DASS)*. New South Wales: Psychology Foundation Monograph.

McEvoy, P., Schauman, O., Mansell, W., & Morris, L. (2012). The experience of recovery from the perspective of people with common mental health problems: Findings from a telephone survey. *International Journal of Nursing Studies*, *49*, 1375–1382.

Mansell, W., & Carey, T. A. (2009). A century of psychology and psychotherapy: Is an understanding of control the missing link between theory, research and practice? *Psychology and Psychotherapy: Theory, Research, and Practice*, *82*, 337–353.

Mansell, W., & Taylor, J. L. (2012). What is CBT and what isn't CBT? In W. Dryden & R. Branch (eds), *The CBT Handbook* (pp. 5–24). London: Sage.

Mansell, W., Carey, T. A., & Tai, S. J. (2012). *A Transdiagnostic Approach to CBT Using Method of Levels Therapy*. London: Routledge.

Marken, R. S., & Powers, W. T. (1989). Random-walk chemotaxis: Trial and error as a control process. *Behavioral Neuroscience*, *103*, 1348–1355.

Marken, R. S., & Mansell, W. (2013). Perceptual control as a unifying concept in psychology. *Review of General Psychology*, *17*, 190–195

Martin, D. J., Garske, J. P., & Davis, M. K. (2000). Relation of the therapeutic alliance with outcome and other variables: A meta-analytic review. *Journal of Consulting and Clinical Psychology*, *68*, 438–450.

Merikangas, K. R., Jin, R., He, J-P., Kessler, R. C., Lee, S., Sampson, N. A., Viana, M. C., Andrade, L. H., Hu, C., Karam, E. G., Ladea, M., Medina-Mora, M. E., Ono, Y., Posada-Villa, J., Sagar, R., Wells, E., & Zarkov, Z. (2011). Prevalence and correlates of bipolar spectrum disorder in the World Mental Health Survey initiative. *Archives of General Psychiatry*, *68*, 241–251.

Miller, S. D., & Duncan, B. L. (2004). *The Outcome and Session Rating Scales: Administration and Scoring Manual*. Chicago, IL: Institute for the Study of Therapeutic Change.

Miller, S. D., Hubble, M., & Duncan, B. (2008). Supershrinks: What is the secret of their success? *Psychotherapy in Australia*, *14*(4), 14–22.

Mineka, S., & Thomas, C. (1999). Mechanisms of change in exposure therapy for anxiety disorders. In T. Dalgliesh & M. Power (eds), *Handbook of Cognition and Emotion* (pp. 747–764). New York: John Wiley & Sons.

Moncrieff, J. (2009). *The Myth of the Chemical Cure: A Critique of Psychiatric Drug Treatment*. Basingstoke: Palgrave Macmillan.

Mundt, J. C., Marks, I. M., Shear, K., & Greist, J. M. (2002). The Work and Social Adjustment Scale: A simple measure of impairment in functioning. *British Journal of Psychiatry*, *180*, 461–464.

NHS (2013). *Your Choices in the NHS*. Retrieved 26 June 2014 from: www.nhs.uk/choiceintheNHS/Yourchoices/allaboutchoice/Pages/Allaboutchoice.aspx.

NICE (2009). *Depression: The Treatment and Management of Depression in Adults*. London: National Institute for Health and Clinical Excellence.

Norcross, J. C. (2000). Here comes the self-help revolution in mental health. *Psychotherapy*, *37*, 270–377.

O'Donohue, W., & Fisher, J. E. (eds) (2009). *General Principles and Empirically Supported Techniques of Cognitive Behavior Therapy*. Hoboken, NJ: Wiley.

Ohayon, M. M. (2000). Prevalence of hallucinations and their pathological associations in the general population. *Psychiatry Research*, *97*(2), 153–164.

Pekarik, G., & Wierzbicki, M. (1986). The relationship between clients' expected and actual treatment duration. *Psychotherapy*, *23*, 532–534.

Perry, S. (1987). The choice of duration and frequency of outpatient psychotherapy. In R. E. Hales & A. J. Frances (eds), *Annual Review* (Vol. 6, pp. 398–414). Washington, DC: American Psychiatric Association.

Pilgrim, D., & Carey, T. A. (2010). Contested professional rationales for the assessment of mental health problems: Can social theories help? *Social Theory and Health*, *8*, 309–325.

Powers, W. T. (1973). *Behavior: The Control of Perception*. New York: Aldine.

Powers, W. T. (1992). *CSGnet Archives, 26th March 1992*. Retrieved 26 February 2014 from: ftp://ftp.pctresources.com/.

Powers, W. T. (2005). *Behavior: The Control of Perception* (2nd edn). New Canaan, CT: Benchmark.

Powers, W. T. (2008). *Living Control Systems III: The Fact of Control*. Bloomfield, NJ: Benchmark.

Powers, W. T., Clark, R. K., & McFarland, R. L. (1960a). A general feedback theory of human behavior: Part I. *Perceptual and Motor Skills*, *11*, 71–88.

Powers, W. T., Clark, R. K., & McFarland, R. L. (1960b). A general feedback theory of human behaviour: Part II. *Perceptual and Motor Skills*, *11*, 309–323.

Robertson, R. J., & Powers, W. T. (eds) (1990). *Introduction to Modern Psychology: The Control-Theory View*. Gravel Switch, KY: Control Systems Group.

Rosen, G. M., & Davison, G. C. (2003). Psychology should list empirically supported principles of change (ESPs) and not credentialed trademarked therapies or other treatment packages. *Behavior Modification*, *27*, 300–312.

Ryle, A., & Kerr, I. B. (2002). *Introduction to Cognitive-Analytic Therapy: Principles and Practices*. Chichester: Wiley.

Schauman, O., & Mansell, W. (2012). Processes underlying ambivalence in help-seeking: The loss of valued control model. *Clinical Psychology: Science and Practice*, *19*, 107–124.

Scottish Executive (2003). *Partnership for Care: Scotland's Health White Paper*. Retrieved 26 June 2014 from: www.scotland.gov.uk/Publications/2003/02/16476/18734.

Shapiro, D. A., Barkham, M., Rees, A., Hardy, G. E., Reynolds, S., & Startup, M. (1994). Effects of treatment duration and severity of depression on the effectiveness of cognitive-behavioral and psychodynamic-interpersonal psychotherapy. *Journal of Consulting and Clinical Psychology*, *62*(3), 522–534.

Skinner, E. A. (1996). A guide to constructs of control. *Personality Processes and Individual Differences*, *71*, 549–570.

Slade, T., Johnston, A., Oakley Browne, M. A., Andrews, G., Whiteford, H. (2009). 2007 National Survey of Mental Health and Wellbeing: Methods and key findings. *Australian and New Zealand Journal of Psychiatry*, *43*, 594–605.

Spratt, C. G., & Carey, T. A. (2009). Can a control model approach assist case formulation in psychotherapy? *The Cognitive Behaviour Therapist*, *2*, 197–210.

Stevenson-Taylor, A. J. K., & Mansell, W. (2012). Exploring the role of art-making in recovery, change, and self-understanding: An interpretative phenomenological analysis of interviews with everyday creative people. *International Journal of Psychological Studies*, *4*(3), 104–130.

Stiles, W. B. (2009). Responsiveness as an obstacle for psychotherapy outcome research: It's worse than you think. *Clinical Psychology: Science and Practice*, *16*, 86–91.

Stiles, W. B., Barkham, M., Connell, J., & Mellor-Clark, J. (2008). Responsive regulation of treatment duration in routine practice in United Kingdom primary care settings: Replication in a larger sample. *Journal of Consulting and Clinical Psychology*, *76*(2), 298–305.

Tai, S. J. (2009). Using perceptual control theory and the Method of Levels to work with people who experience psychosis. *The Cognitive Behaviour Therapist*, *2*, 227–242.

Talmon, M. (1990). *Single-Session Therapy: Maximizing the Effect of the First (and Often Only) Therapeutic Encounter*. San Francisco, CA: Jossey-Bass.

Timimi, S. (2011). *Campaign to Abolish Psychiatric Diagnosis Systems Such as ICD and DSM (CAPSID)*. Retrieved 17 October 2011 from: www.criticalpsychiatry.net/?p=527.

Treynor, W., Gonzalez, R., & Nolen-Hoeksema, S. (2003). Rumination reconsidered: A psychometric analysis. *Cognitive Therapy and Research*, *27*(3), 247–259.

van de Rijt-Plooij, H., & Plooij, F. (1993). Distinct periods of mother-infant conflict in normal development: Sources of progress and germs of pathology. *Journal of Child Psychology and Psychiatry*, *34*, 229–245.

Velmans, M. (2009). *Understanding Consciousness* (2nd edn). London: Routledge.

Wampold, B. E. (2001). *The Great Psychotherapy Debate: Models, Methods, and Findings*. Mahwah, NJ: Lawrence Erlbaum Associates.

Watkins, E. R., Mullan, E., Wingrove, J., Rimes, K., Steiner, H., Bathurst, N., Eastman, R., & Scott, J. (2011). Rumination-focused cognitive-behavioural therapy for residual depression: Phase II randomised controlled trial. *The British Journal of Psychiatry*, *199*(4), 317–322.

Westin, V. Z., Schulin, M., Hesser, H., Karlsson, M., Noe, R. Z., Olofsson, U., Stalby, M., Wisung, G., & Andersson, G. (2011). Acceptance and commitment therapy versus tinnitus retraining therapy in the treatment of tinnitus: A randomised controlled trial. *Behaviour Research and Therapy*, *49*(11), 737–747.

Whiteford, H., & Groves, A. (2009). Policy implications of the 2007 Australian National Survey of Mental Health and Wellbeing. *Australian and New Zealand Journal of Psychiatry*, *43*, 644–651.

World Health Organization (1992). *The ICD-10 Classification of Mental and Behavioural Disorders*. Geneva: WHO Press.

World Health Organization (2008). *The Global Burden of Disease: 2004 Update*. Geneva: WHO Press. Retrieved 12 October 2011 from: www.who.int/healthinfo/global_burden_disease/2004_report_update/en/index.html.

Zigmond, A. S., & Snaith, R. P. (1983). The Hospital Anxiety and Depression Scale. *Acta Psychiatrica Scandinavica*, *67*, 361–370.

Index